SURVIVAL KIT FOR TEACHERS (AND PARENTS)

Goodyear Education Series
Theodore W. Hipple, Editor
University of Florida

Change for Children
Sandra N. Kaplan, Jo Ann B. Kaplan, Sheila K. Madsen, and Bette K. Taylor

Crucial Issues in Contemporary Education
Theodore W. Hipple

Current Strategies for Teachers
Robert L. Gilstrap and William R. Martin

Early Childhood Education
Marjorie Hipple

Elementary School Teaching: Problems and Methods
Margaret Kelly Giblin

Facilitative Teaching: Theory and Practice
Robert Myrick and Joe Wittmer

The Four Faces of Teaching
Dorothy I. Seaberg

The Future of Education
Theodore W. Hipple

Mastering Classroom Communication
Dorothy Grant Hennings

Open Sesame: A Primer in Open Education
Evelyn M. Carswell and Darrell L. Roubinek

The Other Side of the Report Card
Larry Chase

Popular Media and the Teaching of English
Thomas R. Giblin

Race and Politics in School/Community Organizations
Allan C. Ornstein

School Counseling: Problems and Methods
Robert Myrick and Joe Wittmer

Secondary School Teaching: Problems and Methods
Theodore W. Hipple

Social Studies as Controversy
R. Jerrald Shive

Solving Teaching Problems
Mildred Bluming and Myron Dembo

Teaching, Loving, and Self-Directed Learning
David Thatcher

Value Clarification in the Classroom: A Primer
Doyle Casteel and Robert Stahl

Will the Real Teacher Please Stand Up? A Primer in Humanistic Education
Mary Greer and Bonnie Rubinstein

A Young Child Experiences
Sandra N. Kaplan, Jo Ann B. Kaplan, Sheila K. Madsen, and Bette K. Taylor

SURVIVAL KIT FOR TEACHERS (AND PARENTS)

Myrtle T. Collins, M.A.
University of Hawaii

DWane R. Collins, Ed.D.
University of Hawaii

GOODYEAR PUBLISHING COMPANY, INC.

Library of Congress Cataloging In Publication Data

Collins, Myrtle T
    Survival kit for teachers (and parents).

    (Goodyear education series)
    Bibliography:. p.
    1. Classroom management.   I. Collins, DWane R.,
joint author. II. Title.
LB3013.C55   371.1'02   74-10230
ISBN 0-87620-882-0

Library of Congress Catalog Card Number: 74-10230

ISBN: 0-87620-882-0
Y-8820-6
Current printing (last number):
10 9 8 7 6 5 4 3 2 1

Printed in the United States of America

To our daughters, Beth and Anne,
who are special

CONTENTS

Appendix, 197

PREFACE

Discipline-classroom behavior-classroom management (the hyphenation is intentional) is a major and universal concern of teachers, administrators, parents, *and students* in the schools of nations around the globe. This fact surfaced in our contacts with school personnel in more than a dozen countries. We have written *Survival Kit for Teachers (and Parents)* because we want to help these concerned people and because we find the subject relevant and stimulating.

The *Kit* contains probably the most comprehensive combined listing and treatment of behaviors ever published. Inservice and preservice teachers, counselors, administrators, and parents will find the list of 324 behaviors, alphabetically arranged in the Index of Behaviors, a ready reference for coping with student behavior. The behaviors, or concerns (called "Capsules"), were gleaned from live surveys of classroom teachers, a systematic review of professional periodicals and books over the past fifteen years, and a recall of the combined 112 years of our own school experience as students, teachers, counselors, and administrators at elementary, junior-high, high-school, and university levels. The 134 behaviors that are treated are listed in the Table of Contents. There are more than one thousand "Options."

The Preamble and Beliefs set the tone of our approach and help our readers get acquainted with us. The Capsules written for the behaviors are vignettes dealing with the psychology of the behavior as found in school settings. The Options immediately following each Capsule provide specific alternatives for coping with the behaviors. Each Option is introduced by a transitive verb and is alphabetized by the verb; there is *no priority value* attached to the order or sequence of the Options; nor are they finalities, even though they are specific. They will be most helpful to the practitioner if used as stimulants or as reminders of techniques perhaps previously used and forgotten. Users may combine several of the Options; they may experiment with one new to them; or they may reject all of those listed in favor of newer and better ones. In the latter case, the authors and publisher will appreciate sharings.

In addition to its usefulness to the classroom teacher, this book can provide solid discussion material for faculty meetings and workshops. Its use as a communication medium during parent-teacher conferences is also suggested. Another suggestion is to share the Capsules and Options with the child whose behavior is upsetting and let him choose an Option as a resolution to his difficulty. Finally, pages projected by an opaque projector would provide useful course content for a parent study group.

The Appendix includes concise descriptions of twenty-six procedures frequently referred to in the Capsules and Options. They are listed in alphabetical order.

The Bibliography provides selected reference materials for further study by users of the *Kit* who wish to read in greater detail about a behavior or to learn how others cope with the behavior.

ACKNOWLEDGMENTS

We have thought about this book for many years, but serious collection of data began in Laos where the senior author, as principal of the American School of Vientiane, and the junior author, as a consultant to the Lao high school teachers, asked instructors for lists of student behaviors that caused them concern. Data collecting from teachers and parents, reading, synthesizing, writing, and re-writing took place during a sabbatical leave and during our travels to India, the Near East, Europe, Mainland U.S., Hawaii, and back to Laos. Writing the book, even though demanding, has been a satisfying and exciting joint effort.

We are indebted to many, many people: teachers of much experience; practice teachers and their supervisors; parents; hundreds of children; University of Hawaii colleagues; fellow authors; helpful librarians at Arizona State University in Tempe, Arizona and at the University of Hawaii; publisher advisers; and our own children and grandchildren. Special acknowledgment must be given to Topsy Franco who read and reacted to the manuscript and to our three helpful and cheerful typists: Johannes Magelssen and Flo Tanigawa of Honolulu and Nicole Desmaret of Vientiane. To them, a special *Mahalo nui loa*.

M.T.C. and D.R.C.
Honolulu, Hawaii

PREAMBLE

Discipline, from the point of view of the authors, relates to *disciple*—derived from *discere*, meaning *to learn*. If neither the teacher nor the pupil learns from an effort to solve a problem, the procedure needs careful scrutiny. We believe that innovative techniques can be created that, when brought into play with the cognitive, affective, or psychomotor equipment of a child, will help the child learn new and more effective self-fulfilling behaviors. Our approach to discipline is based on learning theory, our emphasis is on the teaching or training of specific behaviors.

BELIEFS

The authors of *A Survival Kit For Teachers (and Parents)* believe that:

1. The teacher is intelligent and quite able to innovate ways of working with children. (Many of the techniques described in this book will serve as reminders of techniques once used but forgotten about, or will show that other professionals agree with your approach.)

2. The teacher has already learned many things that work with children and many that do not.

3. The brunt of maintaining sound discipline rests on the classroom teacher.

4. No one technique works for all students; a given technique may indeed be ineffective with the same student the second time around.

5. The best disciplinary measures open to the teaching profession are preventive ones.

6. The school has the capability of organizing some kind of regularized case conference procedure, sometimes including only the teaching staff and principal, but often including counselors, social workers, psychologists, nurses, physicians, and reading specialists, if available in the school system.

7. A student's misbehavior is a signal—an SOS—for the teacher and administrator, who are in prime positions to administer aid.

8. To help a child the adult must honestly feel that the child is asking for help through this mode of behavior and that he can, indeed, be helped.

9. The wise teacher does not confuse academic evaluations with discipline.

10. The best approach to helping people is to explore the reasons for particular behavior patterns and then to explore alternative choices for effecting change.

11. No behavior is by chance (the principle of causality) and each is, therefore, significant.

12. The humane teacher's goal is to find ways of working with students that will produce the greatest benefit and the least damage to children.

13. Because every student is unique, ways of working with each student will be unique.

14. Whatever is done reinforces behavior one way or another.

15. Most forms of punishment prompt feelings of hatred, vengefulness, and disrespect; they deprive the child of his dignity and leave him less equipped to cope with the next encounter.

16. While punishment may work in a particular instance, it is rarely effective; it is an alibi for not solving a problem, rather than a step toward solution.

17. Irregular and disruptive behavior in a social context carries with it inevitable consequences.

18. Utilization of extrinsic rewards in modifying behavior does not prohibit the student's chances of developing high intrinsic values.

19. The teacher's conduct tells the students how they are expected to behave—student behavior and teacher behavior are highly related and reflective of one another.

20. The teacher is the key modifier of a student's behavior.

21. The teacher's ability to work effectively with individuals is challenged and complicated by the fact that the individual is a member of a group and that the group is affected by the treatment of the individual members.

22. Changes in attitude, rather than in superficial behavior, are the goals of the teacher.

23. It is more important to teach a child *how* to learn than *what* to learn.

24. Consistency of discipline is of prime importance—more important than severity.

25. All correction should be administered in terms of the student's life to date.

26. Correction is related to the act rather than to the individual.

27. Pure discipline recognizes the need for everyone to build self-confidence and conscientiously endeavors to open doors that will enable the student to find ways to develop his own self-direction.

28. Our swiftly changing world dictates an approach to discipline more flexible and pragmatic than ever.

29. No learning is singular and pure; rather it is a composite of facts, skills, and attitudes.

30. It is treatment, not revenge or punishment, that effects lasting, desirable results.

31. The optimum goal of educators and students is self-discipline.

32. Participation and responsibility are prerequisites to self-discipline.

33. A person who thinks well of himself will discipline himself.

34. A teacher who has his own values clarified is better able to help students work through conflicts and confusion.

BEHAVIORS

ABRASIVENESS
(*see also* Acting Out; Talking Out)

CAPSULE: An abrasive personality is one that rubs us the wrong way and makes us want to scream or sets our teeth on edge to such an extent that we find ourselves trying to avoid contact with him. One person may be abrasive because of his pompousness, another because of a rasping voice that never ceases, another because he does not exemplify what he exhorts others to do—and he is always exhorting! Some describe their most abrasive acquaintance as "one who has all the answers." Coping with abrasiveness is like chasing a phantom, but perhaps some of the following will at least help you live with the abrasive one in your classroom.

OPTIONS: **1** Allow the student to feel he has some control over the situation—perhaps by drawing up a simple agreement that focuses on diminishing the abrasive behavior.

2 Analyze reasons for the student's abrasiveness. This means getting to know something about his abilities, experiences, background, and physiological and psychological drives and consulting those best qualified to help. For instance, a speech teacher might help if it's a voice problem.

3 Anticipate and check the undesirable behavior with a diverting comment. ("Jim, you were about to _____ .")

4 Ascertain whether he is patterning his behavior after someone. Then talk to him about the effect this "imitation self" has on others.

5 Ask yourself questions like the following: Does his abrasive personality really interfere with his or the others' performance? Am I magnifying the effect his abrasiveness has on the group? Should I talk this over with another teacher to gain some perspective? What kind of attention is he seeking? How much does he deviate from the norm?

6 Assign responsibilities that require attentiveness and merit praise—preferably solitary activities in a strategic location.

7 Group the abrasive one with students who can help him. Your sixth sense must tell you whether to place him with the quiet, thick-skinned students who will put up with him or the testy, vocal group that will tell him why he rubs them the wrong way. If you choose the latter, be ready to move in with dispatch and capitalize on your information: "Jim, I couldn't help overhearing the group putting you down because you upset their work by _____. Let's talk about that sometime when you drop by after school."

8 Make brief notations of the child's abrasive behavior. Does a pattern appear?

9 Provide the student with opportunities to discover for himself his apparent abrasiveness. One way is to videotape the class and share the film in a class meeting.

10 Reinforce nonabrasive behavior, making no mention of abrasive deportment.

11 Sandwich your corrective statement between two compliments. For example, "George, I couldn't help noticing how *carefully* you put your work away, then how you managed to bump every desk on your way to the front of the room where you *thoughtfully* stopped to pick up wastepaper and put it in the trash can. Your batting average is improving!"

12 Talk with the child about his abrasiveness after school every day for a week. Keep a record of your talks, and each day review the previous day's conversation. This may help him detect the common denominator of the talks. Acknowledge creditable gains in efforts to be less abrasive.

13 Try using bibliotherapy (see Appendix). Several prominent athletes and politicians are accused of being abrasive; perhaps stories about them may give the student some insights.

ABSENCES

during Testing

CAPSULE: Teachers can become very testy about having to accommodate students who miss exams! School administrators, aware of the inconveniences incurred by absences at such times, often help by systematizing make-up schedules. If the make-up testing is left to the discretion of the teacher, the following suggestions may be helpful.

OPTIONS: **1** Arrange for private testing, mutually agreeable to you, students, and others.

2 Formulate, *with the class*, the procedure that will be followed throughout the year with regard to make-up tests. Establish the limitations and penalties that are fair. Be sure that a student is not penalized for circumstances beyond his control.

3 Give an oral examination. (This provides an excellent opportunity to get to know the student better.)

4 Use a token system (see Extrinsic Rewards, Appendix) to encourage students' attendance. "All students present on exam days will be rewarded with . . . "

ABSENTEEISM
(*see also* Truancy)

CAPSULE: Absenteeism and truancy are not synonymous. Truancy connotes idleness and conscious, willful absence of a sporting nature, while absenteeism is simply excessive absence for any number of reasons, ranging from school phobia to parents' demands that the student stay home to help with the family's business. Often the problem is related to sickness and finances. Most schools, for liability reasons, have established procedures for recording and reporting absences, so it is easy to survey and analyze each student's pattern of attendance. The chronic absentee soon distinguishes himself among faculty and students. If illness is not the cause, a high number of absences probably indicates a potential dropout. One thing is sure, the student needs some help because the consequences of long periods of absence are major, even for the ablest.

OPTIONS: **1** Confer with the absentee and interpret for him the real reasons he chooses to stay away from school. ("Bill, it's pretty clear that staying home is more pleasant than coming to school, because your mom is gone and you can watch TV all day. Did it ever occur to you that the headaches you have every morning help you achieve your goal?")

2 Contact the student's family and work closely with them to alleviate, if not eliminate, the problem.

3 Discuss the absentee in a team meeting (see Appendix). The pooled information may be used to construct a behavior change program for him (see Option 5).

4 Individualize and personalize his instruction so that long periods out of school take less of a toll (see Flight Plan, Appendix).

5 Institute a reward system (see Extrinsic Rewards, Appendix) to decrease absenteeism. ("Under our present token system, every day you are in school you will earn credit for ten tokens toward attendance at Field Day at Washington School.") *Note:* The reward event must be meaningful, possible to attain, and announced well in advance.

6 Refer the student to the school counselor, nurse, or doctor. (If a team meeting has been held, these specialists will have been there.)

ABUSED CHILDREN

CAPSULE: Although it is impossible to know the extent of child abuse in our society, it appears that awareness of this problem is becoming keener among doctors who treat extreme cases and educators who deal with the children in school. According to some studies, the highest incidence of child abuse occurs among boys in grades one through six, after which the greatest incidence is among girls. Speculation regarding the factors that give rise to child abuse include (1) absence of father in the home, (2) unstable adult living arrangements (such as a mother with transient lovers who regard the child as a nuisance), and (3) rising costs of living and the attendant frustrations regarding feeding a family.

The child who comes to school with welts on his body, who hangs around before school or after everyone else has gone home, or who tells you of the lickings he gets may very well be an abused child. The quiet, subdued, frightened child may be the object of abuse, too, but his deportment is less arresting. As you become acquainted with your students, you will catch overtones of oppression if they are indeed being abused. Perhaps some of the following ideas will suggest possible courses of action if there is an abused child in your class.

OPTIONS: **1** Arrange for a conference with the parents. They may ask for help in coping with their child. Be prepared to recommend sources of information, such as parent-education courses and free or inexpensive counseling on handling problems with children.

2 Assign an abused child to an older student of the same or opposite sex (see Junior Counselors, Appendix). If abused by the mother, for instance, the child may need a satisfying relationship with another female so that he doesn't feel all women are bad. The junior counselor can function as a confidante and/or a surrogate parent.

3 Deal with the child in a friendly, unsolicitous manner. Your warm, fair manner of dealing with him may convince him that not all adults are slobs who beat their kids.

4 Go to see the parents of the abused child, not to complain or scold them but to get acquainted. Most parents who violently abuse their children refuse to come to the school.

5 Help the student put some perspective into his judgment of adults, including the one who beats him. Use a values exercise (see Values Clarification, Appendix): "List ten things adults do that annoy you; list ten things adults do that please you. By each item put the initials of the person you immediately identify with that thing. Now make statements that include the item listed, plus a "but" statement, such as, 'I am annoyed (or I hate) being beaten by ———, but I like him when he's not drunk.' " *Note:* Such an exercise can be used with a group or on an individual basis.

6 Report the case to the proper authorities. Consult your administrator, who will advise you regarding the procedure to follow. Most, if not all, states now have reporting laws.

7 Use sentence completion (see Appendix) to learn the child's feelings. (My mother always . . . My father is . . . Adults are . . . My stepfather . . .) *Caution:* Use this technique judiciously; remember, you are not a moralizer or a judge. However, knowledge of how the child feels toward adults can be very helpful in dealing with him and his problems.

ACNE

(*see also* Health Problems; Self-Concept)

CAPSULE: Acne seems to have reserved itself for teenagers. The junior-high or high-school student who remembers his smooth, pimple-free skin in the sixth grade, when he wasn't too interested in the opposite sex, is patently annoyed at nature's trick on him! Secretly, he tries lotions, salves, and cover-ups, when the best thing he could do is keep his hands off his face after cleaning it well. The range of causes of acne is great. Some teenagers break out in bumps after one piece of chocolate, others after drinking a can of carbonated soda, eating greasy foods, or subsisting on junk diets. In addition, suppressed psychological problems account for some cases of acne. Usually, acne disappears once the youth is well into puberty, but impatience may cause him to pick and squeeze his face—often resulting in scars that won't go away. There are ways that you, as his teacher, can help the acne victim.

OPTIONS: **1** Discuss skin problems in a class meeting (see Class Discussions, Appendix). Sharing concerns verbally sometimes decreases self-consciousness.

2 Recommend that the student consult a dermatologist.

3 Show films on proper care of the skin, proper diet, and exercise for healthy skin.

ACTING OUT

(*see also* Hearing Problems)

CAPSULE: Acting out is aggressive, overt behavior precipitated by covert feelings. Although acting out is common among elementary-school students and usually reaches its peak around age nine, it is not restricted to that age level. Consider the behavior a symptom of something that needs attention, and accept it temporarily, while you consider the following questions: Is the student being rejected by his peers, and, for this reason, acts out? Is the acting out telling something about the *group*, as well as about the particular student? Is this "just a phase" that the student is passing through? How much does the student's behavior really interfere with his and the others' performance? Are you being consistent and self-disciplined? (Vacillating behavior on your part can actually prompt acting out!) Are you motivating the students or manipulating them? These, and other questions will help you gain a proper perspective.

Having conducted your personal inquiry, turn your attention to other matters. Pay attention to attitudes expressed in nonclassroom matters (conversations with friends, notes, scribbles on notebooks). Recognize the law of readiness in dealing with the student. Take care that privileges are not hastily and heatedly withdrawn—most people have long memories where hasty, unfair action is taken.

Finally, remember that withdrawal of a certain privilege, in an effort to change a pattern of behavior, often intensifies the aggressive misbehavior, so if you feel your theory is sound, don't flinch. "Things get worse before they get better" is often applicable where acting out is concerned. It may be the student's last gasp in an effort to foil divorce from his gratifying old patterns! Since acting out is among the chief concerns of teachers, a rather exhaustive list of options is offered.

OPTIONS: **1** Agree with the student upon a silent signal that can serve as a deterrent. ("O.K., Jenny, after this when you start to act out I won't say anything to you in words, but I'll quietly place an eraser on its end at the end of the blackboard tray." A nod or a smile can do as well.)

2 Agree with the student upon certain times when his kind of acting-out behavior may be acceptable.

3 Allow the student sufficient opportunities to release tension. ("Max, would you help Mr. C. lift those boxes?")

4 Anticipate and divert acting-out behavior with a question, a chore, a command. ("Jake, were you about to make a contribution?")

5 Ask the child to "occupy this space." There is something ominous about one's body filling a designated space! Better that than "Sit down and shut up!"

6 Avoid definitive statements like, "Martha, you're *always* acting out." Instead, try, "Martha, I've been noticing how sportsmanlike you've been behaving in gym lately."

7 Avoid responding with anger or sarcasm, which only reinforces the notion that the method works. Rather, react with, "Judy, you made me feel very upset when you did that."

8 Capitalize on an opportunity to change an undesirable behavior into a new train of thought. ("Joe, you just gave me an idea when you knocked the pencil sharpener on the floor! We can use the pencil shavings in our art project this afternoon. Please sweep them up and save them in this container.")

9 Combine punishment and reward. ("Jim, you know we don't permit shoving others in line, so please take your place at the end. When we have all gone into the auditorium, will you please close the door and turn out the lights? Thank you.")

10 Confer with such important people as the parents, former teachers, the school nurse, physicians, and counselors. Study available school records, then act according to your best judgment (see Team Meeting, Appendix).

11 Confer with the student in a private environment, conveying the idea that it is the *behavior,* not *him,* that is unsatisfactory. It is highly important for the teacher to be clear about the goals to be sought. At the close of the conference the teacher should be able to recap what has been arrived at and to state what the next step should be. A minimal plan of action should be clear to both, and a specific plan for assessment should be set up. The conference should help the student realize he *is responsible for his own behavior.*

12 Consider denying certain privileges, but offer alternatives; then be aware of opportunities to reinforce improved behavior. Make sure the child is *not* denied the very activity he needs most, such as, "O.K., since you've been acting out so much today, no P.E.!"

13 Control the student's environment with established limits that offer security but that give him some latitude for being himself. ("Jim, I know you're very upset, but dropping the books and throwing the chalk won't do here, so take these erasers outside and clean them by knocking them against the post. Thank you.")

14 Enlist the cooperation and support of the class when a student acts out, but avoid a self-pitying posture. ("Class, right now I am faced with trying to get Jim to stop _____; perhaps you can help me.")

15 Establish, with the class, guideline penalties for acting-out behavior. *Caution:* Fixed penalties are sometimes dangerous and are not in keeping with the philosophy that purports to accept each student on an individual basis.

16 Examine the seating arrangement. Try seating the student in a rear corner or by your desk as your assistant.

17 Exchange classes with another teacher for a period, a day, or longer, and then exchange observations (see Observation Technique, Appendix).

18 Have the student tell you *what* he is doing, not *why*. Later ask him to write a letter to his parents, telling them what he did. If the student is too young to write, perhaps he can draw a picture that will tell his parents the story of his acting out.

19 Interpret for the student what he has done. ("Joe, do you realize that by losing your temper and flailing your arms about because your shoelace broke you have spilled Jenny's ink and soiled her slacks?" A more sophisticated interpretation would be, "Joe, you are asking for the attention of the class and me, but we must get on with our work, so please wait in my office until I come to you.")

20 Isolate the student in a nearby place so that you and the rest of the class can get on with the lesson. Be sure the class and the student understand why he is being isolated. *Caution:* There is always the possibility this treatment is exactly what the student wants.

21 Isolate the student in the main office. *Caution:* Now the problem is being transferred to another authority, who really has no information upon which to act unless there is some communication from you.

22 Keep brief anecdotal records of the student's behavior and review them periodically with someone you trust, such as a fellow teacher, school counselor, or a doctor.

23 Note, and remember for future reference, the things that seem to trigger acting out. Is the student worse when classmates bring things from home to share? When other students' parents visit class? When a field trip is planned?

24 Order the student, without rancor, to stop what he is doing.

25 Praise the student about something that carries the inference he's *competent,* not just behaving well. ("You have a lot of manual dexterity, Jim; a lot of boys would have dropped that huge pile of plates before getting to the counter.")

26 Recognize the student when he's "good," not "bad." For example, write students' names on the board when they're *not* acting out.

27 Reflect the feelings of the student ("You're feeling pretty upset with the gang for booing you when you socked Jim.")

28 Remind the student, firmly and in a friendly manner, that what may be acceptable elsewhere is *not* acceptable here.

29 Reprimand the student privately and coolly.

30 Resort to prescribed suspension. This means the student is allowed to stay in school as long as he behaves, but when he oversteps certain bounds he is sent home. The student thereby virtually writes his own ticket.

31 Reward the students on a regular basis until the desired pattern is set (see Extrinsic Rewards, Appendix).

32 Role play (see Appendix). Have another student, or a teacher, play the student's role. Role playing can be ostensibly amusing but inwardly sobering to the disruptive child.

33 Suspend the student. This means temporary elimination from class. The student is sent home, to return when accompanied by a parent. This treatment has the advantages of giving the pupil time to reflect on the matter and of getting the parents involved immediately, which could mean that strong emotions and tempers will surface. A school procedure guide is helpful so that both students and parents have some assurance that all students are treated fairly. *Reminder:* Suspension does not treat the causes of the acting out—keep in mind that further action is required.

34 Use a filmstrip that depicts acting out.

35 Use peer pressure. ("Jim is not quite ready; when he is, we'll go to the puppet show.")

36 Use a questionnaire (see Appendix) with the entire class to gather useful information.

37 Videotape the class when the student is acting out; use the tape for objective evaluation privately or with all the students in a discussion.

ADOPTED CHILDREN

(*see also* Bilingual Children)

CAPSULE: Your children are not your children. They are the sons and daughters of life's longing for itself. And though they are with you, yet they belong not to you. You may house their bodies but not their souls for their souls dwell in the House of Tomorrow which you cannot visit even in your dreams.

Kahlil Gibran

Adopted children are no longer a rarity in the classroom. With the ravages of war, the intermingling of cultures through increased travel, the emphasis on population control, and many couples electing to "have one, adopt one," the child who is adopted finds himself a member of an increasingly large select group. While "You were chosen, so you're special," may become a cliché to the adopted child, it is nevertheless true and gives credence to the fact that his parents evidently selected him to meet a felt emotional need.

Despite the happy overtones that pervade adoptions, anxiety is a natural corollary to the new family undertaking. Any family union is chancy at best. The adoptive parent runs the risk of creating a high-pressure family climate that is understandably, but not excusably, related to a desire to provide the best for the child. He also runs the risk of overindulgence and inconsistent treatment, due sometimes to faulty modes of expressing affection and, quite possibly, to fear of losing the child's affection. For the adoptee (whom research places in the above-average IQ bracket), there is the risk of getting unfit parents! But, then, doesn't every child take that risk?

Some adopted children meld inconspicuously and happily into the family pattern, while others become inordinately consumed with "Who am I?" to the near exclusion of "What am I?" Understandably, adopted children fantasize a great deal, especially if their roots and background are not satisfactorily explained to them. It is not uncommon for one adoptee to become acquainted with another in school and to compare notes on their lots in life. In the past, before laws required that the child be told of his adoption, there were many unfortunate incidents of children first hearing the fact in school. It is no secret that children can often be cruel. One can expect them to understand kindness, but maybe it is a bit much to expect the young to understand that having different genes is no liability or that having the same genes does not guarantee love.

The best antidote for doubts and upsets with regard to adoption is a delicate balance between assurance of affection and some ready ways to cope when questions arise. Often a troubled adopted child feels more comfortable discussing his concern with a teacher than with his own parent. For this reason it is important for you to acquaint yourself with the family and its composition.

(Are there siblings? What are the ages of the parents?) Perhaps some of the following suggestions will be helpful.

OPTIONS: **1** Discuss adoption and the legal process involved (see Class Discussions, Appendix).

2 Encourage the adopted child to talk freely about his role in the family. Be discreet. Baiting children into sharing anxieties, without skill in heightening and broadening their value judgments, is not only damaging, but also unprofessional. Be mindful that the adopted child has the same need and right to question, challenge, and resist his parental guidance as any other child!

3 Give the student opportunities to relate the story of his adoption via various forms of expression: stories, poems, songs, drawings, scrapbooks, and photographs, for example. Young children enjoy sharing the story of their childhood with a class; older children consider it a private matter.

4 Show the child by your attitude that you not only think that *he* or *she* is special, but that *all* children are special.

ALIBIING

(*see also* Forgetfulness)

CAPSULE: Alibis are pleas of negligence intended to convince the listener of the speaker's good intentions. Some students become such clever purveyors of plausible poppycock that it's difficult not to believe them, even when you know better! It's easy to become impatient with the child who has an excuse for everything. One wonders what, indeed, his major goal is. Is he begging for attention, pleading helplessness, asking for sympathy, trying to get even with someone outside of school, or getting even with you? The student is a victim of a well-set pattern, so experiment with ways to rescue him.

OPTIONS: **1** Counsel the student, with emphasis on collecting clues to his problem. Do his alibis usually involve certain people (mother, sister, servant)? Do they proliferate at special times (before tests, during bad weather, after vacations)?

2 Discuss chronic alibiers in a class discussion (see Appendix): "Today you have chosen to discuss a fictitious classmate, Alibi Ike."

3 Establish an out-of-school relationship with the student to see how he handles himself away from the classroom. For example, invite him to attend a community function with you. Is he late with a ready-made excuse, or is he punctual? Use his conduct as the topic for a future rap session.

4 Give clear assignments with deadline dates and well-defined penalties for defaulting. Class agreement on suitable penalties will give this tactic some weight.

5 Have the student submit all his alibis in writing, and use them for a credit in a course. ("Ben, I haven't time to *listen* to your excuses every day, but I'll be glad to *read* them as part of your English assignment.")

6 Help the student identify the causes of his habit. ("Think of three things that delay you in the morning and of one solution that you could try tomorrow.") Listing the ideas on a note pad and giving it to the student adds dignity to the counseling session. A simple agreement (see Commitment Technique, Appendix) might be a natural result of the conference.

7 Include another student in the solution process. ("Elmer, Jack and I have agreed we'd like you to help him break his habit of alibiing. When he has an excuse for something, he'd like to try it out on you, and if you think it's a good one he'll pass it on to me.")

8 Telephone the parent, in the presence of the student, to assess the validity of his alibi. This could bring about an instant cure!

9 Tell the student that your patience has run out. ("For a month now I've accepted excuses for your late work. I'm weary of it. Beginning tomorrow I shall turn my deaf ear to you, so let's hear your final excuse right now.")

ANGER

CAPSULE: Anger is a strong emotion that everybody knows quite well. It can be useful, as well as destructive. The challenge is not one of eliminating anger altogether, but of conquering it so that it won't destroy us.

Recognize the symptoms of anger: flushed face, taut throat, and tears, for example. Be aware that anger usually occurs as a result of failure to accomplish a goal, of feelings of inferiority, of feelings of abuse, of guilt, or of having had something taken. It may represent legitimate rebelliousness toward unfair, intolerable conditions.

When a student is angry he needs a cool-headed listener. Adding your anger to the scene won't help. From what he says, make a mental note as to whether it was one person or a group that made him angry. Deal with the anger in private, if possible. Allow the student sufficient time to sulk, cry, or retreat before expecting him to return to the group.

OPTIONS: **1** Develop, with the student, a mentally rehearsed, plan of action, to put to use if a similar incident recurs. ("When he makes me angry again, I'll ... ")

2 Discuss the psychology of anger in class (see Class Discussions, Appendix). Help the student recognize the phenomenon as a part of his personality that can be useful when controlled. "Let's begin with listing things that make most people angry. Now list specific things that make you angry. Now let's work in buzz sessions [see Appendix] and talk about ways to cope with anger."

3 Encourage the student to practice stating his anger using first person, rather than second or third. ("*I* am so mad," instead of "*You [he, she]* made me do this!")

4 Have the student list ten things that made him angry during the past week. Have him identify persons he thinks contributed to his anger. An analysis of such a list might help the student see that he must be responsible for his own behavior.

5 Role play, shortly after the fact, an incident involving anger (see Role Playing, Appendix).

6 Tell the student how you cope with your anger. ("I have two pet ways of coping with my anger. Shall I tell you or do you want to see if you can figure them out as the semester goes along?")

7 Use a positive reinforcement technique to decrease angry outbursts (see Extrinsic Rewards, Appendix): "Tom, last week you were credited with ten angry outbursts that made you and a lot of others feel terrible. This week I'm going to keep track of your flareups, but for a special reason. This yellow token is worth 300 points, or a prize worth $3.00 in the school store. Every time you lose your temper you will forfeit 50 points. If, at the end of the week, you have lost no points you may collect a prize worth

$3.00. If you lose 100 points you may still collect a $2.00 prize."
Note: There are as many versions of reward systems as there are
people, so invent your own! Keep it simple.

ANXIETY

(*see also* Fearfulness)

CAPSULE: Anxiety can best be described as uneasiness. A moderate degree
of anxiety serves as a splendid motivator; an excessive degree
immobilizes.

Common comments of an anxious person are, "I have butterflies
in my stomach," "My hands are sweating," "My head is
splitting." The familiar ring of such comments indicates the
universality of the emotion. Conspicuous in the areas of jobs, sex,
and school, anxiety is impelled by desires to succeed or avoid
failure; the closer the person hovers near failure, the more likely
he is to behave recklessly. Lack of structure and fear of the
unknown generate anxiety. Quarrelsomeness and pressure outbursts are common symptoms of anxiety in adults.

Certain psychologists believe much anxiety in children is the
result of parents' imprudent evaluation of their youngster's conduct and products during his first six years. Often the causes of
anxiety are not manifest, and all one sees are the symptoms, such
as tics, blinking, subvocal throat clearing, hair twirling, sucking,
and the like, all of which are distress signals and safety valves.
Medication is often used in connection with anxiety, but it can
only reduce the symptoms.

As a teacher, expect to deal with anxiety in many forms. Your
sensitivity will eventually sharpen your awareness to the stresses
that emit anxiety signals, and being the professional you are, you
can respond helpfully.

OPTIONS: **1** Acknowledge the student's creditable gains in dealing with an
anxiety-causing situation. ("Mr. Field tells me you handled your
fear of the water with real courage today. Tomorrow you'll do
even better.")

2 Acquaint yourself with the history of the child's anxiety. (See
cumulative records; consult former teachers and parents.)

3 Anticipate the fears of the student and share with him your appreciation of his anxious feelings. Encourage him to speak openly. ("Jim, I know you worry about the report to your parents, so why don't we go over it before it goes to them?" or "Since you get so anxious about taking tests, would you like us to make some special arrangements for you until you are better able to cope?")

4 Ask another teacher to observe the anxious student. Discuss your mutual observations.

5 Ask yourself how much you feel he deviates from the norm. To what extent are you more aware of his behavior than that of others? In other words, are you overreacting?

6 Avoid embarrassing the student with regard to the anxiety symptom. Handle embarrassing moments with dispatch and courtesy. For example, divert the attention of the class in cases of ridicule of the anxious one.

7 Change activity or routine, if possible, when anxiety symptoms become evident.

8 Check the level of difficulty of the academic material you are using. Consider the goals of the student as established by you, the parents, and the student himself. Are they realistic?

9 Consult a counselor or the school nurse, who can suggest proper referral procedure.

10 Keep anecdotal records of the situations that make the child most anxious. (Dec. 1, 19——: Danny came to my desk three times this morning, asking if he would have to take the swimming test today. Dec. 3, 19——: Danny went to the toilet and a classmate reported that he had vomited. When he returned to the room he was pale and the first thing he asked me was if he would have to take the swimming test, since he had been sick. Dec. 8, 19——: The following boys forgot their swim trunks at home: Dick, *Danny*, and Sam.)

11 Lead the child through a threatening situation, gradually increasing the intensity of the stimuli, until he or she feels secure. A student who is anxious about taking showers after physical education could be involved in constructing a gradual induction plan, step by step. (Monday Mary will sit in the shower room, but take no shower; Tuesday she will go with a friend to turn on the shower, but take no shower; Wednesday she will take a shower with her friend; Thursday Mary will shower alone.)

12 Listen to what the student talks about with friends during free periods, at lunch, and so forth. You might pick up a clue to his anxiety.

13 Seek opportunities to enhance the student's opinion of himself. ("We were all proud of you for finishing your speech, even though we knew you were a little nervous.")

14 Use the student's name often, kindly, and without threat.

ARGUMENTATIVENESS

(*see also* Attention Seeking; Talking)

CAPSULE: One wife commented about her husband: "He always wants to argue!" Further observation of the couple made it clear that the wife considered *any* remark the husband made to be arguing. Many students are likewise mislabeled.

Healthy argumentation livens up a group, but unfortunately it is often a threat to teachers and parents. Perhaps this is tied to a long-held notion that there must be a winner and a loser in every intellectual skirmish. It takes skill to minimize this competitive spirit and to encourage openness to bizarre and unsettling ideas as well as to vapid and familiar ones.

Arguers usually come on strong. They may have learned the control power of arguing. Some arguers are intellectually motivated; others are cantankerous. All are talkers who enjoy disputes and debate more than most. They may be amusing, cocky, overconfident, overbearing, threatening, but they are *not* evil! The student in your class who always wants to argue could be the key to a memorable semester—with your judicious guidance.

OPTIONS: **1** Allocate certain times in your class schedule for argumentation. This way the students can anticipate that time and other tasks will not be jeopardized.

2 Ask the student, on occasion, to write his arguments, instead of speaking them. Have a student he respects react to them.

3 Focus the student's attention on improving his logic and judgment and away from always winning an argument. ("Next time the umpire calls a foul, Ted, try to imagine yourself in his place.")

4 Require the student to preface at least some of his statements with, "I agree with you on ..." He may need experience in seeing that others also have sound ideas.

5 Speak candidly about the arguer's penchant for overwhelming the other students with his argumentativeness. Suggest that he might enjoy his mental gymnastics even more with added participation of others. Constantly listening to one's own ideas can become quite dull!

6 Use the Ann Landers technique (see Appendix). Presenting ideas before a large group can have a modifying effect on a student who finds it easy to subdue a small group.

ARROGANCE

(*see also* Domineering Children; Self-Concept)

CAPSULE: Someone has described an arrogant person as "the self-made man who worships his creator." A less stinging statement might be that he is an enigma. His peers call him "stuck up," "opinionated," "a know-it-all," "conceited," and "overbearing." He explains himself very simply as "basically shy." Who is right?

It seems reasonable to conjecture that the arrogant individual received a generous helping of adulation and praise at a time when it was deserved but that the worth placed on the accomplishment became grossly exaggerated in his mind, so that now he sees himself as generally superior to others. At least that is the message that he emits through his comments about himself and others, his bearing, and his speech—his total attitude. Those around him reject his message for reasons that may be as invalid as his view of himself; he continues, however, to be called "stuck up," "snooty," "high hat," and much more. It is safe to say that he wants friends as much as anybody, but not having had much luck in cultivating them, he's found it safer to promote behaviors such as aloofness and braggadocio, which guarantee him some protection. When his self-concept is more in line with reality he will lose his arrogant posture.

OPTIONS: **1** Counsel the student, using some values clarification skills (see Appendix): "List ten adjectives you think others would use to describe you. List ten qualities you like about yourself."

2 Encourage the student to improve his skill in activities that make him uneasy but that are required (such as swimming, or speech, for instance). Devise an improvement program that has success built into it by virtue of attainable goals (see Flight Plan and Extrinsic Rewards, Appendix).

3 Enhance the student's self-image by giving specific evaluative praise instead of a general laudatory statement. ("Your solution to that problem gave me a clue to a problem I've been struggling with for weeks," *not* "You're good at solving difficult problems." The first statement implies that he is not only a good thinker but also helpful to others.)

4 Help the arrogant one examine his motives. ("Tom, could it be that your boastfulness about your test scores is an attempt to compensate for not being very good in ———?"

5 Interest the student in tutoring younger students. Getting involved in helping someone else is a quick way to take the spotlight off yourself.

6 Verbalize what the arrogant one is obviously trying to impress upon you. ("You really *are* the best informed student on the Russian Revolution.") Hearing *you* say it may indicate that now *he* can stop.

ASSEMBLY DISRUPTION

CAPSULE: Large-group activities generate human turbulence. Therefore, develop a tolerance for a normal amount of noise where large groups are involved. Anticipate what might cause an eruption so that you can channel energies elsewhere, but try to assume that there won't be any trouble. Remember to look upon negative conduct as a symptom of something that deserves attention, not something that should be taken personally by you. Be aware of the "high intensity" times in school (just before a tournament, before holidays, before lunch, at times of conflict between groups of students or students and faculty, for instance) and adjust your level of tolerance accordingly. If trouble lurks, pray for the wisdom of Solomon to discern whether it is a minor infraction that may never recur or whether it is major. Establish a proper tone by using an opener that commands respectful attention (such as singing the national anthem, or saluting the flag). Likewise, use an appropriate closer (dismissal by the student body president, for example). Establish a tone, through your own deportment, that is conducive to acceptable behavior and that emphasizes standards of conduct instead of school rules. *If* all the props, audio-visual aids, and so forth are in readiness for the assembly, *if* the physical climate of the auditorium is correct, *if* teachers are seated among the students (instead of in a huddle in the rear), *if* you have circulated and periodically reviewed acceptable assembly conduct, and *if* the content of the assembly is worthwhile, it is highly unlikely that any problems will arise.

OPTIONS: **1** Assign helping roles to potential disrupters: controlling traffic at the auditorium door, passing out programs, and so on.

2 Avoid singling out and embarrassing students who misbehave. Use a face-saver, at least for the first offense.

3 Capitalize on an opportunity to turn an undesirable activity into a pleasant experience. For example, if the student is making airplanes out of assembly programs: "Dave, I've never really mastered the art of folding and flying those 747s you're sending up. How about meeting me after the assembly and we'll plan a contest for those who are interested?"

4 Chat with the student privately after the assembly and listen to his comments. You may learn something very important.

5 Consider demerits, which are sometimes effective with the disrupter if your school is committed to such a system. This is more popular in military schools than in other private and public institutions.

6 Consider taking away the privilege of attending assemblies. Loss of a privilege may help the student realize that his conduct affects the group's effectiveness. Many students are accustomed to this form of control at home. However, care must be taken that the student is not denied the very thing he needs most. Once the debt is paid, forget the incident.

7 Detain the student with the teacher, an administrator, or in study hall. *Caution* This approach must be used judiciously since transportation and security problems preclude spontaneous detention. Parents should be notified.

8 Ignore the student or act immediately following a warning. ("Jim, please report to the office immediately and see me after the assembly.") *Caution:* Any action that embarrasses a student is risky and loaded with potential repercussions. Learning when to ignore a disruption is a matter of sensitivity and judgment. Just because school personnel are trained to observe doesn't mean they must *do* something about every observation!

9 Involve the student in planning and executing the next assembly.

10 Move near the student and remain there until all is quiet. Refrain from talking over the students' voices. Raise your hand and wait for silence.

11 Observe the assembly with the aid of an appointed observer (see Observation Technique, Appendix). Consider asking a potential disrupter to be an observer.

12 Perform a surprise act to dissolve the disruption. Some examples: whistling between your fingers, doing a jig, switching the lights off and on, playing a chord on the piano.

13 Refer the student to a counselor for individual or group counseling.

14 Refer the student to the principal.

15 Reflect the feelings of the student when conferring with him. ("You were really enjoying popping your gum when I spoke to you in the auditorium.")

16 Reinforce positive behavior. ("I'm sorry to have to remind you again not to give wolf-whistles when the pretty new teachers walk across the stage, but I want to compliment you for not dragging out your applause.")

17 Remove the disrupter from the auditorium. *Caution:* Be sure the student knows why he is being asked to leave. "Get out!" is rarely effective. Remove him only when it is in the best interests of the group. Consider alternative techniques before dismissing the student. Sometimes sending him on an errand gives temporary relief.

18 Role play (see Appendix) with a select group sometime after the assembly.

19 Suspend the student if your particular school's guidelines seem to justify such treatment for the misdemeanor.

20 Talk to the assembly about large-group conduct and rehearse routines. Avoid a nagging posture.

21 Tape-record the students as they enter the auditorium and replay later at an appropriate time.

22 Threaten the student. This is risky, but sometimes inevitable and effective. *Caution:* The teacher who threatens tends to overuse the technique, and it becomes empty talk. An occasional threat, with evidence of sure follow-through, might be quite in order, however.

23 Use nonverbal reminders. Some examples: a shake of the head, a finger to the lips, a wink, a smile.

24 Use positive reinforcement habitually. ("The sixth graders came into the auditorium 200 percent better today, so why don't we dismiss them first?")

25 Use prescribed suspension. For example, a student who is a chronic disrupter is allowed to attend assemblies as long as he obeys the rules, but when he oversteps his bounds he's sent home (after the office has notified the parents). The student thereby writes his own ticket.

26 Use student courts (see Appendix) to try offenders. *Caution:* Students can be too severe. The method can be highly successful, however.

ATTENTION SEEKING

(*see also* Loneliness; Tattling)

CAPSULE: Every student needs attention, seeks it, and gets some. It's the glutton we dread! Once out of bounds, heaven and earth seem incapable of quelling the whistler, the hummer, the giggler, the wisecracker, the whisperer, the swearer, the gossip, the clown, the crier, the dawdler, or the chronic telephoner, all of whom are saying, "Look at me! Listen to me! Pay attention to me!" Passive, seemingly innocuous behavior is also a form of attention seeking, though many fail to recognize it as such. Try to help the student who calls so much attention to himself to understand how he is trying to control those around him. You may be amazed at his insight. What he is doing may be quite all right—in small doses. Good humor and skill in recycling the student's energy will make him less demanding and you more serene.

OPTIONS: **1** Ask the entire class to engage in the attention seeker's gimmick and then call a halt to the activity. For example, if a student groans when a pop quiz is announced, say, "Let's all do a harmonic groan together before we start the quiz. Take a deep breath . . . frown . . . sigh . . . *groan!* Great! Jim (student who started it), please pass out the papers. Thank you."

2 Do a flip-flop. That is, turn an attention-getting device into a learning experience. For example, if a boy is making and shooting paper planes through the air, say, "Ross, I've always wanted to learn how to fold paper airplanes. Would you teach all of us now, and then we will continue with our lesson?"

3 Ignore whatever the child is doing.

4 Praise the child for something that has *nothing whatever* to do with his bid for attention.

5 Talk to the child privately about his or her ways of asking for attention. It may not have occurred to the student that that was what he (she) was doing. Between the two of you, devise a check plan that will help him (her) realize the extent of the attention-getting behavior. ("Sue, I'll bet you don't realize that you ask to borrow things at least five times every day, and I've come to believe it's your way of getting my attention, because your exams show that your memory isn't that bad. Let's tabulate, for a week, the times you ask to borrow things." Note that Sue's memory was praised at the same time that a corrective measure was suggested.)

6 Use the child's name kindly and often. This gives him a modicum of attention, so he may not seek much more.

ATTENTION SPAN, Brief

(*see also* Anxiety; Eye Problems;
Health Problems; Hyperactivity)

CAPSULE: Teachers and parents often mention the child with a "short attention span," rarely realizing that, for the level of material and conditions prevailing, perhaps his span is as good as can be expected.

Brief attention spans may be related to physical discomforts (vision and hearing problems, hunger, or fatigue) as well as to the

academic material at hand. It is important to maintain a comfortable room temperature, and to permit the child ample opportunities to get drinks and go to the bathroom if you want him to
pay attention to you or to whatever is going on. Having done this,
it is your job to provide learning experiences and tasks that are
commensurate with his ability. Just think for a moment how
your own attention span wanes when the discussion level of your
friends gets too far over your head or when it hits a level so
disgustingly simple and you've heard it all before! Luckily for
adults, they can excuse themselves without anyone accusing them
of having brief attention spans!

OPTIONS: **1** Allow the student some choice in the order of the subjects he
will study.

2 Ask the school nurse or counselor to observe the student in
the class setting.

3 Ask the student to run an errand for you *after* he completes
what he is now doing.

4 Become a master at knowing when to accelerate, decelerate,
change activities, raise your voice, lower it, place your hand on
the child's shoulder, and so forth—in other words, when to
"recharge" the student just enough to maintain his attention.

5 Maintain an accurate check on the inattentive child's behavior
(see Observation Technique, Appendix).

6 Reinforce with a token (see Extrinsic Rewards, Appendix)
every five minutes of attention. Allow the student to trade the
tokens for an object of his choice at the end of a determined
time. Gradually withdraw the extrinsic reward.

7 Remind the student of what he had hoped to accomplish in a
given time. This may glue his attention to a task a little longer.
("Flo, you wanted to have this birthday card finished for your
mother by noon.")

8 Show the inattentive student precisely how he can do better.
("Pat, you are bogged down in this problem because you made a
little error in subtraction here.")

9 Teach the student how to use the listening formula, FALR
(see Appendix).

B

BAITING The Teacher

(*see also* Note Passing)

CAPSULE: Students sometimes enjoy the game of "Baiting the Teacher." Usually the student's attitude and facial expressions belie his intent, but the clever student can lay a subtle trap for the unwary. Good humor and honesty in conducting your class are better antidotes to baiting than playing a continuous game of one-upmanship. Actually, the art of questioning is the soundest and most profitable form of preparedness (see Inquiry Process, Appendix).

OPTIONS: **1** Confront and surprise the baiter. ("Jim, you're baiting me. We're all quite aware that you already know my stand on the subject of _____. However, in the past month I've modified my views somewhat. Can you guess how?") This approach openly settles the matter of baiting, without rancor. At the same time, it engages the student in a guessing game that few can resist.

2 Ignore the baiting and thereby extinguish the student's ploy through lack of reinforcement.

3 Respond to a question with a question. (*Student:* "Mr. B., why do you question the right of _____ to _____?" *Teacher:* "Why shouldn't I?")

4 Submit to the student, in private, the possibility that he uses baiting more to impress his classmates than to befuddle the teacher. If the student concedes the correctness of this analysis, he will have interpreted his own conduct and the behavior will undoubtedly diminish.

5 Tell the student, privately, that he is making only partial use of one of the best tools for becoming a success—astute question asking. Suggest that he may be spoiling his mode of inquiry with insincerity and preoccupation with trapping someone. If you are sincere, the student will record your advice for future, if not present, use.

BATHROOMITIS

(see also Anxiety)

CAPSULE: The bathroom holds a special fascination for students of all ages. For the student who is bored, unsure of himself, or just "seatsick," it is a plausible retreat. It provides an umbrella of temporary asylum for the dawdler, the evader, or the mischief-maker. For the little ones, the fascination of running water, of rolling paper, and of slathery soap offsets anything stenchy. For the older student, the john is the last place most teachers will look for him and the best place for a clandestine meeting or a quick smoke. Also, asking to go to the john is the surest way of getting permission to go someplace else!

It is important to be sensitive to students' toilet needs and to avoid treating the matter of elimination with severity or rigidity. If you are matter-of-fact and good natured, it's almost a surety that excessive running away to the bathroom will not plague your class. If, however, students are going more often than seems reasonable, do some sleuthing and use common sense in stopping the exodus.

OPTIONS: **1** Ask your administrator for help. (It is not uncommon for administrators and teachers to neglect proper supervision of toilets until there is a hassle or to deal with the matter so rigidly that they unwittingly name the battleground between students and faculty.)

2 Begin class activities promptly, and generate so much interest that the students won't want to leave. An atmosphere of aimlessness breeds wanderlust.

3 Check discreetly whether, in fact, the need is there. If it's a ruse, what's the motivation? Could the student be reacting to aversive behavior on your part?

4 Plan with your students, during your class organization (see Appendix) the first week of school, how you will handle your "basic needs" problems. Peer pressure will then govern the students' use or abuse of any privilege.

5 Refer problem students to medical personnel.

6 Talk informally with the class about the problem. ("Too many are going to the toilet during this period. I wonder what the reason is and how we can curtail it," or "I'd like some help with a problem this class has.")

7 Use a sign-out sheet, allowing only one student out at a time.

8 Use a wooden pass that carries the number of the room or the name of the student's teacher. Possession of the pass indicates that the child has permission to go to the toilet.

BILINGUAL CHILDREN

(*see also* Migrant Children, Self-Concept)

CAPSULE: Many classroom frustrations spring from overcrowded classes that include non-English-speaking minorities, such as Filipinos, Chicanos, Samoans, Puerto Ricans, Asians, and others. The concept of "equal opportunity" is really put to the test in such classrooms. However, there is a wealth of opportunity and personal satisfaction due the teacher who is willing to approach the challenge with an open mind and a good measure of empathy. Resist the temptation to expect the student who is learning English as a second language to be totally enamored of all that is new in his school and country. The fact of the matter is, he's probably scared stiff. Show him you are not frightened by him or the challenge he represents, but assure him by your attitude that you are a teacher in the highest sense of the word—and "teacher" here means "reacher." Don't forget that he very likely comes from a culture that holds teachers in high regard, which behooves you to provide a good model in general conduct and speech. Refrain from imitating his speech pattern (so easy to do!), from speaking in an overly slow and laboriously unnatural manner, or from using pidgin English, especially during the period when he is first becoming acquainted with his new language. (He will be learning the pidgin from his peers, regardless of your efforts; by exposing him to standard English you are broadening his language skills.) Don't be surprised if a child coming from a highly structured school system begins acting out when he finds himself in a freer setting. He is, in fact, responding to a form of culture shock. The commonest negative behavior problems generated by non-English-speaking students fall in the extreme areas of acting out and withdrawing, both dramatic indicators of frustration. There are many ways to reduce adjustment and behavior problems that stem from language communication problems. One of the first

things you might do is to select another student to orient the
newcomer to his new surroundings.

OPTIONS: **1** Build the ego of the child by often using his name in connection with a simple request. ("Zi Ping, please turn out the light.")

2 Contact the family of the child in the way appropriate to his culture. (Among the Samoans, for example, the best contact is the Chief or an uncle, not the natural parents.) Assure the family you are interested in them.

3 Engage the child in puppetry activities. The very nature of this medium combines speech practice and reduces self-consciousness since the puppet's lines are spoken backstage and audience distractions are minimal.

4 Exhibit good work of the child. It need not be much, just a sample of a good effort.

5 Give the student an assignment to become teacher and teach his classmates some of his native vocabulary. *Note:* If you, the teacher, will learn some key words in the language of the bilingual child, he can teach you how to say them and you will become learners together.

6 Pair the new student with one who knows the language, and reward the tutor for the gains made by the non-English-speaking student (see Extrinsic Rewards, Appendix). There are several commercial games that teach basic concepts and are pleasantly competitive. Consult your latest professional literature.

7 Provide many opportunities to do group activities that are minimally verbal. Some examples: art work, group body-language exercises, and games involving clapping, numbers, or names. Such activities often generate laughter and allow the student to inconspicuously and happily participate.

8 Send friendly, simply stated notes to the parents, since they are doubtless also learning the new language. ("Dear ———, Maria is happy in school and enjoys her new friends. I hope you will visit school some day and meet the children in Maria's class.")

9 Start the student on reading and writing *after* he has sufficient background in speaking.

10 Teach about the native country of the new student. Introduce English words that sprang from his native tongue; show art work or pictures of art of his country; tell stories of successful people from his culture; show films of his country.

11 Teach meaningful concepts and give the student practice in grasping the concepts in many different ways. For example, teach the multiple meanings of a certain word or idiom (such as *train, train of thought*) via dramatization, visual aids, and first-hand experience.

12 Use bibliotherapy (see Appendix). A child can readily identify with a famous literary character out of his own culture who was also confronted with adjusting to a new country and a new language.

13 Use linguistic-approach materials for teaching the sounds and structure of language.

BLUFFING

(*see also* Arrogance; Self-Concept)

CAPSULE: The bluffer knows he's not going to succeed forever. He's the great pretender, the staller for time, the fantasizer. In the classroom he pretends to know the answer when he doesn't, to have more information than he in fact has, and to have skills that he hasn't. "Insecure" describes him. He has a poor self-image. He is more brash and outspoken than the habitual liar, with whom he differs in that he's pretty sure that if he can delude someone (teacher, parent, priest, classmate) just this once, he can correct his deficiency and no one will be the wiser. A characteristic comment is, "I bluffed my way through that class, but now I'm really going to study." He needs help in sound ways of learning and retaining information so that he won't feel compelled to bluff.

OPTIONS: **1** Allow the student to save face, but also let him know that you know he's bluffing. ("You are skimming the surface of a good point, Pat, but how well have you thought the problem through, really?")

2 Call his bluff. ("Ed, you and I both know that you are not prepared to perform the experiment, so why don't you stop bluffing?")

3 Tell the student, in a private conversation, that you've noticed that he pretends to have read and studied so much more than he obviously has. Let him know that you can help him cope successfully with his lessons so that he won't have to bluff any more (see Study Skills, Appendix).

BLURTING OUT

CAPSULE: Blurting out annoys because it is disruptive, noisy, incongruous, and attention getting. It should be viewed as a behavior that needs toning down for the sake of the class.

OPTIONS: **1** Ask well-phrased thought questions instead of simple recall questions (see Inquiry Process, Appendix).

2 Have the student spend a day silently following a counselor or the principal around the building and grounds—not talking, just sitting and walking. Such a day may prove to him that he can, indeed, live through a day without blurting out.

3 Help the student select some restrainers to help him control his blurts. ("Every time you blurt out, write the time on this card that has your name at the top. We'll use a new card every day, and at the end of the week maybe we can detect your blurtiest times. Perhaps you have a better idea.")

4 Use rewards (see Extrinsic Rewards, Appendix) to change behavior. ("Let's consider trying to control our blurting out by working for a prize. These tokens represent money that can buy things in our school store. For instance, if I place a green token in this manila envelope that is your bank and has your name on it, you have 400 points, or the right to select an item worth $4.00. Every time you blurt out, you lose 50 points and $.50 is subtracted from your original amount. At the end of [time-to-be-determined] you may select a prize worth the amount of money you have left in the bank." [Recommended for upper elementary students.])

BODY ODORS
(*see also* Health Problems)

CAPSULE: It has frequently been said that of all our senses smell is the most easily fatigued. When in the vicinity of fecal, urinary, and ordinary body odor, most people would say the rate of toleration is not rapid enough. Offensive body perspiration odors generate withdrawal from the source. The most considerate associate finds it difficult to refrain from grimacing, talking through his nose, feigning a nasal drip, or taking refuge near a window. Even though applied psychologists have made our society so B.O. and cologne conscious that "the sweat of our brow" is in jeopardy of extinction, body odor problems persist.

Our responses to smells are not only deeply imbedded in our culture, but are also quite resistant to change. Depending upon the circumstances, one may be lucky or unlucky to have a keen sense of smell—lucky when his senses pick up the smell of smoke, gas fumes, burning cookies or roses; not so lucky when his senses pick up the reek of an unbathed body in unwashed clothing or of excessive excretion of overactive glands clad in fresh clothing on a daily bathed body. The person who smells because he hasn't bathed or washed his clothes has a simple problem to solve, but the individual whose body chemistry works against him can rightfully despair. The malodorous ones in the classroom will be one or the other. In either case, they ought to be dealt with delicately until you have decided how to approach this problem. Be frank. Try to avoid embarrassing the student. And need we inject how important it is that you provide a good example of cleanliness yourself?

OPTIONS: **1** Ask the physical education teacher to assist the student.

2 Capitalize on a time to comment somewhat facetiously on "fumes of the figure." For example, during the first minutes of class when the boys have just returned from a hard game of football say, "Alas! Our gridiron heroes have not only brought victory to themselves but have diffused among the entire class the reeking essence of B.O!" This proclamation might generate a healthy discussion about ways for students to make themselves even more "winning."

3 Consult a trustworthy friend of the student with body odor or halitosis. ("Jan, I have a problem. Several students are complaining about Tina. Can you suggest a tactful solution?")

4 Consult school health specialists. They will find tactful ways to approach the immediate problem, as well as the underlying cause.

5 Emphasize awareness of the body—its beauty, its capacity for change, and its care. ("Toni just got a new motorcycle and I see her polishing it and taking very good care of it. Would you say you take as good care of your body as you do your motorcycle, Toni?")

6 Learn about the eating habits of the family and gauge your expectancies accordingly. The student whose mother puts garlic in the Jell-O is going to exude it, no matter what!

7 Present a hypothetical case for students to react to. ("I once had a boss who had such strong body odor I could scarcely be in the same office with him. What would you have done?")

8 Remind students that the skunk is the last to know that he is not "heaven scent." ("Jenny, I'm about to tell you something that I think you aren't aware of. We all have our unique body odor, but yours seems to be stronger recently. Are you aware of it?")

9 Show films on proper body care.

10 Talk directly, honestly, and privately with the student. ("Jim, everybody has problems and I'm taking the liberty today of talking to you about one of yours. The students and I are often aware of your bad breath. Do you have a clue as to what's causing it?")

BOREDOM

CAPSULE: Boredom has become a highbrow excuse for not performing a given task. The statement "I'm bored" is potent because it has accusational and intimidating overtones. To be a party to boredom means one is not stimulating, motivating, or exciting. Who, besides a pewter pot, wants to be dull? If your students speak of boredom or reflect boredom in their attitudes consider the following questions: Are the assignments nearly always the same? Are you overdoing programmed materials? Do you require an excessive amount of memory work? Are you rehashing old stuff on a too-easy level? Are you talking too much? Have you included the students in the planning at all? Are you concerned too much with fixed, pat answers that have no emotional quality, and not enough with imaginative, contemplative thinking that excites and disturbs? Do you really value the student, or are you primarily interested in picking up your paycheck? When was the last time your class witnessed you being excited about an idea? If you have to think hard to answer these, you may have your number-one clue to your students' boredom.

OPTIONS: **1** Allow the class to feel that it has some control over the situation. ("This English class can be conducted in a number of ways: Lecture/exam; individual flight plans [see Appendix]; group-study/project approach; or traditional daily assignments." After briefly describing each possibility, conduct buzz sessions [see Appendix] for discussion and recommendations.)

2 Capitalize on the interests and talents of the students when teaching basic concepts. ("We've observed that the different amounts of water in the glasses produce different tones. Jenny [the bored, musically talented one], will you reproduce the vocal tone of each glass as you strike it?")

3 Provide puzzles, word games, and art supplies that are available and for use without special permission.

4 Reflect the student's feelings. ("American history bores you.") Decipher the response and pursue clues. If the student charges the course with irrelevance, seek out a way to make it relevant, using the student's suggestions—even if they hold little fascination for you.

5 Surprise the students with an unexpected activity. ("I promised you a quiz on *Hamlet* today, but instead we're going over to Mr. Gray's house across the street, and Arnold Frost, who is now playing Hamlet in summer stock, is going to talk with us about the role"; or with primary students: "Instead of using our workbooks today, as we usually do, let's take a walk and see how many things we can find that are oval, round, triangular, square, or rectangular."

BULLYING

(*see also* Self-Concept)

CAPSULE: Bullying is common among children, and unless the pattern is checked or replaced it continues into adulthood. Because the bully is often loud-mouthed and large, he can scare off the weak and intimidate those who hang around, but the fact of the matter is he is scared and crying to himself that the world is cruel. More likely than not, the bully is responding to punitive adults in his life. (Who's bullying *him?*) He needs polite, consistent firmness in his models. In your classroom or school you can curb bullying by providing ground rules that define conduct expected of all students. (These will work better if the students have a part in formulating the rules.) Consider carefully some immediate and long-range efforts to help the student; these could range from deliberately separating him physically from those he bullies to guiding on an intellectual level his understanding of his own behavior.

OPTIONS: **1** Combine a reprimand with a dignified command. ("Jeff, stop bugging Pete and bring me the science kit from the round table.")

2 Construct a sociogram (see Appendix) to learn where the bully's preferences and dislikes lie. Use this information judiciously in grouping and in activities.

3 Discuss the bully in a team meeting (see Appendix) with or without his presence. Try to pinpoint his fears and hold positive reinforcement.

4 Discuss the problems of bullies with the class. Present a hypothetical or real case for discussion, such as "A few years ago I had a student who delighted in bullying those smaller than himself. One day . . ." (see Class Discussions, Appendix).

5 Fight fire with fire. ("Okay, Tim, I've watched you bully Fritz for two weeks now. For the next two days I'm going to give you a taste of what it's like to be bullied.") *Note:* This is a risky technique, but you may be just the one to pull it off successfully.

6 Help the bully interpret his own behavior. ("Jim, the movie we saw showed bullies who wanted attention, bullies who wanted to get even with someone, and bullies who wanted to show who was the boss. Which one did you feel you understood the best?") Then proceed to establish a strategy to follow the next time he feels like playing the role of the bully. Use *his* ideas, instead of yours.

7 Hold out a reward for limited control of bullying (see Extrinsic Rewards, Appendix). Increase the time spans as control improves.

8 Isolate the student. *Caution:* If you isolate him in "the office," those in charge deserve to know why the bully is isolated and what your expectations of them are. This is not a very sound practice, really.

9 Keep a record of the student's bullying incidents and discuss each one matter-of-factly with the bully after a cooling-off period. ("Joe, this incident is different from the one we discussed Wednesday. Let's see how the two are alike and different.")

10 Reinforce the student's good behavior with an observation that may come as a surprise to him. ("Frank, you treated that little girl so gently after she fell off her bike!")

11 Role play (see Appendix). The bully may, for instance, play the role of the one who is bullied. Avoid preaching. Let the activity speak for itself. He may, for the first time, appreciate what his behavior causes another to feel.

12 Study his art work for clues to his inner self.

13 Use bibliotherapy (see Appendix). Assign selected readings (about nonbullies) to help change the student's attitude.

14 Use buzz sessions (see Appendix) to discuss an incident and share group ideas.

15 Use movies or filmstrips to reinforce acceptable playground behavior.

16 Withhold a privilege, demonstrating the fact that the bully reaps the consequences of his behavior. At a softball game, for example, say, "Sam, you have bullied and teased Mack during the entire fourth inning. Please sit on the sidelines for the next two." *Caution:* This is risky, since such an approach is sure to incite anger in Sam and may be harmful to Mack.

BUS CONDUCT

(*see also* Dangerous Conduct)

CAPSULE: Kids love to ride the buses with their friends, and it's not uncommon for rowdiness and even hazardous activities to take place on school buses. It takes a level-headed person, and preferably one slightly hard of hearing, to live with the job of bus driver for very long. The school can make the driver's job easier by planning ahead. This would include setting down guidelines for bus conduct before school starts and making sure the guidelines are made clear to parents and students through letters, homerooms, newspapers, posters, and so forth. If possible, it's wise to limit the length of school bus routes, because discipline problems are bound to arise if students are on buses too long. Whenever possible, have students of comparable ages on buses. And, for goodness' sake, be sure to include student representatives (and, if possible, a bus driver) when drawing up the rules.

OPTIONS: **1** Confer privately with involved students. Ask the right questions to redirect anger. ("Can we list some ways to cope with the problem?") This eliminates taking sides and hurling insults. It also reduces the teacher's temptation to moralize or become vindictive.

2 Consider having a teacher ride the bus as a part of his contractual agreement. (This is applicable to only certain kinds of schools, obviously.)

3 Consider having parents ride the bus on a rotation basis.

4 Establish a hierarchy of treatment for unseemly bus conduct.

- First offense: Hold a conference including the bus driver, the student, and a school official.
- Second offense: Hold a conference including the bus driver, the student, a school official and a parent.
- Third offense: Hold a conference including the student, a school official, and the parents, to consider the student's removal from the bus for a stipulated period of time.

5 Use acceptable bus conduct as a means of accumulating credit toward a reward (see Extrinsic Rewards, Appendix).

6 Use brainstorming (see Appendix) for generating solution ideas among the students. Remember, no ideas are rejected!

7 Use student monitors with prescribed responsibilities mutually agreed upon by students, the school administration, and parents.

C

CARD PLAYING

(see also Gambling)

CAPSULE: Card playing has invaded many schools on an epidemic scale. How it is dealt with depends entirely upon the place the students and administration feel it has in the school program. If cards are a lunchtime diversion, that is one thing. If learning to play cards (bridge, rummy, and so on) is a part of a recreation or activity period, that is another. If cards are used for gambling, that is still another. When cards become an obsession and vie with the curriculum for attention, it can safely be said that they are a problem. Some people categorically reject cards as time wasters, if not the work of the devil! It is certainly true that cards are often associated with gambling, even if the stakes are small and the game is a ladies' luncheon affair.

If card games are a nuisance in a classroom it is almost safe to wager that there is some deficiency in the teaching or the course content. Administrators can render support to all of their teachers by arming them with a well-publicized policy statement regarding card playing, but they probably won't make much of an impression unless the students are involved in formulating the statement. Let's face it; those who play cards enjoy it,—some of them so much that they become addicts. Cards consume time, so unless one has time to spare, card playing can become a student's occupational hazard.

OPTIONS: **1** Be supportive of existing regulations and still enlighten the students regarding democratic avenues for making changes (student council, petitions, and so forth). Even though the outcome may not be favorable to the card players, they will feel that at least they were heard and will be made aware of the consequences of card playing. If the verdict is favorable, they will have the satisfaction of having experienced a proper procedure for effecting change through the democratic process.

2 Discuss card playing in a group meeting (see Class Discussions, Appendix). You might begin with a question like, "Is there a place for card playing in the school setting?" or "Is it possible to play cards without getting hooked on them?"

3 Encourage the student to use a game of cards as a reward for having completed a school assignment, rather than playing cards first and running out of sufficient time to prepare his lessons well.

4 Have the student maintain a record of how he spends his time for one week. If card playing is conspicuously cited on the record and grades, health, and work are suffering, the student needs guidance in planning better use of his time.

5 State your position regarding cards. ("There will be no card playing in this class," or "Cards may be played in this class at certain times; I'd like your suggestions regarding those times.")

CARELESSNESS

(*see also* Forgetfulness; Vandalism; Wastefulness)

CAPSULE: A common complaint of teachers and school administrators is that the students are careless about the equipment and materials in the school. They are careless about library books, about the amount of paper and water they use, and about the care of the buildings in general. Furthermore, they complain that reproaches are often met with "I-don't-care" responses.

Similarly, parents are hard put to control the loss of sweaters, baseball mitts, tennis shoes, rackets and so on. Lost and found departments in schools are known to have enough unclaimed goods to start a well-stocked thrift shop. It is not uncommon for a mother to inspect the accumulated goods for one thing and to find her long-lost monogrammed cashmere sweater among the heap! Unfortunately, mealtime is often the battleground for feuds over lost or mislaid items.

In the face of attacks from teachers and parents, and not knowing the value of things, children take one of two routes. They feign or feel indifference, or they dissolve into penitent tears. In the former case, the adult is likely to respond with belligerence and threats, and in the latter, with overindulgence and overprotection. Neither is good for the child. The best approach is to teach the child that this cold world requires that he be responsible for his own actions, that adults will not always be around to bail him out even if it were good for him, and that a mature person, once he gets the hang of it, enjoys being held responsible for the logical consequences of his behavior.

OPTIONS: **1** Avoid preaching, scolding, or nagging when carelessness is the problem. Unless his experiences have created a pathological indifference, the student is reproaching himself sufficiently.

2 Be friendly but firm about the fact that he must face up to the consequences of his carelessness. ("I'm sorry, Jim, that you left one of your tennis shoes on the bus, but there is no way to get it now and there are no extra shoes, so you'll have to sit on the sidelines today.") Mothers who rush to the store for another pair of shoes are teaching the child that carelessness is not detrimental; they perpetuate the very behavior they say they want to eliminate.

3 Find opportunities to praise the student for his or her improved attention to the care of things. ("Jill, I've noticed how much better you've been taking care of your books and the things in your locker lately.")

4 Use common sense about entrusting something of extremely high value to a young person, such as sending a collector's item with a child to school. Losing or damaging it might incur the wrath of adults. It is better to assume the responsibility yourself, thereby conveying the value concept as well as your willingness to share the rare object with others. Values are absorbed; they are not forced.

CHEATING

(*see also* Deviousness; Fearfulness; Grades)

CAPSULE: Cheating is a product of pressure. It is not enough to say, "Everybody does it—so what?" The fact is that *not* everybody does it, though cheating does occur to an alarming degree throughout our schools and universities. Students cheat for many reasons—some to compensate for a physical disability, some to compensate for failure to study, and some to compensate for a poor memory, but all because they are afraid. A system that overvalues acceptance in "the best schools" or that prizes a letter grade over competence to perform a task plants the seeds of its own destruction, and widespread cheating has proved to be the consequence. The guilty are legion—students, parents, teachers, and the general public—who tenaciously embrace the grading system that plagues most students and annoys many teachers. In an era of lunar explorations it appears that educators can only be graded R (retarded) if they cannot lead the students and their parents out of the abyss that generates cheating and kills inquiry and creativity. However, there are things you can do to minimize the practice with your students. Begin by checking up on your expectations of the students in light of their backgrounds and potential by teaching them some valid study skills and by discussing the psychology of fear and how it manifests itself in times of stress. Alert them to the fact that you are aware of the pressures that sometimes compel people to corrupt behavior.

Sometimes the old query, "How would you like the doctor who cheated his way through medical school to do open heart surgery on you?" gives students pause. Convey the attitude that you expect your students *not* to cheat. If you transmit the message that they're a bunch of cheating slobs, you have blown the whistle for an exciting race—one in which they're primarily interested in seeing how many can avoid getting caught this time! Here are some specific things you can do to reduce students' temptations to cheat and to restore positive attitudes toward any kind of evaluation.

OPTIONS: **1** Ask the students to contribute the questions for the exam. ("Next week's exam will be composed of questions formulated by you students. Work in pairs and submit two recall (memory) questions, two hypothetical problems, and two multiple-choice questions.")

2 Consult others, such as a counselor or a favorite adult friend of the student, who can help you work with the student who needs his self-confidence bolstered.

3 Control the testing environment by moving the furniture and separating students who "help" each other.

4 Discuss the problem with the cheater privately. Learn how he can be freed of the need to cheat, then experiment with some of the ideas the two of you discussed. ("Pat, you say written exams scare you to death and that your dad insists that you get good grades, so you feel forced to cheat—even though you know it's dishonest. As a result of our conference, we've agreed to administer two kinds of tests for awhile—the regular written one and an oral one, with the higher grade going on your record.")

5 Discuss the subject of cheating (see Class Discussions, Appendix). Agree upon ways to deal with the problem. Later, if the problem occurs, you will have some guidelines that were jointly drawn up. ("Jim, according to our agreement, your paper is disqualified and you will be tested tomorrow during study hall.")

6 Engage the students in sharing and in trying many ways to cheat on an exam. ("Yesterday we talked about cheating and nobody really thought it was *right,* but everyone admitted he'd either cheated or thought about it. Today I'm going to give you a different assignment. You are to prepare for the science test for next Friday with the idea of cheating *without getting caught.* See how many ingenious ways you can conceive.") *Note:* This may be your most creative lesson of the year; don't be put off by calls from parents who think you're immoral!

7 Give credit, where applicable, for the *process* as well as for the final answer.

8 Give open-book or group-participation exams. The former emphasizes skills other than rote memory, and the latter emphasizes a cooperative approach to problem solving.

9 Give some oral exams, where cheating is more difficult.

10 Move inconspicuously to the student to curtail the effort to cheat. For example, if Sally is reading the notes written on her palm, whisper to her, "Sally, why don't you wipe those answers off with a tissue now and later I'll give you some help with those problems. Go on and do the easy ones now."

11 Show a film on cheating and discuss it without preaching.

12 Use alternative versions of a test so that students sitting next to one another have different sets.

CLIQUES

CAPSULE: To many students, security means being in a clique. It is a hedge against loss of identity—a safe niche. People are accepted in cliques for a variety of reasons: because, for instance, they have a car, a beach home, a job, or easy access to money. Inclusion may be subtly or openly based on religion, race, or social mores. Cliques are a social phenomenon. Members slip in and out of them as life shapes them, so accept cliques and be prepared to lend a shoulder to the bruised one who gets pushed out.

OPTIONS: **1** Discuss values with the student and try to interest him in analyzing his feelings about being included or excluded. ("List the names of those in the clique. Beside each name write what you feel each member contributes to the group, then beside each name put an M if your mother approves of the person, a W if he contacts you on weekends, a $ if he borrows money from you, a T if he telephones you.") Such an exercise may clarify the student's thinking and alter his feelings (see Values Clarification, Appendix).

2 Lead the entire class into a discussion (see Class Discussions, Appendix) of cliques and their *raison d'être*.

3 Read or produce plays that deal with being in or out of a clique. The students can write their own scripts.

4 Use role playing (see Appendix).

CLOWNING

(see also Mimicry)

CAPSULE: The class clown might very well be your most misunderstood student. He says, by his conduct, "I want attention; I know how to get it, but I'm also worried about what others think of me, and I'd like to be taken seriously." All of this is hard to believe when the rascal has sabotaged a perfectly good plan and temporarily stripped you of control.

For a starter, ascertain, if you can, who the clown's model is. Then consider his strengths that could be affirmed with a natural diminution of the clowning. Instead of the easy put-down, try for some shrewd understanding of why the student needs to clown so much. It's a fact that clowns usually live up to the expectations of their teachers, so first moves by you might include silent recognition of his funniness—perhaps only a fleeting smile. If you opt for sarcastic warnings, expect to herald encores. The battle is on.

Examine objectively such management details as seating arrangement, your mode of handling routines (roll call, lunch count, and so on), and the class schedule. Above all, scrutinize the pace of your teaching approach. One can actually promote horseplay by being disorganized or insensitive to the flow of activities. It's much simpler to revamp classroom routines than to "declown" a student. Finally, you will have to decide whether the student is a clown or a real troublemaker, in which case you may need outside help.

OPTIONS: **1** Build into your schedule (whether a period or a full day) release times when it's O.K. to be the class clown without censure.

2 Draw up a flight plan (see Appendix) with the clown, designing it to meet his comic needs yet showing him how he can control them. The flight plan might begin with a study of famous comics' lives and culminate with the student's one-man show.

3 Give the clown responsibility that demands concentration. Find an isolated place for him to work. The task should make him feel important as well as convince him that you take him seriously. ("Fred, these science cards are all mixed up and they need to be sorted before Mr. K. calls for them. A few are missing, so please place the numbers of the lost ones on the board. Thank you.")

4 Interpret the clown's goals for him. ("You crave attention and you feel clowning is the best way to get it.")

5 Laugh with the clown but refrain from overdoing your appreciation; the latter makes the other students impatient with your overindulgence and doesn't help the clown. It's better to be direct and make the limitations clear. ("That moment of levity should brace us for the seriousness of the next few minutes. Get ready for your quiz.")

6 Praise the student about something that carries the inference that he's sensitive, not just a clown. ("Dick, your clowning around is fun for all of us in moderate doses. I'm glad to see you establish your own limits.")

7 Preempt and redirect the student's disposition to clown. ("Lance, you act as though you have a good idea brewing. Tell us about it.")

8 Reverse roles with the clown. ("Jeff, your imitations of the animals in the zoo are amusing. We'd like to join your menagerie. You be the teacher, I'll be Jeff, and we'll all have a turn.")

9 Show a film that focuses on the class clown. Discuss it objectively.

10 Use a questionnaire (see Appendix) to learn more about the student. Revealing questions might include: Who are your favorite TV characters? Who is your favorite relative? What's the funniest thing that ever happened to you? If you could have three wishes, what would they be?

11 Use dramatics in some form. Resist the temptation to always cast the clown in a comedy role. State your faith in his competence to handle a straight role. ("Ted, because you seem a natural for the role of the comic, the casting committee has recommended that you take the part of the priest, where your acting ability can really be demonstrated.")

12 Use puppetry as a mode of expression. The clown may perceive that he doesn't have to be "out front" in order to entertain.

CLUMSINESS

CAPSULE: The clumsy child is as upsetting to himself as he is to things and persons around him. Dishes and silverware get in his way. Chairs and tables seem to walk right up to him. He can't play catch or rollerskate very well. Falling off a horse or a bike is easy. One doesn't blame him for holding a healthy disdain for people who seem to glide through life. He gets yelled at for being so clumsy, and often he strikes back in ways that don't increase his popularity. He's a student with motor-coordination problems who may elect to compensate for his clumsiness by spending his time doing safe things like reading and sitting around.

According to some literature, one-fifth of our elementary-school students have significant motor-skills problems. The family physician may be able to identify the reasons the child has coordination problems, but the important thing is to help him get to know his body and what it can do—with grace.

OPTIONS: **1** Arrange for small groups of children with similar problems to work under the direction of the physical education teacher or dance instructor. *Note:* The physical education teacher can apprise the classroom teacher of the hierarchy of skills the student should attempt.

2 Engage the child in sit-down eye-hand coordination activities, such as marbles, or jacks.

3 Give him gradual experience handling inexpensive breakables. Praise his success, no matter how small.

4 Seat him in an uncongested area, away from breakables and near big kids who can resist the bumps.

5 Share embarrassing moments in class discussion (see Appendix) and mention clumsiness as one of the reasons. ("I'll never forget the time I felt I had two left feet . . .")

6 Talk good naturedly about his awkwardness. ("Rob, you're a racer—just like a greyhound—and I notice when you crash into things you feel terrible. What do you say you try moving like a sloth for a change?")

COMPLAINING, Chronic

(*see also* Attention Seeking; Jealousy; Self-Concept; Tattling)

CAPSULE: The chronic complainer is an unhappy first cousin of the tattler. Things rarely go right for him because if they did, he'd be stripped of his attention-getting device. Chances are he's unconsciously imitating someone in the home or neighborhood. In addition to suggestions mentioned in other sections, you might find the following helpful.

OPTIONS: **1** Ask the complainer to refrain from voicing his unhappiness but to submit his complaint in writing.

2 Have an all-school or classroom suggestion box for students so they can register complaints freely. Deal with the complaints in a democratic manner.

3 Help the student become aware of his or her complaining attitude by requesting that he (she) state something positive with each complaint. ("Eve, you may not be aware that you are falling into the complaining habit, but the rest of us are. Suppose you allow yourself the luxury of your complaints but always include a plus with your minus—like 'The cafeteria food is lousy, *but* the silverware is clean!' ")

4 Rephrase the student's complaint in a declarative sentence. ("Mr. J. is the worst chemistry teacher in the school; he never gives a fair grade.")

5 Tabulate the student's complaints and present them to him. ("Tom, today I recorded the things you complained about. Here they are—twelve of them.") The list could be the basis for a private conference.

COMPULSIVENESS

(*see also* Stubbornness)

CAPSULE: Compulsive people come in all shapes, colors, and ages. In the classroom, they are the ones who view anything that is loosely organized, free, or spontaneous as a threat. They find comfort in clinging to preciseness and detail—deviations upset them. Consumed with detail, this type of person is sometimes labelled rigid, perfectionist, intolerant. As might be expected, many compulsive children have learned their behavior from a fastidious parent who places order well above divergent thinking. Compulsive students not only fare well but often "overachieve" in highly structured classrooms. There is nothing "wrong" with being compulsive. As with any other quality or behavior, it is the *degree* that is significant. Watch for opportunities in your classroom to help children experience the harmlessness of trial and error, of taking a chance, or of hazarding a guess.

OPTIONS: **1** Accommodate the student's need for certainty in one subject and demonstrate the success one can have by trial and error in another. ("Phil, you have learned your rules for decoding well, and this lesson is perfect. Now let's turn to this science problem. Try to find three possible solutions . . .")

2 Confer with parents to learn to what extent perfection and order are expected at home. Diametrically opposed expectations in the home and in school can confuse a student.

3 Engage the student in activities and assignments that do not put a premium on minute detail and exactness.

4 Refer the student to the school counselor if compulsiveness seems excessive.

5 Tell the parent you would rather have the child explore more and learn to accept errors than to limit himself because he doesn't want to err. (The parent may receive new insight, and the pressures at home may be released.)

CRUSHES

(see also Demonstrativeness)

CAPSULE: Crushes are most common among high-school and college students who are drawn to their teachers for reasons other than scholarship. They also occur on the elementary-school and junior-high levels. There, they are usually brief, and, with common sense and courtesy on the part of the teacher, they pass naturally into oblivion.

Symptoms of a "bad case" include feigned inability to understand a lesson, requests for additional help after school, missing the bus, hanging around, helplessness, and acting out in class—most anything to get attention.

The new teacher, just out of college, is vulnerable. His zeal for openness and his desire to be liked are sometimes misinterpreted. Usually, peer pressure keeps the case within bounds in the classroom, but when the postman brings you love notes and you receive telephone calls at your home, you will know you have a problem! There is always the off chance that a "spurned" student will make a real or imagined charge against a favorite teacher, so be on your guard!

OPTIONS: **1** Avoid situations that create opportunities to be alone with the smitten student. The slightest, most casual touch can be grossly misunderstood.

2 Have a professional colleague of the same sex as the student talk to him or her if the behavior is excessive or embarrassing.

3 Ignore the student's overtures.

4 Talk privately, aware of the risk involved, with the student.

CRYING

CAPSULE: Crying is a form of hostility and may be interpreted as saying "I feel left out," "I want to punish you," or "I want to be boss." Resist the temptation to show the child who's boss, because you will most certainly lose. Become an expert in analyzing the differences among types of crying—crying caused by sympathetic feelings for another person or a pet, crying caused by physical hurts or illness, or crying caused by the need for attention or revenge. The latter type is usually the product of a successful tactic both at home and in school. Because tears are among the most powerful of weapons, consistency in dealing with them is absolutely necessary. It is of utmost importance that a united family and professional approach be used. The male crier deserves to be reminded that it is not unmanly to cry, that it is important to show one's real feelings, and that crying is one of those ways. Deal warmly and firmly with the student. Remember that any behavior that has become habitual will not be relinquished instantaneously, so be patient (and maybe long-suffering) for the good of the child.

OPTIONS: **1** Ask the student to use the first person when expressing himself. ("I am so mad," instead of "*You [he]* made me do it.") This will check, to some degree, his penchant for blaming others and feeling sorry for himself.

2 Change the activity and tempo of the class, diverting attention away from the crier. Play a march, for instance, and have everybody march or clap his hands.

3 Consult professional help.

4 Convey the idea that it is the behavior, *not* the student, that is unsatisfactory. ("I like Jimmy, but I get upset when those tears start flowing.")

5 Devise a prevention game with the crier. ("As soon as you feel a cry coming on, come to my desk and ask for the tissue box. That will be a signal to me that you are feeling upset. It will also be a signal to me to leave you alone until you've dried your tears and we can talk about your feelings.") This places some responsibility on the crybaby and tells him you'll be talking later. Keep notes on your talks.

6 Exhibit, without comment, the good work of the child.

7 Establish an alliance between the crier and an older student in one of the upper grades. Keep the relationship uncluttered—just friendly (see Junior Counselors, Appendix).

8 Hold a class discussion (see Appendix). Discuss why the student cries. ("Jimmy is upset and has been crying most of the morning. I wonder why he is crying.") The insights of the students will astound you! Plan together as a class how to best help the crier.

9 Hold a meeting of all teachers who deal with the crier (see Team Meetings, Appendix). *Caution:* It is very important that no member of the team "cheat" by digressing from the strategy the team agrees upon, or all will be lost and the crybaby will correctly say, "See! It works!"

10 Interpret for the crybaby why he behaves as he does. ("You are bidding for my attention and trying to make me feel guilty when I don't stop everything and give it to you," or "You feel you can't do the work, but you've already shown me you really can, so you must be crying to get my attention.")

11 Listen to what the crybaby says in his noncrying moments. Look for clues to feelings about failure, favoritism, or friends. Is he modeling his behavior after someone else? Restate his feelings in simple, declarative statements.

12 Place the crier, temporarily, with a different class and a different teacher.

13 Provide tissues and leave the sobber alone, allowing time for the natural aftermath of the problem.

14 Reinforce normal (noncrying) behavior without any reference to the habit of crying. ("Sandy, Jim, and Sue were good sports about being moved to the other team at the last moment. Let's give them a hand.")

15 Show films that deal with crying and ways of diminishing it.

16 Tally and graph the incidence of crying, and periodically show the student the progress being made.

17 Tape-record the sobber. A replay of the child's histrionics might prove a deterrent. (They may, however, encourage the student to outdo himself, so play it by ear and use good judgment!)

18 Use a reward system (see Extrinsic Rewards, Appendix) to change the crybaby's behavior. ("Sally, you have cried for ten minutes today. From now on I'm going to keep a record of how many minutes you cry. When you get your crying down to eight minutes, I'll give you a token. When you cry only six minutes, I'll give you another; four minutes, another; two minutes, another; and when you're down to a sniffle, another. When you have five tokens, you can exchange them for a prize.") *Note:* Once the crying has been eliminated, be sure noncrying is rewarded through social approval (a smile, or a pat).

D

DANGEROUS CONDUCT

(*see also* Attention Seeking; Bus Conduct; Self-Concept)

CAPSULE: The bold, daring one thrives on dangerous conduct. He's the one who climbs out the classroom window, walks the ledge, and seconds later waves at you from the top of the flagpole. His conduct is a blatant call for attention and help—perhaps an effort to compensate for feelings of inadequacy. Sooner or later he may discover the folly of his conduct, but the price, as well as the fall, may be very high. It is the duty of teachers and parents to caution children not only to be aware of potentially dangerous situations but also to know the difference between the normal risks of daily living and foolhardiness.

OPTIONS: **1** Brainstorm (see Appendix) possibilities of dangerous conduct that could take place around a school. Remember that the brainstorming method of evoking ideas is rapid-fire, and there will be many zany ideas, but they are not to be censored. Exposure of a fascinating, bizarre stunt is not likely to move a student to try it unless he already has psychotic tendencies; in fact, the fantasy privilege would, if anything, lessen any desire to try the act.

2 Establish, with the help of the students, safe conduct guidelines.

3 Hold a class discussion (see Appendix) that focuses on dangerous conduct in and out of school. The lead question might be: What is the most dangerous thing you ever saw anyone do? Other possibilities are: What's the most dangerous thing you ever did in your life? What compels people to dangerous conduct? What are some ways to discourage others from doing foolish and dangerous things?

4 Invite a member of the fire department rescue squad to talk about preventing dangerous situations.

5 Reward obvious efforts to practice safe conduct or to constrain someone who is behaving recklessly. If the students go for a token or point system based on a self-management program (see Appendix), they may want to include "safe conduct" as one of the categories that earns points.

6 Take the class on a tour of the school, with the express assignment of detecting zones that might stimulate dangerous conduct. Return to the classroom and discuss your observations.

DAWDLING

CAPSULE: Some look upon the dawdler as a relaxed, creative thinker. Perhaps the majority feel he is a time waster who likes to deal in trifles. Most will agree that the dawdler has developed a clever way to forestall detection and scolding because he is physically in motion, doing his "own thing" at a snail's pace. To "Hurry up" he says, "I'm coming." To "Clean you desk," he says, "I'm sorting my crayons." In addition to being poky, he can figure out the kinds of activities that are just commendable enough to keep you from saying they're not important. After studying the dawdler through the usual means—past record, health history (How's his hearing?), conferences with those who know him best—there is one best thing to do, and that is to *retrain* him. The following approaches may suggest some ways to do this.

OPTIONS:

1 Design a flight plan (see Appendix) so that the dawdler can see how one task leads to another and culminates in a satisfying creative activity. The age and interest span of the student must dictate the complexity of the flight. Sufficient emphasis must be put on successfully meeting time limits and target dates so that he is neither discouraged nor immobilized.

2 Focus on successful attainment of goals within limits. ("Joan, you should be able to finish your graph in ten minutes," instead of "Joan, why are you dawdling so when you know you have only fifteen minutes to finish your graph?")

3 Give him many opportunities to engage in art activities. A study of his art work will give clues to his interests, moods, patterns of behavior. Care must be taken, however, not to read too much into a child's art work unless one is professionally trained to do so.

4 Pair one dawdler with another. Watch which one emerges as dominant, then acknowledge him or her. Ignore the more dawdly one, but don't discourage him (her) from listening in on your conversation. ("Mary, I noticed you didn't fritter away so much time during science today, and look how much you accomplished!")

5 Pair the dawdler with a more organized child. Reward the organized child (see Extrinsic Rewards, Appendix) for increments made by the dawdler. ("Gary, every time this week you are able to get George to gym class without dawdling you'll receive ten points toward the next Field Day.")

6 Prepare the student for the possibility of being excluded from an activity sometime in the future if his dawdling continues. Having given him fair warning, you will not be unjust to leave him behind. ("John, you knew that the bus would leave at 9:40 for the Art Center and you continued to dawdle. Since you are not ready and the bus must leave, I've made arrangements for you to work in Miss Bennett's room until we return.") Reaping the consequences of his conduct may sharpen the student's awareness of his problem.

7 Talk to the dawdler about his pattern of behavior and *listen* to his ideas about his conduct. (Is he bored? Tired? Hungry? Lonely?)

8 Use rewards to challenge the student to diminish dawdling (see Extrinsic Rewards, Appendix).

9 Use the observation technique (see Appendix). Consider adjusting activities for the dawdler in light of the findings. If the observations reflect more concentration between 9:00 and 11:00, for instance, then structure the lessons accordingly.

10 Use videotaping to show the students how they behave. Seeing yourself as others see you can be a powerful motivator for change!

DEMONSTRATIVENESS

(see also Crushes)

CAPSULE: Students smitten with "puppy love" or deeper feelings often manifest their affection with little inhibition on the campus, on the bus, in the hallways, and in the classroom. Any reminder, no matter how tactful, might be met with disdain. What can a frumpy old schoolteacher possibly know about "young love"? The Victorian handshake and a peck on the cheek have become passionate clinches, with or without audience. Often, insecure youth latch onto a "steady" and feel obliged to convey the "hands off" message by being ultrademonstrative. When the romance is over, you can expect them to be in the doldrums, making "never again" pronouncements. What should one do when demonstrativeness actually interferes with the student's learning and with your teaching procedures? Approach the matter with good humor and excellent teaching, which are deterrents, if not cures.

OPTIONS: **1** Discuss acceptable social conduct in groups (see Class Discussions, Appendix).

2 Hold an Ann Landers meeting (see Appendix). The first questioner might say, "I'd like to know what some of you think about showing affection for each other in school." Count on conservative as well as "boundless" points of view to surface.

3 Show the students that your heart isn't cold by good naturedly referring to their demonstrative behavior. ("Jan and Don, you're going to need all four hands for this next assignment, so why don't you move your desks apart and grab ahold of this string that's being passed around?")

4 Use a listing exercise (see Values Clarification, Appendix) to help solidify feelings regarding what is acceptable behavior for each student as an individual. ("List *x* number of things that embarrass you," or "List *x* number of ways one can show affection for others.")

DEPENDENCY

(*see also* Playing Dumb; Self-Concept)

CAPSULE: The dependent child hesitates to act before he has the teacher's approval. He may have been conditioned to behave this way by overprotective or critical parents. Somehow he has come to feel that he can't trust himself and must depend on others. It is not uncommon for overly dependent children to resist learning to read. While this kind of behavior is most evident from ages four to six, it can persist into adulthood. Eventually, such a person may come to hate those who fostered this dependence, because he was robbed of precious time, during which he should have been thinking for himself.

OPTIONS: **1** Confer with the parents and agree upon strategies that will develop the child's independence. If it becomes clear that the parents handle the child inconsistently, perhaps you should refer them to the school counselor or psychologist.

2 Encourage the student to identify something that troubles him and that he would like to find the answer to, then help him to independently cope with his problem. You may begin by (1) naming the problem, (2) determining the cause of the problem, (3) predicting the solution that might succeed, (4) trying out the favored hypothesis. *Note:* This approach may be used on any age level.

3 Praise obvious efforts to become more independent. ("I was glad to see you walk home from school by yourself today, Gina.")

4 Seat the child by an independent worker who will not "help" the child but will provide a good model.

5 Show the student how he can use what he has learned. ("Bill, you have learned your multiplication tables; now use them to solve this problem.")

6 Wean the child away from his dependency by establishing a hierarchy of steps and moving him through it (see Option 2 in *School Phobia*).

DEVIOUSNESS

(*see also* Cheating; Lying)

CAPSULE: To be labeled devious is highly uncomplimentary, for it implies manipulation and deception. The devious student has lost trust in adults. He feels that he can deal with them best through chicanery. He expects adults to respond adversely to his wily ways, perhaps because some have conveyed to him that they think he's sneaky and crooked. He may even want them to think so, so that his negative view of adults can be confirmed. Adults working with the devious student have the task of convincing him that he can achieve his goals via more direct routes.

OPTIONS: **1** Be generous in your praise of the student who is habitually devious but who surprisingly breaks his pattern. The student may catch the message that directness carries its reward. ("You gave a very direct answer to Mr. Z. when he questioned you about _____ and it was easy to see that he admired you for it.")

2 Refuse to submit to the devious student's effort to trap you into open rejection of his behavior. (Instead of, "That's Tricky Ricky for you!" try "Thanks for being so open about _____.")

3 Show the student you prefer straightforwardness instead of beating around the bush. ("Give it to me straight now, Ron. Save the detours for another time.")

4 Trust the student. If you cannot, tell him why and demonstrate that you are ready to help him cope with problems less deviously. Your honest concern for him will break down some of his defenses.

DISCOURAGEMENT

(*see also* Fearfulness, Self-Concept; Underachievers)

CAPSULE: Several years ago one of the authors was asked by a family member for some ideas on a topic. The given responses met with, "No, that won't work," "Sorry, that's no good," "Not too bad, but not good enough," until a feeling of uselessness took over and the suggestion was made, "Instead of turning down my ideas as fast as I come up with them, why don't you just say, 'That's an idea!' and I'll be encouraged to continue?" Since then, "That's an idea!" has been a Collins byword. The moral of this story is that definitive rejection kills; a spark of recognition kindles.

In addition to recognition, the discouraged student needs help in distinguishing between short- and long-range goals. It's quite possible that the long-range goals set forth by the adults in his life are so far-reaching and frightening that he can't even do anything about the immediate goals. Student involvement in establishing objectives diminishes this kind of stress; it also makes teaching easier and more fun.

The discouraged child must be helped to conquer the fears that dominate his behavior. He may cower in a cloak of average or respectable performance rather than endeavor to excel, because he is afraid of failing, afraid of appearing silly or stupid, afraid of being made fun of by people who rate high with him, afraid of calling attention to himself—afraid, afraid, afraid. The renowned bacteriologist, August von Wasserman, we are told, failed over 600 times before he succeeded in producing the serum that bears his name. What a pity if he had stopped just one try short of success! Teachers must become experts at helping students accept errors as parts of problem solving instead of as stigmatic seals of disapproval. When errors become stepping stones instead of ledges on which to perch unhappily, they may be more effective than a series of rapid-fire successes.

The discouraged student also needs to be shown how an idea can transform inactivity into power. Witness the transformation that takes place when an otherwise indolent, slow moving housewife receives a call from an old acquaintance who will be there for lunch in half an hour. The adrenalin flows at such a rate that a full day's work is accomplished in that half-hour! Never underestimate the power of an idea; it is potency personified. Its place is in the classroom.

Discouraged students become hopeful through (1) recognition of their honest efforts, (2) a vision of attainable goals, (3) elimination of fear of failure, and (4) a promise of experiencing something that has special significance or value to them. You may add ideas of your own to the following, which may be used with the discouraged student.

OPTIONS: **1** Acknowledge the student's contributions without put-downs, sarcasm, or half-hearted acceptance. ("That's an idea!")

2 Ask a discouraged child to teach others how to do something. ("Eric, Shawn would like you to teach him how to tie his shoe-laces," or "Sue, you are the only one in the class who knows anything about Japanese paper folding; could you teach these boys who want to learn to make folded fish?")

3 Devise a flexible schedule (see Appendix) for the student.

4 Display samples of the student's work that will call others' attention to his capabilities. Peer motivation is potent.

5 Enlist the discouraged student's help in tutoring younger children, and hold him responsible for recommending techniques that will work. Some of the discouraged one's ideas may then be turned into useful ways of working with *him*.

6 Help the student analyze possible reasons for his state of discouragement through lead questions such as, "Who are you most like, your mother or your father?" "What subject holds your interest the longest and why?" "If money were no object, what would you like to do for a living?"

7 Individualize and personalize some of the student's assignments (see Flight Plan, Appendix). The graduated progression built into the lessons should encourage him.

8 Talk to the student, in an informal setting outside the classroom, about his hopes and aspirations. Restate some of them so that he knows that you understand and can help him clarify his thinking. ("You like playing your sax and drums more than anything else in the world. Making a living playing in a band is your big dream.")

9 Use a listing technique to identify concerns. ("List twenty things you resist, resent, or fear." When the student has done this, ask him to label each item with an S, H, or C, indicating whether the concern is localized in School, Home, or Community in general.) Listing is a nonthreatening way to get students to look at a problem analytically. With little children who cannot yet write well, ask them to tell you what to write for them. The list for young ones will be shorter.

DOMINEERING CHILDREN

(*see also* Abrasiveness; Bullying)

CAPSULE: Domineering describes the person who behaves arbitrarily, and overbearingly and who wants to be boss. Whatever the explainable reasons for this attitude, he is usually unpopular. Perhaps his physical size, his place in the family (first, middle, or last child), or his model of conduct (domineering father or mother) contributes significantly to his attitude. Very often he is aggressive on the athletic field and, at the same time, a poor loser because the family has placed unrealistic emphasis on winning or on upholding the family's record. Whatever accounts for his loud, dogmatic approach to dealing with others, he needs to reduce his intensity of conduct, and the way that holds out the most hope is to help him identify his goals. The following suggestions will help you help him.

OPTIONS: **1** Counsel the domineering student. ("Pat, you create some problems for yourself with your domineering attitude.") Suggest then that he may be dominating situations because he wants to be the "big shot," that he wants to "put some people in their place and even a score," or simply that he craves attention and doesn't know how else to get it. When the student is able to state what he feels his goal is, you will be in a position to help him attack his problem. The initiative for change must come from him.

2 Establish time limits for talking or using materials. Children who announce "Glen's time is up!" exercise greater influence than the teacher.

3 Reinforce any small sign of improved behavior. ("Russ, you are working like a good team member.")

4 Solicit from your students, through class discussions (see Appendix), ways of coping with abrasive behaviors, which could include a domineering attitude, and agree to try some of the approaches if incidents ever arise. For example, the class may decide that a domineering student will be asked by the class chairman to leave the room until he can be a contributing member of the group. Peer pressure is often more effective than adult pressure.

5 Tell a young child who is dominating an interest center that others aren't having a chance as long as he is there, so he can play in another spot by himself until he is ready to rejoin the group.

6 Videotape small-group activities that may reveal very clearly that the domineering student is inclined to take over. Discuss the film objectively, asking each student to evaluate his own behavior, not that of others. Expect observations like, "I didn't realize that I talked so much!" or "I didn't realize I'm so mousy."

DOODLING

CAPSULE: Doodling is an analyst's delight when the squiggles and scrawls disclose something significant about his patient's personality. Doodling in the classroom is an irritant to some teachers, who feel that only direct attention to them manifests guaranteed thinking. Doodling is a harmless expression of something—but of what? It could mean deep concentration or the first blushes of a new idea. Detectives and historians collect doodles. The manner in which you deal with the doodler will probably depend upon whether or not *you're* a "doodle bug."

OPTIONS: **1** Have the students display their doodles for others to enjoy and study.

2 Request that students keep a certain section of their notebook for doodling so that they don't cover their assignment papers and desks with their doodles.

3 Talk about the doodling done by such well-known public figures as J. F. Kennedy, Kissinger, and Nixon. Conjecture about the significance of their favorite formations with pen and pencil. Playing amateur psychologist can be amusingly diverting.

DRESS PROBLEMS

CAPSULE: It's amazing how one's tolerance for dress and general grooming modes keeps broadening! Certainly the public's tolerance for exposed anatomy has been accelerated by the "a-peeling" garb of the Age of Aquarius! But note, as well, how the pendulum brought in the "layered look," with garments atop garments. It's true that dress codes, which were once standard procedure in most schools, are dwindling in public schools and are being challenged in some private schools. For most private and military schools dress problems do not exist.

School authorities should remember that unless they have planned cooperatively with the students, parents, and faculty on how to deal with the dress and grooming problem, they may have trouble. Further, if the same authority cannot be happy without dictating the code, he'd better look for a safe retreat. Rigid regulations regarding dress and grooming bespeak a single-value system and nullify lofty claims to "recognition of individual differences." This is not to say that controls regarding school dress are completely passé; it is rather a plea for emphasis on standards of conduct, not school rules. This approach minimizes friction over proper school dress.

Pertinent reminders: If a dress code exists, it should be widely publicized through school news media (handbook, newspaper, daily bulletins). Parents should be apprised of the dress code by means of an official communication. When dress matters are discussed with an offender, the adult who has the best rapport with the student should handle it, and that may *not* be the vice principal! Furthermore, the student's attire shouldn't affect his grades one way or the other. A rule of thumb might be: Fads come and go. Don't let them throw you. If the fads don't interfere with learning, don't do anything, unless you're very sure that you're the best judge or that you must be boss to that extent.

OPTIONS: **1** Apprise students of areas in which rules are firm, and at the same time remind them of areas in which they may establish their own rules and of how to go about doing so.

2 Be firm, but kind, when it becomes necessary to withdraw a student from class (or school) because of indecent apparel. ("Ginny, may I say without offending you that your dress is very fitting, perhaps too much so for school? Mr. Black says the boys just can't concentrate on their chemistry experiments because of your outfit, and I believe I can count on you to get the class back on an even keel.")

3 Compliment the student in question when he or she is pleasingly attired, but be matter-of-fact. ("That's a smart outfit, Susie," instead of "Wow!")

4 Discuss the psychology of fashion—how everything we do tells something about our inner drives and motivation. This kind of discussion is a natural in social studies, literature, and psychology classes.

5 Enforce consistently any rules of dress, good speech, and so forth that have been adopted.

6 Engage the skills of the sewing teacher to work with students who would like to sew simple garb. Don't exclude the boys!

7 Hold a fashion show in the spring, featuring acceptable apparel. Students will be buying or making their wardrobes before school starts, so if you wait until September it will be too late.

8 Review the dress code with the student and jointly conclude whether or not there has been an infringement. Then consider alternatives.

DRINKING

(*see also* Drug Use; Health Problems)

CAPSULE: With relaxed campus rules becoming more prevalent, it is virtually impossible to know the extent of alcohol consumption on school premises. Drugs and drinking are not strange bedfellows. Acquaint yourself with the vocabulary and symptoms of a drinker. Remember to keep your cool and acknowledge that you recognize a problem that ought to be approached rationally and from an educator's standpoint, not a preacher's. Booting a drinker out of school when you are angry may backfire and help no one, so be sure you are the best person to do anything before acting. Try to emphasize health instead of school rules.

OPTIONS: **1** Comment matter-of-factly to the student with liquor on his breath, "Jim, please don't drink before coming to class."

2 Confront the student privately and point out that alcohol has no place in the school setting, then *listen* to him for clues that will tell you something of the degree of the problem. Does he bring a flask to classes? Where does he get the money for it? Does liquor flow freely in his family? Is the family fanatically anti-booze? Is he having academic, romantic or economic problems? Find out whether the drinking incident is a one-shot deal, or whether drinking is a problem at all. If in doubt, go easy and be sure to let him know you are his friend.

3 Consult school health personnel and recommend a team meeting (see Appendix) be held to discuss the student.

4 Demonstrate and uphold the idea that every act carries its own consequences. ("Jim, you know alcohol has no place in our basketball training program, and our code of conduct, which you fellows helped me write, states pretty clearly that you are now out of Saturday's game. I'm sorry, because we need your speed and accuracy against Monmouth, but that's the way it is, and I doubt that it will happen again.")

5 Encourage students to make their own studies of problems stemming from drinking through data available from local agencies, news media, and professional people. Give them the privilege of choosing and inviting speakers for the class.

6 Invite students to your home and use appropriate values clarification techniques to encourage peer communication and exploration of ways to cope. (See Simon, Howe, and Kirschenbaum, 1972.)

7 Make available the viewing of films and filmstrips in a club setting, free of a "tight and teachy" atmosphere. Also, library carrels or resource centers provide excellent places for students to privately view films or listen to tapes.

8 Suspend the student from school for a limited time and readmit him when his parents or guardians accompany him to school. Suspension is handled by the administrators, not the teachers. *Caution:* The longer the student is out of school, the farther behind he will get in his work. Suspension doesn't treat the cause of the behavior, only the symptom. However, suspension *does* compel the student to reflect on the problem, and parents become involved. This fact can almost assuredly bring latent and some not-so-latent emotions to the fore and calls for experienced and skillful counseling. A further caution goes to teachers who might be tempted to drop the student's grade a letter because he has been drinking. You can record his "swigging" behavior in the citizenship evaluation, but give him his full academic credit.

9 Take (or create) opportunities to convey, through your teaching, the idea that drinking is a common way of attempting to solve problems. ("Several literary and political figures severely curtailed their careers, and in some cases wrecked their lives, by attempting to solve their problems with liquor. Who comes to mind?") As you discuss the reasons these people turned to alcohol, the students may internalize, empathize, and consider a personal response if or when confronted with alcohol.

DROPOUTS, Potential

(*see also* Loneliness; Underachievers)

CAPSULE: There are multiple reasons for students dropping out, but the prime ones are academic, environmental, and physical. The elementary teacher would do well to soberly remind himself that at this very moment he may inadvertently be preparing a future dropout, since frequent analyses of dropouts reflect the beginnings of failure in the elementary grades. Dropouts are usually lonely, disillusioned people. Ask yourself whether your smiles and nods of acceptance have contributed to their hanging in there as long as they have or whether your scowls and judgmental attitude have pushed them out! If you're dead serious about helping a potential dropout, you won't expect an overnight change, but you'll be able to note change and make the most of it.

OPTIONS: **1** Arouse the student's ambition to realize an attainable goal. Capitalize on a talent he has, such as singing, or assembling motors, and enable him to use this skill in meeting a specific assignment in a class. ("Today during science we'll all go to the local garage and Phil will demonstrate how to take a motor apart.")

2 Ascertain the student's present and potential level of achievement through tests or retests, either formal or informal, as the situation dictates. ("Jim, you're ready to drop out because of your grades. What do you say we arrange for a brief battery of tests to be given you and then discuss your scores in light of your potential?") This will enable you to accent his strengths and encourage him to build on them.

3 Consider a flexible work-study schedule for the student. ("Bill, if you can arrange to work for Mr. J. at the filling station every Thursday morning, we can adjust your class schedule.")

4 Consult the school records to identify clues and patterns, then openly discuss your findings with the student. Most students fear what the files hold; this is your opportunity to assure them that they merely hold some clues and nothing conclusive about anyone.

5 Deemphasize conformity; rather, emphasize the strengths of the individual. ("You're the only one in the class who can play the guitar.")

6 Expose the student to the flight-plan approach to studying (see Appendix), then set up an irregular schedule for the student, mutually worked out.

7 Hold a team meeting (see Appendix) to garner all possible pertinent information, and select the most competent and empathetic person to follow through with the team's recommendations.

8 Recognize the student's goals as he talks to you, and restate them for him. ("What you seem to be saying is that none of your course work will ever help you be what you want to be. Let's consider some alternatives in your case.")

DRUG USE

(*see also* Drinking; Loneliness; Underachievers)

CAPSULE: Drug addiction is the product of unresolved conflict. The use of drugs is highest among failing students and those who see little or no relation between their studies and life in general. This fact alone should motivate educators and parents to reexamine their goals. Furthermore, drug addiction is a family affair. To the user, the drug scene is exciting and tantalizing because of its dramatic mode of registering hostility. It is commonly felt, among those who study the drug problem, that loneliness is the single strongest reason anyone goes on a trip and that drugs cause youth to experience a false freedom. Warnings that he may be adversely affecting future generations usually go unheeded by the student. Teachers and parents are frightened by the prospect of being among those touched by drug abuse. The entire scene is a threat to them because of their inability to pinpoint anything until it is very late. Three things parents and teachers can do are: (1) acquaint themselves with the vocabulary or slang terms used in the drug culture; (2) observe the friendships developing—rarely will a user trust a nonuser enough to associate with him; (3) be aware of dramatic changes in attitude, attendance, scholarship, personality, dress, friends, best friend, and sports participation. Teachers, remember that your chief role is that of an educator, not one of a surrogate parent. Also remember that it's better to emphasize health than laws. The following suggestions may be helpful, either as prevention or cure.

OPINIONS: **1** Arrange (with the cooperation of students) a continuous drug education program on all age levels (from fourth grade up). There are several package programs that are generally popular; the Department of Health, Education and Welfare, Washington, D.C., can give help, if requested.

2 Consider the possibility of holding drug education meetings *away* from the school building, since it sometimes makes the experience too "schooly."

3 Consult the school nurse, physician, or social worker regarding the wisest move and work as a team (see Team Meeting, Appendix) in taking action. *One* professional person dealing with the parent or student is quite enough.

4 Encourage students to make, within the context of the regular class, simple, scientific research studies on the subject of drugs.

5 Engage the services of ex-users if possible. (They are usually more influential than others.)

6 Get to know the student on an informal basis. Frequent the halls, gyms, and playgrounds. Discern, if you can, possible reasons for the student's turning to drugs (family, grades, friends, unpopularity, health, fears, and so on.)

7 Have an older student counsel with a younger one who is experimenting. The school counselor can give numerous tips on approaches, but certainly the reflective technique is one of the best. ("You're really curious about a marijuana high," or "You feel left out of the gang and you think smoking pot might get you in.")

8 Make films, filmstrips, tapes, and records available to students. Turn the media over to a reliable key student and trust his judgment as to the use of the material. The important thing is that the students get together and use the equipment without someone always checking. ("Stan, you've been rather free in sharing your past experiences with marijuana and speed, and the students like and respect you. Would you consider taking charge of the audio-visual aids on drugs and figure out a way to get them used?")

9 Provide a "hot line." Students' problems in school may diminish if pressures are released through this means.

10 Provide meaningful outlets that carry responsibility and might supplant the need for drugs (theatre, sports, art, for example).

11 Recognize the stoned student. Clues are the following: redness and watery eyes (glue); red, raw nostrils (cocaine); profuse perspiration and body odor, constant licking of lips to keep them moist, and tremor of hands (amphetamines); runny nose (heroin, morphine, codeine); long-sleeved garments to hide needle tracks (heroin, Methedrine); sunglasses worn at inappropriate times to hide dilated pupils (LSD); and staggering, and disorientation (barbiturates). Remember that many of these symptoms also identify other ailments.

12 Recommend that another student (perhaps a former drug user) take the stoned one for a walk.

13 Refer an identified drug user to a counselor or to medical personnel, all with the utmost discretion. The path to follow will be different in each case, and only you have the wisdom to discern which route is best.

14 Try group guidance techniques, with an adult consultant. Have students bring in outside data on drugs and, through free discussion, discover ways of coping. The greatest dividend comes from the increased peer communication. (See Simon, Howe, and Kirschenbaum, 1972.)

E

EATING PROBLEMS

(*see also* Anxiety; Health Problems)

CAPSULE: The student who doesn't eat well, or who regularly gags or vomits during lunchtime is emitting a message to be interpreted. Most likely, the child is so fear-ridden that his body is not able to handle its input. There are studies that suggest a relationship between picky taste preferences and personal adjustment. The finicky eater has more emotional problems. The student who is turned off by the unfamiliar dish or something that isn't "Mama's cooking" may opt to chuck it all instead of eating the lunch.

It could be, however, that the child is not reacting to the food at all. He may be reacting to the climate of the lunchroom. As a preliminary to your action, stand back for a moment and watch the crowded cafeteria lines, the quantities of "fillers" shoved at the students, the time limits on eating, the rules, the policing, the din or the quiet, or the exclusiveness, the drabness, and the sameness. Most certainly the child does not need to be told to eat "because it's good for him" or to "hurry, because the next class is coming." He knows these things. Something has to be unlearned, as well as it has been learned.

OPTIONS: **1** Ask the student which person he'd like to sit by while eating and discreetly arrange it.

2 Confer with the parents, the school nurse, or a physician.

3 Consult the child's school record for clues.

4 Elicit from the student, privately, his mealtime worries. Be nondirective. ("To you, lunchtime isn't a very fun time of the day.") If you make the mistake of asking a question you will have to be satisfied with a "yes" or "no," period!

5 Give the child some options regarding the food. ("Max, will you have half an apple or a whole one?") This not only gives the child an opportunity to make a choice but places some responsibility on him.

6 Have an older student eat with the child (see Junior Counselors, Appendix).

7 Hold a team meeting (see Appendix). The obvious benefit will be consistent treatment.

8 Permit the student to earn tokens or points toward purchase of a prize in the school store (see Extrinsic Rewards, Appendix).

9 Present a hypothetical or real case for class discussion (see Class Discussions, Appendix). One example: "I once knew a student who got very upset during lunchtime in school. Sometimes he even gagged and threw up. It took us a long time to find out why. What do you think might have been the matter?"

ECCENTRICITY

CAPSULE: The eccentric student is different from the rest. He may be whimsically so because of his penchant for a unique wardrobe, or he may be different enough to suggest mild mental aberration. He may be very lonely or he may be the happiest one in the lot.

Very often the eccentric child is pressured by adults to be more "well rounded and typical," which he clearly does not prefer. Respect the eccentric child for his differentness. His ideas may be offbeat, but his very eccentricity may spawn a great revolutionary idea!

Children, being what they are, can be both charitable and cruel. It requires the sensitivity of a concertmaster to deflect unkind comments regarding eccentricity. Your attitude of general acceptance will provide the best model for your students.

OPTIONS: **1** In a class discussion (see Appendix), encourage your students to recognize and appreciate the uniqueness of people. ("In what ways are Tom and Joe *alike*? In what ways are they *different*? In what ways are they *unusual*?)

2 Get acquainted with the eccentric child's family, so that you can better understand him. This should be the case with any child, but it may be particularly necessary in the case of the eccentric.

3 Give the eccentric a special task that nobody else could (or would) do quite as well: photographer for the yearbook, for instance, or water boy for the football team.

4 Help the eccentric pursue his studies through individualized, personalized lessons (see Flight Plan, Appendix).

5 Recognize a product, a special talent or a deed of the eccentric one. For example, buy one of his art works that may be in an exhibit, ask for a copy of a poem he wrote, or write him a note of appreciation for a deed.

6 Show the eccentric student, in inconspicuous ways, that he is important to you. A smile, a nod, a touch, a request to do an errand, or a listening ear will all be effective.

EXHIBITIONISM
(*see also* Obscenities; Self-Concept; Sexual Concerns)

CAPSULE: Exhibitionism is not one of the most common problems encountered in schools, but it does occur. When the high-school senior flexes his muscles and his friends call him an "exhibitionist," they are, of course, being facetious. If he were an exhibitionist, his behavior would be of an obscene, psychosexual nature.

News of the exhibitionist usually gets around—in whispers. To be sure, cases of obscene conduct should be reported to the proper person, but they should be factual, firsthand reports. On-the-spot reprimanding and embarrassment will add nothing to the correction of the behavior.

Little children's early explorations of the world, which include their own bodies, may include masturbation and childhood exhibitionism of the "I'll-show-you-if-you-show-me" variety, which scarcely qualifies for the traditional "show and tell" agenda. At any rate, there are numerous studies that show this kind of behavior diminishing around age five.

The classroom is the least likely place for exhibition, but there are other protected areas around a school where crowds cluster and supervision is minimal. Should you be confronted with this kind of a problem, keep your cool and rely on your relationship with the student to handle the matter with dignity.

OPTIONS: **1** Be sensitive to other students' reaction to the exhibitionist, but don't make the subject a conversation matter.

2 Speak to someone you can trust about the incident and divert the problem into professional hands.

3 Talk to the student privately sometime after the incident, preferably at a time when other students are not aware of the conference. Expect his greatest fear to be your reporting him. Explain that his conduct must be reported, solely for the purpose of getting help for him. If he is under the care of a psychiatrist, tell him you will let him share the incident with his doctor.

4 Tell the student he is excused. Do nothing more at that time.

EYE PROBLEMS

(*see also* Health Problems; Tics)

CAPSULE: Surprisingly or not, six out of ten schoolchildren who need eye attention are not getting it, or they are getting it too late! The popular eye-screening tests used in schools are designed to test only the keenness or sharpness of what the child sees; they do not tell how well he uses his eyes or how well he sees material near at hand. To be sure of your students' eye capacities, it is wise to consult an ophthalmologist or local agencies and service clubs that make sight saving their special concern.

Today, many more children come to school wearing glasses than did a decade ago. Contact lenses and stylish eyeglasses as glamour accessories have eased the problems of students who habitually lose glasses or resist wearing them for vanity or inconvenience reasons. Small children, however, still wear framed glasses and still have the usual problems of breaking them (though plastic products have lessened this), misplacing them and flatly refusing to wear them. Parents have a responsibility to apprise the teacher of the child's particular problem. School nurses can be helpful where eye exercises are required of the child during the school day.

There are always some children who show symptoms of eye problems—squinting, frowning, inattentiveness, losing their place, holding reading material too close to their face, or complaining of headaches. It is the teacher's responsibility to share his or her observations with people who can help.

OPTIONS: **1** Allow the child to wear a status symbol (such as a pretty "dog collar" or a special badge) if he will keep his glasses on. (Usually the child feels so much better, and sees so much more, with his glasses on that he's happy to wear them. The child who rebels may have glasses that are ill-fitted, may have frames too heavy, or may be using this as a means of getting your attention.)

2 Check the print size of the child's study materials. Print that is too fine can put an undue burden on the child's eyes.

3 Comment on how nice the child looks in his glasses.

4 Expect the child to wear his glasses. Withhold something the child enjoys until he puts his glasses on.

5 Place the child with eye problems in a strategic place in the classroom so that he will not suffer eye strain.

6 Refer the child to the school nurse or a physician.

7 Reward the child when he wears his glasses. ("Glen has worn his glasses all day. Let's give him a hand!")

F

FARTING

CAPSULE: It is not uncommon for a group of pranksters to take delight in diverting their classmates (and particularly the teacher) by unrestrained gas leakage, especially after the cafeteria has featured baked beans or bean soup. Students take delight in both the audible and the inaudible, and when the natural gas supply has been exhausted, there is always the Bronx cheer. It's best to be philosophical, knowing that "this, too, will pass." Chances are, the students will agree with you that it's a gas and let it go at that. Keep your sense of humor as keen as your sense of smell.

OPTIONS: **1** Ascertain the identity of the "instinkator" and speak to him privately and firmly. ("O.K. Joe, we've had our little game. Now I'm counting on you to help discourage this kind of behavior in the future.")

2 Deodorize around you or the pranksters with aerosal spray, open a window, or turn on a fan—but *don't* overreact.

3 Make a matter-of-fact statement and then drop the subject. ("Boys, please contain yourselves.")

FEARFULNESS

(*see also* Anxiety; School Phobia; Test Phobia)

CAPSULE: Some experienced and knowledgeable observers state that most student behavior in the classroom is based on fear, rather than on a desire to learn. Risk taking is dangerous in most classrooms. The "right/wrong" atmosphere that permeates our schools, and the consequences of either position, put stress on all children—and an excessive amount on some. Most students spend their minutes in classrooms fearful of being called upon to recite or answer a question, of being wrong in reply, of what the teacher will do, of the other kids making fun of them, of their parents hearing about their errors (or seeing their grades), of the punishment they may receive (or privileges denied), of actually being dumb, and so on. The student is fearful both in and out of the classroom about whether others do or do not like him and about whether he will be included in their activity, group, or clique.

Fears produce stress, and excessive stress immobilizes. However, immobilization is not always traumatic; it may be only fleeting. In fact, some stress is necessary for purposeful living, so our concern is the amount of fear and stress any one student is subjected to and how to deal with it. Our major effort must be to maximize the success experiences for each child. Even then, there will be occasional wrongs, errors, or defeats. Negative teacher reactions, in the form of sarcasm, tirades, anger, and punishment, increase the stress and the resultant immobility; positive reactions, such as encouragement and specific helps to the student, turn the failure into a learning experience.

OPTIONS: **1** Be supportive when failures come. ("You're right in there, Johnnie, but we need to restudy the unit on frogs. Try checking your answer against what you see in the aquarium [or pond].")

2 Commend consistently, but not effusively, any success of a fearful child.

3 Display appreciation of the capabilities and humaneness of a fearful child. ("I couldn't help admiring the way you helped Sue during _____ when I knew you were just a little less scared yourself.") He will learn, then, that you know he is struggling with his fear.

4 Establish, if you can, the origin of the fear. Share your information discreetly so that the child may receive help.

5 Help the student develop friendships. Friends ameliorate the trauma of failure.

6 Match the difficulty and relevancy of subject matters and your requirements to the capabilities and interests of the student (see Flight Plan, Appendix).

7 Refer the student to an appropriate counseling service.

8 Work out a performance ladder or a desensitization plan with the student that will help him overcome a particular fear (see Option 2 in *School Phobia*).

FISTFIGHTING

(*see also* Bullying)

CAPSULE: Slugging it out spells bravado for many students. For the teacher the watchword should be *prevention.* Prevent fights by establishing some ground rules, such as, "When two people are slugging it out, the audience will not egg them on by laughing, booing, taunting, or shouting." Periodically review with the students the school guidelines regarding warnings, the recording of fights in student files, and the consequence of fights. When a fight occurs, keep cool and size up the situation. Use common sense in determining how long to let a fight continue or whether to interfere at all. Ideally, your interference should take place only when mortal danger is involved. Hazards to be noted are eyeglasses, dental braces, and sharp objects. Ask yourself what forms of explosion are permitted within the framework of your classroom. Avoid taking sides or demanding apologies when such action is clearly forced. Consider each student's involvement on an individual basis. It is not always necessary to notify the parents. Sometimes such action only aggravates the situation. For future reference, note and remember what it was that triggered the fight. (Did Jim call Bill a thief? A cry baby? His mother a whore?) Avoid treating the matter with anger. This only reinforces the notion that anger works. Once the fight is over, remember to allow for its natural aftermath—give the participants time to cool off and maybe to sulk a bit.

OPTIONS: **1** Consider settling differences with Indian wrestling. Ask your physical education teacher about this. He may help referee matches if you can't.

2 Consult the physical education teacher regarding opportunities for students to use gloves, punching bags, or other aids to acceptable fighting.

3 Have each fighter write his side of the story. If he can't write, have him draw a picture, dictate, or tape his side for you. Upon reading or listening to his own words he may reevaluate the situation.

4 Isolate the fighters in a private room and hope for a joint, private resolution to their differences. Provide them with a tape recorder and an acceptable noisemaker, such as a drum, for dramatic sound effects. Don't insist upon a report unless they want to share the experience with you.

5 Use appropriate films and filmstrips to promote objective thinking about fighting.

6 Use brainstorming (see Appendix) to elicit creative ways to handle the urge to fight. ("In the next ten minutes let's share all the ways of fighting we can think of.")

7 Use the incident as a springboard for discussion in a class meeting (see Appendix) at a future time, when the incident has cooled and the fighters are more objective.

8 Use the listing technique to help the student identify his feelings. ("List ten things that make you lose your temper," or "List ten things that used to make you very mad.")

FORGETFULNESS

CAPSULE: One who forgets may be saying many things: "I get attention by asking to borrow," "I'm stingy so I'll use others' materials," "I'm irresponsible." It's amazing how well people can remember to forget, especially if the consequences are gratifying. Establish in your classes sound habits of preparedness and reinforce the behavior of those who are trying to remember.

OPTION: **1** Demonstrate that we must suffer the consequences of our own behavior. ("I'm sorry you forgot your gym shoes, but that means no basketball today.") *Caution:* Be aware that there are those who purposely forget so that they won't have to do a chore they fear or dislike. This calls for individual counseling and eventual facing up to such strategies.

2 Have a supply of stubby, eraserless pencils for the one who is always forgetting a pencil, and collect them at the end of the class.

3 Have the student maintain an assignment book. Initial the student's correct recording of the assignment. Ask the parent to initial the completed work.

4 Identify (via observation and reputation) the student who forgets because he fears or dislikes an assignment. ("Scott, I've noticed that you've forgotten your swim trunks three days in a row now. Something tells me you either don't like the water or don't like some people connected with swimming.") If the student corroborates your appraisal, construct a hierarchy of steps, leading him toward success. ("Monday, bring your swim suit to school; Tuesday, suit up, but sit on the sidelines; Wednesday, suit up and go in the water for five minutes . . .") This approach can be applied to any number of fears.

5 Thank and reward the class for remembering. ("Thank you for remembering your donations to the Heart Fund. Since everyone remembered, let's treat ourselves to ten extra minutes on the volleyball court today!")

6 Use tangible reminders; a string around the wrist, a pinned-on note, polish on a fingernail, a note on a telegram blank, a marble (which the student may keep) in his lunch pail to remind him (and his mother) and why not give him a second marble if he remembers? Or why not take something that belongs to the child and hold it in your "hockshop" until he remembers whatever he forgot?

G

GAMBLING

(see also Card Playing)

CAPSULE: Lawmakers have difficulty trying to solve the problem of gambling, so there is little wonder that school administrators are perplexed! Among legislators coping with the question, there are many cogent arguments for and against legalized gambling. In states where gambling laws are on the statute books, school authorities have a reference base but no assurance that the students will have the same regard for the statute, which is always subject to interpretation. (Are raffles and bingo gambling? Are private penny ante games against the law?) External controls of gambling are difficult indeed. There is no way to be sure students are not quietly taking bets on anything from athletic game scores to the number of rainy days there will be in November! Internal controls are the more desirable, but the odds are against their impact when children become so accustomed to raffles and pinball machines in public places that placing a bet on a horse or dog race is the next logical step. Rigid prohibitory regulations have a chance of success *only* when the morale of the student body and faculty is extremely high. In fact, imposing regulations without teaching students some understanding of behavior controls is contrary to sound educational principles. Students are prone to testing rules to see if they are, in fact, operative. Your role is that of an educator, not a moralizer or penalizer. If your efforts help the student weigh the pros and cons of gambling and then decide for himself how he will behave, you have helped him mature.

OPTIONS: **1** Hold group discussions on gambling (see Class Discussions, Appendix). Possible lead questions: How do you interpret the gambling law in our state? What penalties should be imposed on law breakers within the school? Convey the feeling that it is important for everyone in the group to hear what others think about the matter. Become expert at tossing the group's questions back to them, and among them, rather than giving them pat answers.

2 Keep the school curriculum so relevant that there will not be time to explore such activities as gambling to fill the void.

3 Use some values clarification techniques (see Appendix) to think about gambling. ("List twenty things you would not be willing to gamble on." "List twenty things you would be willing to gamble on.") The students may find that they would not gamble on their health but that they would gamble on a game score. Soon they will see not only what they value the most but also what their friends value.

GANGS

(*see also* Drinking; Drug Use; Name-Calling; Vandalism)

CAPSULE: What some psychologists call the "gang stage" emerges during the junior-high years. Students at that time go for clubs, secret societies, and "in" and "out" groups. Loyalties are intense, and often big prices are paid for a smattering of recognition.

Although some of the gang fever manifests itself in innocuous, short-lived clubs, more sinister gangs often infuse the school proceedings. They are the ones who travel in packs, yet are as elusive as quicksilver. To be sure, there must be an electrifying security in being a gang member when sheer numbers and intrigue spell power and the limelight. Whether traveling afoot, on motorcycles, or in automobiles, the unity of the gang is evident through secret signals, passwords, hand clasps, hair and clothes modes, and special lingo. Every gang has its leader and its second-in-command. Loyalty is the virtue most sought by the leaders; members know that disloyalty carries a heavy price. Once in, it's hard to get out.

A gang thrives on targets. When a gang sets out to "get someone," its armor is the psychology of fear. As simple an operation as challenging a victim in a bathroom or on the sidewalk can go undetected for weeks because the gang's psychology works so well. They may force a boy who enters the toilet to "fork over his money" or "get $5.00 before noon" and threaten to "get him" if he tells. They may tell a student to appear for a rumble at a designated battleground after school and that if he fails to show up they'll "knock the whey out of his old man." The student thus used is caught, unless extricated by a force more powerful than the gang. In some cases, police and detectives are called in.

As a precautionary measure, school administrators need to get out of their offices and walk the halls and grounds to find out what is going on in their schools. When students don't dare go to the toilet for fear of molestation or "hijacking," there is a reign of terror for sure.

OPTIONS: 1   Be aware of any sudden friendships that indicate subservience on the part of the "newest friend." He may need help but not dare ask for it. Do some sleuthing on your own.

2 Determine, if you can, where the leadership of the gang lies. The faculty member who gets along best with the leader should probably be the one to work with him on redirecting his creative energies.

3 Discuss various subversive activities (airplane hijacking, kidnapping) from a psychological point of view. Providing students opportunities to talk about subversive behavior may help them think about how to cope if confronted with a similar situation.

4 Engage a psychologist or psychiatrist to speak to your class on the psychology of fear or on mob psychology.

5 Explore with the gang member the "win/lose" concept in light of his gang membership. What chance does he have of winning or of losing? What risks must he take if he elects to split with the gang now? Professional counseling may be necessary to enable the student to make the break safely.

6 Keep tuned in to the language and conduct of the students. Often one can detect the overtones of intrigue by subtle hints, such as overly polite requests to go to the bathroom, a weapon hastily flashed in the halls, a guilty, nervous look, "high signs," or significant body language.

7 Visit the bathrooms, locker rooms, and clubrooms regularly. Make it a habit from the first week of school. Waiting until there is a crisis is waiting too long.

GIFTED CHILDREN

CAPSULE: For several decades now IQ scores have been used as the chief indicator of the gifted. In recent years, the word "creativity" has crept into the psychologist's vocabulary when describing the gifted. Since there is a low correlation between IQ scores and creativity, and if creativity is indeed a mark of the gifted, the IQ test has lost some of its prestige as a gifted child indicator. Therefore, when discussing the gifted it is important to differentiate between the *intellectually* and the *uniquely* gifted. The former holds a *general* capacity to excel, the latter a *special* capacity or talent.

Significant efforts are being made to create culture-free tests that do not penalize the disadvantaged, or the so-called poor, in the measurement of IQ. Discovery of the uniquely talented child is still largely a matter of luck. Deplorably, research literature reveals that classroom teachers identify *less than half* of the gifted children they teach! Immediately, one can assume that the unidentified child is probably unmotivated and that the teacher needs some outside help, for certainly the children deserve more than a 50-50 chance of being identified and encouraged to develop their gift!

There has been much speculation about the differentness of the gifted. It is well established that the gifted, as a group, are appreciably superior to others in health, longevity, physique, social adjustment, mastery of schoolwork, and moral attitudes.

Early identification of the intellectually and/or uniquely gifted in your class is paramount. Perhaps some of the following ways of identifying and working with the gifted will generate even better ones of your own.

OPTIONS:

1 Allow the students to work in groups based on friendships as well as on ability.

2 Allow time in the day's schedule for fantasy, browsing, quiet, and doing nothing. These are the times that new ideas surface!

3 Become acquainted with the family's life style through conferences or home visitation. Consider your findings when arranging the student's schedule.

4 Challenge the gifted student with tasks that more mature students find easy.

5 Consider acceleration. Do, however, carefully consider social and physical maturity. Promoting a child a grade or two is often advantageous. In nongraded or open classrooms the gifted student should have a decided advantage.

6 Consider a flexible schedule (see Appendix) for the student. ("Sue, we can arrange your course work in school to accommodate your art classes with Mr. Z. on Tuesdays and Thursdays.")

7 Consider holding some segregated classes for the gifted. Those identified as creative writers, for instance, might have regularly scheduled sessions with a writer—not necessarily a member of the school faculty.

8 Encourage the student to compose and invent products (music, poetry, plays, essays, stories, games, puzzles, models, and so on). Encourage him and help him submit his work to publishers and manufacturers.

9 Enlist the assistance of artists in many fields to observe students from the same ethnic and socioeconomic background (in a nonthreatening environment, which may be away from the school) and to identify the gifted. ("Mr. Eusebio, I'd welcome your assistance in identifying my Filipino students who are gifted in dancing.") *Note:* While the gifted dancer, for instance, will undoubtedly be recognized as coordinated and rhythmical by physical education and music teachers, the special talent could go undetected in school for years without the liaison person from the child's own ethnic group.

10 Have the gifted one tutor a slower child. He may be a more successful teacher than you, and he may experience a feeling of compassion for the slower child that will add a precious dimension to his total personality.

11 Individualize and personalize some of the gifted student's assignments, capitalizing on his talents (see Flight Plan, Appendix).

12 Nurture, don't penalize, the student's tendency to question, doubt, and challenge others' thinking.

13 Nurture the student's natural desire to learn independently, but don't use independent study to the exclusion of small-group work and large-group participation. Overuse of any technique or approach spells extinction of that technique's good results.

14 Use a questionnaire (see Appendix) to learn the ambitions of the student. ("What do you enjoy doing most in your spare time?" "If money were no object, what would you like to do or be?" "What do you feel may be your 'hidden' talent?") *Note:* Hobbies are very reliable indicators of giftedness.

GOSSIP

(see also Tattling)

CAPSULE: Gossip is usually a report of an intimate nature that includes some sensational facts. While tattling, so common among the younger children, usually deals with trivialities like "Somebody took my chair," or "He pushed me," gossip flourishes among older students and is frequently related to sex, drugs, pregnancies, venereal diseases, wild parties, gambling, theft, abortions, incest, gangs, and hijacking. The effects of malicious gossip can be devastating.

The most effective gossip deterrent is unwillingness to listen to or to repeat malicious comments about another. This, however, requires the character of a saint, which not one of us has! Teachers, exposed to the stormy overtones of gossip problems in school, walk a fine line that separates the *indifferent,* who just "don't want to become involved" at any price, and the *different,* who temper information thrust their way with common sense and care enough to become involved if the situation demands or warrants it.

OPTIONS: **1** Ask the gossip if he's willing to put into writing the juicy morsel he just peddled to you.

2 Expect students to be positive, instead of negative, in their comments about others. Hopefully, the attitude generated in the regular classes will spill over into the students' purely social contacts.

3 Help students, through class discussions (see Appendix), learn how to cope with gossip when they are the ones gossiped about. They will be able to add to these suggestions: Ignore the gossip; refrain from countercharging; talk to someone you can trust; don't talk to everyone.

4 Play the old gossip game, with each person whispering to his neighbor what he thinks he heard from the one next to him. The end product carries its own message.

5 Put on original plays or skits that are amusing but that also carry the message of the consequences of idle gossip. Discussion is bound to follow.

6 Resist the temptation to get "in on" the gossip that you sense is going around. Promptly discount 90 percent of what you overhear and put the other 10 percent into mental cold storage, just in case it proves significant later on. Knowing what you do, you may, in an ensuing discussion, diplomatically avert embarrassing situations.

GRADES

(see also Anxiety; Self-Concept; Underachievers)

CAPSULE: Many of the behaviors that are dealt with in this book are direct results of the damaging evaluation system that pervades our schools. It is called grading. It is a curious phenomenon that systems that are quick to develop and/or adopt extensive mental health programs adhere to the rigidity of grading.

There is now considerable documented evidence that (1) grades do *not* motivate students to do better, (2) the student with the highest grades does *not* necessarily do better on the job, (3) maintaining a straight-A average can be a heavy psychological burden, (4) teachers dislike the grading system, (5) parents uphold it, and (6) students like grades *if* they are getting A's and B's.

Students with good self-concepts can handle the grading system, but those who are still developing a belief in themselves feel that they must find ways to "beat the system," so they cheat, worry, quarrel with their parents, make deals with their teachers ("I'll get a whipping if I bring home a D!"), play truant, hate school, turn to drugs, develop ulcers, and, worst of all, see themselves in a very negative light.

Many kinds of students are hurt by the system. The gifted child may be as vulnerable as the slow learner. Pressures to have an unclouded record, to do as well as older brother, or to achieve a unanimous Phi Beta Kappa record in the family take their unmerciful tolls. Getting into the "best schools" is another social disease. One sometimes wonders what happened to the old-fashioned idea of getting an education for the purpose of engaging in satisfying work!

These unfortunate things happen because grades stick! Right now, if you will dig into the recesses of your memory, you can dredge up an "unfair grade" you once received. If the letter grade succeeds in convincing the student that he is not yet competent enough in a given area, its validity will not be challenged, but it is often interpreted as an assessment of the student's value *as an individual,* and therein lies its clout.

Because the present letter and number marking systems are so firmly entrenched in most schools and because grading is such an emotion-ridden subject, there are moves by some school administrators to allow parents and students a choice of the kind of evaluation they would prefer. For instance, parents could request only letter grades, only parent conferences with narrative reports, or combinations of letters and written comments. Most teachers would be quite able to comply with the preferred marking system. The idea that entire student bodies must be evaluated in one way because of computerization or for clerical reasons is not a valid reason for resisting improvement in evaluative measures. Neither is there any good reason why all report cards must go out at one time. If you have students who are showing strains of grade-itis perhaps you can help them.

OPTIONS: **1** Agree to mark the student after he has marked himself and you and he have discussed his work. Being able to discuss his performance will help both of you assess his real knowledge of the subject, and he will be more accepting of the result, whatever it is.

2 Encourage parents whose child has a severe case of grade-itis to seek family counseling. It's quite possible that the family may not be aware of the messages they are conveying to the child regarding school performance. A trained counselor can help the family members tune in to one another.

3 Hold a team meeting (see Appendix).

4 Individualize the lessons, using the flight plan (see Appendix). The fact that the student begins with a unit that eliminates failure by immediately guaranteeing at least a D is an incentive to the chronic failer.

5 Refer to the school counselor or psychologist.

6 Use informal self-evaluating devices to help the student get to know himself better and to know what he can reasonably expect from himself. The school counselor can assist you in selecting effective questionnaires, check lists, rating scales, and interest inventories (see Questionnaire and Values Clarification, Appendix).

GUM CHEWING

CAPSULE: *A gum-chewing girl*
And a cud-chewing cow
Are very much alike,
But different, somehow.
(It's the intelligent look on the face of the cow!)

Man has a basic need to chew. In some cultures it's the betel nut that satisfies this need. To the Western culture goes the dubious credit of introducing gum to other cultures around the world. Whether you chew or eschew it, the subject is a sticky one.

A common form of punishment in "the olden days" was to assign a culprit the task of scraping all the dried-up gum wads from the hidden recesses of the classroom furniture. This exercise was intended to make gum so unsavory to the student that he'd give up chewing altogether. It seldom worked. Once the job was finished, he hankered for a fresh stick of Juicy Fruit!

Teacher acceptance of gum chewing varies considerably. Doctors, too, hold varying opinions of the value of gum. Some prescribe gum chewing for certain of their patients. How super it must be for a student to go from the prohibition of gum chewing to having it prescribed for him! On the other hand, the high incidence of braces worn by teenagers these days precludes gum chewing for many.

The teacher who studies his students finds gum chewing an excellent informal indicator of the emotional tenor of the student. Nervous or excited, the student generates rapid chewing motions. Comfortable and unthreatened, he relaxes to such a level that he repeatedly and quite unconsciously extracts a huge wad and reclaims it to his slowly moving jaw. The attention seeker snaps, crackles, and pops bubble gum to the distraction of everyone. And then there is always the silent one who merely houses the gum to "sweeten his breath" and quite honestly says, "I'm not chewing gum."

Gum can be a distinct menace, a minor annoyance, or no trouble at all in the classroom. If you are employed in a school where rules flatly state the expectations regarding gum, it is your responsibility to uphold them and to refer those who defy the rules to the proper authorities. If you are operating in a more relaxed setting, perhaps some of the following ideas will be helpful.

OPTIONS: 1 Consider gum chewing as one way of coping with stress and permit it during exams, with the provision that the student does not clack and chomp the gum to the annoyance of others.

2 Develop some cues to remind the student that he's swinging his jaws more than he perhaps realizes. Imitate him, good naturedly.

3 Discuss gum chewing in a class meeting (see Class Discussions, Appendix). The group may agree upon times when gum chewing is permissible; for instance, at sports events as a participant or spectator (swimmers excepted) or at informal meetings, such as pep rallies. Similarly, the class may question the advisability of chewing gum at such times as applying for a job, making a speech, or being romantic. Peer-group pressure and a common-sense approaches are effective deterrents.

4 Inform the students that among your peculiarities is an abhorrence for gum chewing. Depending upon your plus factors that might balance this idiosyncrasy, you might be lucky in soliciting their abstinence.

5 Inform the students that your main concern is that learning take place in a conducive environment. Unless there are obstructions to that ideal, nothing need be said about gum chewing or any other possible disturbance.

6 Use the subject of gum for light-hearted debate or speeches. Encourage some investigation into the pros and cons of gum chewing from aesthetic and health points of view.

7 Videotape the class when everybody is chewing gum during an exam. You might also videotape during regular, informal class activities. Discussion of the films will certainly elicit comments of delight and consternation at their mobile faces!

H

HAIR PROBLEMS

(see also Dress Problems; Lice)

CAPSULE: Hair presents a range of classroom problems. Common among the very young are hair-pulling incidents, with girls' braids being most vulnerable. In the middle grades girls enjoy combing one another's hair. It is a way of showing affection as well as an opportunity to satisfy one's curiosity about another. (What does her frizzy hair feel like?) In the upper grades hair styles continue to follow the pendulum. The tenured teacher sees them all—teased bouffants and slinky tresses, crewcuts and ponytails. No matter how simple the style, hair seems to claim a fair share of students' time and attention. Time and again it has to be dealt with in the classroom.

OPTIONS: **1** Ask the students to take care of their hair before coming to class, since activities will begin promptly after their arrival and won't allow time for combing.

2 Discuss hair and its attendant problems regarding styles, length, and care at an Ann Landers meeting (see Appendix). This approach is as effective with 300 students as it is with 10 or 30.

3 Discuss informally the socially acceptable conduct related to several subjects, including care of the hair. (Is it bad manners to comb one's hair in public? To clean one's fingernails? To pick one's teeth? Where does one draw the line for doing one's "own thing"?)

4 Provide a stationary mirror in the classroom so that the students can check their appearance when they wish without feeling guilty about it.

5 Request that everybody in the class get out their combs or brushes and in the next minute take care of their hair. Having done that, order them all to put their combs away and to get to work on the lesson.

6 Tell the hair-combing student to finish the task at hand, after which you'll excuse him to go to the toilet to comb his hair.

HANDEDNESS

(see also Handwriting Problems)

CAPSULE: The matter of handedness is less a concern these days than it was during the period of the widely touted cerebral-dominance theory, which seems to be receding into obscurity. By the time the child enters school, he will have a well-developed preference for one hand or the other. Occasionally you will have an ambidextrous student.

OPTIONS: **1** Accord the left-handed student a few common courtesies, including: (1) seating him so that his left hand and his neighbor's right hand don't hitch during writing lessons, (2) seating him judiciously at the lunch table for the same reason, (3) showing him how to place his paper in the correct position so that he won't be forced to develop the crabbed way of writing, and (4) having left-handed scissors for his use.

2 Permit the left-handed child to follow his natural inclination. You might encourage him to use his right hand by giving things to him in his right hand.

HANDWRITING PROBLEMS

(see also Handedness)

CAPSULE: Handwriting problems are often deplored but not explored. Like the lines in one's hands, each person's handwriting is a unique expression of the self. It reflects much of the total personality— one's coordination, attention to detail, visual awareness, and more. Therefore, to expect uniform results from students is foolish. The goal of the student should be improvement in writing legibly at a reasonable speed. The goal of the teacher should be careful guidance, after intelligent appraisal of the learner. Naturally, the teacher's appraisal will include attention to anatomical differences. Did you ever notice how different every hand is? Acceptable handwriting doesn't just happen. Reflect a bit on the child's opportunities to draw and to acquire some motor control of crayons and pencils prior to writing. Children are motivated by examples and by natural desires to read and write. For maximum results, consistent reinforcement ought to prevail in all students' training, but often our mobile society wrenches the student away before his handwriting patterns have jelled. Following are some specific measures that may be taken with the student who has handwriting problems.

OPTIONS: **1** Ask the student to identify the letters he sees he must work on and construct a flight plan (see Appendix) to achieve his goal.

2 Display samples of improved writing, preferably with previous samples so that the changes can be noted by onlookers.

3 Emphasize writing words and phrases, rather than isolated letters.

4 Have the student alternately draw and write on the same sheet, in an effort to encourage free flow of energy.

5 Have the student practice his handwriting using material that he *wants* to write and that has meaning to him. A good place to begin is with his name. ("Tod, let's begin improving your writing by working on your full name, Tod Alexander Bach.") This exercise will afford many opportunities to dwell on proper letter formation and at the same time assure legibility of his signature. Proceed next to his address, the names of family members, and so on.

6 Have the student write stories, poems, or reports that are part of another class assignment. Using meaningful material to teach penmanship makes sense.

7 Use rewards to motivate improvement. ("Jeff, when you can make these letters well you may do your next practice exercise using this special pen.")

8 Use the kinesthetic method to improve formation of letters—tracing on paper, writing in sand, writing with your finger on the chalkboard, or writing in the air.

9 Use window-frame guides for students who write off the page.

HAZING

CAPSULE: Hazing is disagreeable, sometimes torturous harassment used by clubs and fraternities to initiate their new members. Following a spate of news reports, including reported fatalities, about hazing among students in high schools and colleges during the 1940s and 1950s, the practice has been forbidden, or rigidly controlled, in most schools. Clearly, nobody intended to murder or maim the victimized initiates, but lack of leadership and control produced irresponsibility and mass hysteria.

If the school in which you teach allows great latitude regarding initiation procedures, you might be able to influence the students' thinking.

OPTIONS: **1** Caution the students regarding the dangers of uncontrolled hazing. ("Before you push an initiate into the pool, be sure that he's a swimmer or that there's a rescue crew on hand.")

2 Discuss hazing (see Class Discussions, Appendix).

3 Encourage clubs and fraternities to draw up initiation limits before the semester begins. Help the students think of safe ways to have a measure of frivolity and mischief-making without jeopardizing a student's life (see Brainstorming, Appendix).

4 Refer the hazers to the school psychologist.

5 Use the student court (see Appendix) to try the hazer.

HEALTH PROBLEMS

CAPSULE: A says,   "A healthy child is a happy child."
B says,   "A happy child is a healthy child."
C says,   "Sound mental health strengthens the body."
D says,   "Sound bodies generate good mental health."
E says,   "The goal of all is a sound mind in a sound body."

The wedding of man's physical and psychological attributes is such a mysterious bond that physicians, psychologists, theologians, and philosophers cannot resist probing for keys to the true state of the union. Whatever path you choose to follow, health problems will follow you, particularly in crowded schools, where close personal contact and public facilities are common.

Resist the temptation to diagnose ills and prescribe remedies. This is not your responsibility. However, the parents, the school medical staff, and the student's family physician will value your keen observations and accurate reports of the child's symptoms.

You will be among the first to note signs of epidemic illnesses—measles, mumps, chicken pox, pinkeye, impetigo, and so on. You will be in a prime position to note significant clues to previously undetected or unidentified ills, the signs of which might be extreme drowsiness, fatigue, coughing, dizziness, pallor, stumbling and falling, or hyperactivity. Furthermore, you will be in a position to identify the kinds of activities that create anxiety or that provoke allergy or asthma attacks.

For your own benefit, review carefully the health records of each of your students. Studying the students' medical histories might give you your "second sight" very quickly—as well as some alarm—but, being forewarned, you will be forearmed. Second sight brings into focus not a too-fat kid but a diabetic who could go into insulin shock; not a skinny reed of a girl but a borderline anemic who folds midday if she forgets to take her iron; not a lazy, tired student but a hooked pill popper; not a grouchy frowner but a migraine sufferer who does well to get to school at all; or not a robust healthy fellow but an epileptic who could momentarily have a seizure.

In addition to physical ills, you may become aware of certain psychological ills. Masochism and sadism are sometimes evidenced in children's behaviors. Signs of the former include pain-inspired anxiety that becomes pleasurable and is directed toward the self. Signs of the latter include the anxiety-pleasurable sequence, directed toward others. Both behavior types have perverse and desexualized forms and contain three major elements: fantasy, suspense, and demonstrativeness. The teacher often finds it difficult to accept the idea that a child could strive for physical or psychic pain. Behavior of this quality is aberrational and, like all extreme, deviant, or bizarre behaviors that are persistent, should be referred to psychological and/or psychiatric personnel.

Beyond recognizing significant signs and alerting the family, as well as alerting the professionals who can diagnose and treat, you have the added responsibility of sometimes "standing in" before medical help arrives. Your school administrator will apprise you of prevailing school-wide health and accident procedures. Ask the school nurse to review safety measures and health rules with your students. Here are some security measures you may take within the construct of your own classroom organization.

OPTIONS: **1** Arrange the seating for the maximum comfort and convenience of all. For instance, seat the child with a brace or a crutch in an uncluttered area; the chronic hiccuper near the door, for ready access to the drinking fountain; the farsighted, nearsighted, and hard-of-hearing in advantageous spots; and the kidney-problem child near the door.

2 Have a "backstop" arrangement with another teacher or a student whereby emergencies can be met if you are away from the scene. ("If B.J. has a seizure, you should . . . ") *Caution:* Sometimes parents of the helping child resent placing this much responsibility on him, so obtain clearance from both students' families. Instill in all the students an attitude of caring, without chaos.

3 Refer students to school medical personnel.

4 Remember, with normal courtesy, the health-problem children when planning the physical education program, large-group testing, field trips, and excursions. School specialists can be of enormous help in this regard. Don't always think first of "sending him to the library." You're more creative than that!

5 Use the school nurse or physician as a resource person. Remember, they are educators, too! Learning to take proper care of one's body is basic to other kinds of learning.

HEARING PROBLEMS
(*see also* Acting Out; Health Problems)

CAPSULE: School health programs provide some services for screening the students who have hearing problems. However, due to circumstances not always under the control of the system, many weeks pass before students are tested. It therefore becomes necessary for each teacher to learn early in the semester which students may have hearing problems. Some students act out because they can't hear what others are saying. Others withdraw and lose out on things because they don't want to call attention to their condition. The observant teacher will notice the child who tilts his head to favor a certain ear, or the one who talks to fill the void. There are simple tests that a classroom teacher can use to get clues regarding those who have difficulty hearing (see Option 3).

OPTIONS: **1** Consult the parents or guardians regarding the child's health history.

2 Face the child when speaking to him.

3 Give a simple hearing test yourself, if no medical staff is available. Place the student twenty feet from you, with one ear toward you. Ask the student to cover his other ear with his hand. Pronounce words, phrases, numbers, and letters in a range of intensity. Ask the student to raise his free hand when he hears your voice. Repeat the procedure for the other ear, then for both ears.

4 Place the student in the area of the classroom most advantagious to hearing.

5 Refer the student to the school medical staff.

HOLIDAYITIS

CAPSULE: Holidayitis is an acute schoolhood disease marked by quickened pulses and a rash of absences a few days prior to the scheduled holiday. Students are particularly susceptible, but teachers have been known to contract it—especially near Christmas, when great aunts and dear uncles often die of exposure. There are reported cases of sick teachers having fled their sick beds to catch a plane for emergency evacuation.

Some colleges have coped with holidayitis by allowing students to take their exams prior to early departure—if the exam is accompanied by a sizable cash payment. The exodus decreases sharply!

Parents sometimes contribute to the epidemic, for they themselves are not immune to taking a mile when given an inch. There are, of course, times when family plans absolutely necessitate early departures. In those cases it is wise to exact from the student and parent a fair arrangement, so that the student is not penalized for something beyond his control.

Teachers often dread the hyper tone of the school before holidays. However, it is possible to plan learning experiences that become richer *because* of the spirit of the season, not in spite of it. If you are one who is bothered by the festive mood or the

impending vacation interfering with your teaching, make very
sure you plan lessons that won't contribute to the high feeling.

OPTIONS: **1** Ask the students to plan assignments for the period before the
holiday. ("Prevacation days are often wasted because the holiday
atmosphere and the schoolwork seem to work against each other,
so let's make a 'then' plan, now.") Use buzz sessions (see
Appendix) to gather ideas and make plans.

2 Have each student develop his own flight plan (see Appendix)
on a topic related to his vacation plans (such as a trip, or a job).
Remember, personalizing is more important than individualizing
plans.

3 Hold an Ann Landers meeting (see Appendix). It's a prime
time to have happy large-group meetings.

4 Plan activities that contribute to a happy mood without
overstimulating the students. Some examples: puzzle time with
soft music in the background, drawing and painting to music,
dancing, body language conversation, pantomime.

5 Plan field trips that include visits to places where some of the
parents or friends of the students work.

6 Plan visits to other classes. Many students spend years in their
classroom only, without opportunities to visit other rooms.

7 Use cross-pollinated pedagogy. Have students in the upper
grades assist the teachers in the lower grades. The possibilities are
infinite, especially if the older students can be included in the
planning.

HOMESICKNESS

CAPSULE: Homesickness is a pit-of-the-stomach longing for family, friends,
and familiar routines. It often strikes at boarding schools and
camps. The happy-go-lucky child who hasn't previously been
away from home overnight may surprise everyone with a
determination to go home immediately, no matter what. From
afar, the most detestable home condition or chore suddenly takes
on an aura of pleasantness.

Camp directors and private-school directors know the symptoms
well, (moroseness, tears, loss of appetite, feigned illness) and
make plans that minimize homesickness. They take into account

the times that children seem most lost: sundown, bedtime, stormy days and nights, and visiting days when they have no visitor.

Parents can help the child by casually mentioning that he may get homesick but that he will have more to share when he gets home if he stays the entire period and that he should not expect them to come for him.

Most of the following suggestions for coping with homesickness are preventive and usually help. There are times, however, when there seems to be nothing to do but allow the child to go home.

OPTIONS: **1** Allow the students some voice in the selection of roommates or bunkmates (see Sociogram, Appendix).

2 Assign a task that requires attentiveness to the job and that may merit commendation by others if well done. ("Jack, would you and your friends prepare the wood for the bonfire?")

3 Keep the students busy with group activities that nurture friendships and help them discover interesting facets of their personalities. Good humor and the unexpected dispel tears.

4 Tell the students that they will be allowed x number of phone calls during a certain period, and have them select the dates on which they will call. Allow no exceptions unless there is an emergency.

HOMEWORK

(*see also* Procrastination)

CAPSULE: "Not until you've done your homework!" is a conditional pronouncement that has a familiar ring to many students. "I have to finish my homework!" is a familiar response to a parental request.

What is homework and how can it be dealt with satisfactorily? Some feel it is a school bogeyman produced by Sputnik. We believe homework should be purposeful activity, not busywork, and that it should accomplish one of two things: It should provide needed *practice* in a skill well taught by the teacher, or it should allow the student time *to finish* work begun in school.

Homework assignments that confuse and that offer little or no success because the teacher has neglected to lay a proper foundation are marks of irresponsible teaching.

For the upper school levels, it appears homework is here to stay, and goodness knows there's much to learn! For the little ones in the primary grades, the validity of homework is still much debated. Being born imitators and liking to be "like the big kids," the little ones are thought cute when referring to their homework. Overanxious parents believe it's never too early to engender good study habits. This is true. However, common sense must prevail with regard to homework. Some schools, recognizing the absurdity of homework assignments that entail the use of reference materials that students could not possibly have in their homes, have extended the school hours and have freed teachers to function as consultants while the students do their "homework" in school.

While it is sometimes difficult to remain detached, parents are wise to allow the child to be responsible to the teacher for his homework. Too much parental assistance can be disastrous to both student and parent. Teachers should communicate their homework expectations to the parents. "Lost" or "forgotten" papers often create classroom and home conflicts. The following ideas for parents and teachers may be helpful.

OPTIONS: **1** Give each student a well-identified manila envelope in which to keep loose papers.

2 Give the student a choice regarding when he will do his homework: before or after dinner.

3 Have each student maintain an assignment book that parents may also refer to, if necessary.

4 Have the student begin his assignment during the end of the regular class period. This makes the continuation at home less arduous and allows for clarification of questions before school is dismissed.

5 Parents might inject a note of cheerfulness and caring into the homework scene. (Set the timer on the stove, or the alarm clock, then tell the child, "When you hear the buzzer why don't you stop working on your homework and look for the surprise that awaits you in the refrigerator?")

HYPERACTIVITY

(*see also* Acting Out; Attention Span)

CAPSULE: Hyperactivity, more common among boys than girls, is more than excessive activity; it may be the aftermath of early-childhood illness or injury or a symptom of minimal brain damage. Teachers often speak of their hyperactive children and of those with brief attention spans in the same breath. Physicians and psychologists are more prone to question the *degree* and the *quality* of attention the child is getting from others. The teachers and parents of these overly active children find their ingenuity strained because every child is different, and individual approaches are a *must* if the behavior is to be changed. The hyperactive child is in special need of *consistent treatment* (inconsistency may have precipitated the present state!), and for this reason a carefully thought out hierarchical approach is preferred. Since some hyperactive children suffer from vitamin B deficiencies and metabolism problems, they should be referred to a physician. Some doctors prescribe drugs for the hyperactive child.

OPTIONS: **1** Draw up an agreement with the child and have him affix his signature (see Commitment Technique, Appendix).

2 Encourage the family to consult a school or family doctor who can test the child for hyperactivity. Cooperate with the requests of the physician.

3 Encourage the family to routinize the child's activities at home (a certain time for homework, a certain place for his things, meals on schedule, specific TV privileges, and so on).

4 Establish behavior goals and a system of rewards (see Extrinsic Rewards, Appendix). Remember to keep the assignment short enough so that he feels satisfaction and interesting enough so he wants to continue.

5 Examine closely the daily schedule with regard to kinds of activities you have planned. Are the children sitting for long stretches? Are they being overstimulated by too many physical activities in rapid succession? Your hyperactive child could be your quickest index to a flaw in the daily schedule!

6 Give the student a monitor role that requires specific responsible behavior at specified times (taking roll, recording lunch count, and so forth).

7 Grant small privileges to the student, such as permission to walk to the principal's office with a book once a day or to go outside to count something (plants, trees, fence posts) that he will record on a special tablet or a clipboard. (Clipboards really give one status!)

8 Have the child report to someone at regular times to describe his own behavior. (*Tom:* "Miss Gray, I'm reporting on how I behaved this morning. Well, I was pretty good. I just got up and ran out to the drinking fountain and squirted water once, then I went back and settled down.") After a period of regular reporting, free of judgmental responses from the listener, the child will begin to feel free to make some judgments about his own behavior.

9 Hold a team meeting (see Appendix) to assure consistent responses from the adults who work with the child.

10 Take firm, immediate action, followed by explanation of the action and the possible consequences had you not intervened. For example, you might say to a child wielding a sharp or heavy object, "Joan, stop!" then take the object. "If I hadn't stopped you then, you might have hit Fred's head."

11 Talk with others who are dealing with the same problem. Parents can get help through an organized community group, where feelings and facts can be shared without embarrassment. Such groups are springing up in many places and they generate new ways of dealing with the hyperactive child.

HYPOCHONDRIA

(see also Health Problems)

CAPSULE: The hypochondriac uses feigned illness to gain support and sympathy from others. In this way he manipulates them. He may be the last to really comprehend that he is not ill or that he is using pretended illness in order to avoid his basic problems. There are always some hypochondriacs in a student body. You will recognize them by their preoccupation with self-diagnosis ("I think I have an ulcer," "I'm sure I have a tapeworm," "I think I have a rare muscular disease"). The overriding question is; what is his *real* problem? While the teacher may not be the one to settle this question, for it is usually a medical and psychological concern, there are ways in which the student's mental health can be modified in the classroom. If you note students with hypo-chondriacal tendencies in your class, try the following.

OPTIONS: **1** Alert the medical staff of the school; leave the matter to them, unless they enlist your aid.

2 Discuss informally as a class (see Class Discussion, Appendix) the derivation and meaning of "hypochondria". You might lead into the discussion by stating that medical students often imagine that they actually have every disease they study in medical college.

3 Hold a team meeting (see Appendix) to discuss with the teachers, school specialists (including medical personnel) and the parents proper strategies to use when the child feigns illness. ("When Ada says she is sick, she will not be taken home, which is obviously what she expects and wants, but will wait in the nurse's office. When she sees that she is not achieving her goal of having her parents come for her, she may change her tactics.") It is highly important for all of the adults dealing with Ada to under-stand the plan.

4 Listen to the hypochondriac but do not oversympathize, since this is what he craves. Show your concern by recommending that the student contact a doctor. Once a doctor has assured the hypochondriac that he indeed is not ill, find ways to help the student appreciate his good health. ("Your schoolwork has improved 100 percent since you found that you didn't actually have the disease you thought you had. It pays to check with a doctor, doesn't it?")

I

IMMATURITY

CAPSULE: One of the most common causes of failure in school is imma-turity, or placement on a level too difficult for the child. Research confined to children who apparently failed due to immaturity now clearly indicates that repeating a grade pays dividends. Success of retention, so long practiced and later so blatantly denounced, is of course largely dependent on the attitudes of the child and his adult company. Immaturity becomes less of an issue in an open or nongraded organizational plan where one experience leads to the next *sans* a grade label.

There are many behaviors that may be indicators of immaturity. The child who constantly fusses with miniature toys or who wanders away from the group is asserting that the task is either too difficult, too easy, or boring. It is for the teacher and other professionals to decode the message the child is emitting. Clearly, the immature child needs, first of all, to be properly placed so that he can succeed. The following are ways of identifying and coping with the immature child.

OPTIONS: **1** Administer both verbal and nonverbal readiness or reading tests (readiness for the kindergartener and first grader, and reading for those who already know how to read). If your school has a reading consultant, he will be able to render this service.

2 Give the child many opportunities to select his own best work for display purposes. This helps him become an active evaluator of his accomplishments, aware of his own maturing.

3 Give the immature student tasks to do that *teach* him something, such as alphabetizing word cards that he puts away, replacing cards in numerical order, placing related colors together, placing similar shapes together. or counting and sorting objects.

4 Observe the child at play. How does his performance compare with the others on a physical basis? Do most of the children skip while he can't? Do most of the children jump rope while he can't? Consult the physical education teacher, who is an expert in judging where in the body-control hierarchy the child is.

5 Observe the child's choice of friends. During the play period, does he gravitate toward students in a lower grade?

6 Refrain from labeling a child "immature." The word is regarded negatively by students on all levels.

7 Request that the child be given appropriate psychological tests to add to your fund of knowledge about him. Use this information in a team meeting (see Appendix), at which time the pooled information will become the basis for a decision regarding the student's placement.

8 Study the drawings done by the child. The immature student will indicate less awareness of the world around him than the more mature one. Consult an art educator to help you if you feel unsure of yourself.

IMPOLITENESS

CAPSULE: Impoliteness or discourtesy is the result of bad training, anger, or both. The old verse "Politeness is to do and say / the kindest thing in the kindest way" is still an accurate description of that behavior. Conversely, impoliteness is to do and say the rudest thing in the rudest way. Curiously, politeness cannot be demanded without creating resentment. Fortunately, with a good model most students pick up polite behavior. If the climate in your classroom is a healthy one, little need be said about impoliteness or manners. Remember to caution your students not to confuse impoliteness with strange manners or etiquette (surface behavior), since these may be the results of innocent unawareness of certain cultural practices. The following suggestions may not only help redirect the rude one but may actually help him enjoy behaving politely.

OPTIONS: **1** Ask the students to write original plays using impoliteness or manners as the theme.

2 Establish with the students norms of conduct for the class. They may elect to identify specific offensive behaviors and the attendant penalties; for example: unnecessary interruptions—2 points; failure to excuse self—3points; and so on.

3 Practice polite behavior as an integral part of homeroom or of a regular class. ("Tomorrow we'll practice introducing strangers to each other. Ask outsiders for help or refer to your book.")

4 Reinforce, casually, your students' natural acts of politeness. ("Barbara, thank you for offering Mrs. T. your seat when she entered the room.")

5 Role play (see Appendix) a glaring incident of bad manners. ("This is the situation. The class has invited parents to watch a play and have refreshments. Ron dashes in front of an adult, grabs three cookies, and nearly trips the adult.")

6 Show films in which characters behave politely or in which impolite conduct reaps its negative consequences.

7 Take the student aside and talk to him about his impoliteness. First, assess whether or not he was fully aware of his indiscretion—ask him *what* he did (not *why*) and assume for the time being that his own description of his conduct is a deterrent in itself. Forced apologies aren't even for the birds, so forget them.

IMPULSIVENESS

(*see also* Blurting Out)

CAPSULE: The impulsive student is usually energetic and given to solving his problems without benefit of analytic or reflective attitudes. Because he is prone to premature judgment, he needs to be confronted with activities that will slow him down. Generally, he doesn't value academic goals highly. He takes chances and thinks little about the consequences of his behavior. People who ponder their moves bore him. He much prefers to jump to conclusions.

The impulsive child in your class quickly identifies himself by his unpremeditated comments and his penchant for acting on the spur of the moment. It's common to hear him say, "I just didn't think!" He's quick to volunteer, to threaten, or to voice an opinion but short on the follow-through. Propelled by action, he spurts through school, spending too much time trying to undo predicaments he gets himself into. Tests are not his cup of tea; he often hurries through them just to be the first one out the door. He needs a governor built into his locomotive. Perhaps some of the following ideas will suggest things you can do to retrain him.

OPTIONS: **1** Anticipate and check the student at a time when you are sure he is going to act impulsively. ("Ray, you are ready to jump to a conclusion, now hold it a moment.")

2 Commend the student at a time that you know he has constrained himself.

3 Develop a curriculum that curtails the student's penchant for impetuous action. Show him how to use the inquiry process (see Appendix).

4 Go through an assignment or a test with him, step by step, immediately after he has reacted impulsively to a task. The different end results should be impressive.

5 Help him develop a flight plan (see Appendix) that reinforces skills at the same time that it deals with a subject of interest to him and minimizes the competition factor.

6 Try to interest the student in the commitment technique (see Appendix).

INDECISIVENESS

(see also Anxiety; Self-Concept)

CAPSULE: The indecisive student is afraid. His irresolute pattern may have been set by an inordinate number of mistakes, large and small, counting against him. Shouts of "Well, make up your mind!" throw him into a tizzy. Your role, as his teacher, is to give him useful practice in making up his mind and in living with the consequences of his decisions.

OPTIONS: **1** Brainstorm (see Appendix) with the student x number of ways to attack a problem and help him choose one to try.

2 Give step-by-step practice in previewing possible procedures. Follow with rational, not impulsive, decision making. Evaluate what happened as a result of the decision that was made.

3 Suggest (if the student is at a loss) specific ways he can accomplish his goal, and urge him to make a choice from those you have mentioned. ("While you're getting ready to come up with some ideas, may I suggest some?")

4 Use the College Board Deciding Program (see Bibliography).

INSUBORDINATION

(see also Acting Out; Mimicry)

CAPSULE: An insubordinate student is unwilling to submit to authority. He deliberately behaves disruptively because he hates the power structure and the people who wield power. It is highly important to discern what his needs are (Does he seek revenge? Does he want to lord it over you? Does he merely want attention?) rather than to challenge him directly. The insubordinate child may not gain the approval of his classmates, but he knows that he can at least get their attention by his blatant indiscretions. Insubordinate students often enjoy "testing" a teacher to see if they can get a "rise" out of him. For this reason, it is wise to agree upon reasonable classroom expectations early in the semester so that remarks like, "Now's a fine time to tell me that!" don't create a climate of dissension. Examine your conduct as a teacher. Has it been too buddy-buddy? Has it been inconsistent? Actually, insubordinate students often prefer stricter, more serious handling. The last thing you want to do is get into a power struggle with him.

OPTIONS:

1 Announce to the insubordinate student that, instead of engaging in a confrontation now, you are requesting that the class discuss insubordination at the next class meeting (see Appendix). Hearing one's peers discuss a behavior is quite different from hearing a teacher hold forth.

2 Have the student report to someone (teacher, counselor, vice principal) on a regular basis (every hour, every day, every week). Each time he should comment on his conduct and how it is different from the last time he reported. The adult listens only.

3 Ignore the student's behavior for the time being.

4 Interpret for the student what his goals seem to be. ("Ben, by your remark 'Make me do it' you are trying to force me into a contest with you that wouldn't help either one of us. We need to find a way to work together.")

5 Isolate the student until you have time to deal with him.

6 Leave the room if several students are insubordinate. ("I'm going to leave the room for five or ten minutes. When I return we'll continue with Betty's group reporting.") Extracting yourself from the scene holds an element of mystery. (Is he going to the office? Is he so furious he can't stand us any longer?) When you return, continue as if nothing unpleasant had happened.

7 Perform a surprise act of kindness. The insubordinate student is often callous to rebukes; he may flip over a friendly gesture!

8 Praise something he does well, ignoring, for the time being, his rebelliousness.

9 Use a face-saver for the first offense. ("What you just did came across as terribly disrespectful, but I'm sure you didn't mean it quite that way.")

10 Use a three-step procedure for dealing with the insubordinate student. (First offense: confer with him and issue a warning; second offense: withhold some privilege; third offense: notify the parents through administrative channels.)

IRRESPONSIBILITY

(*see also* Carelessness; Forgetfulness; Self-Concept)

CAPSULE: Life goes better when one is working with a responsible individual. He not only brings to the task at hand an interest, a willingness to tackle the job, and a sense of caring but also an understanding of what the assignment entails and a realistic concept (self-concept) of his unique ability to meet the demands of the job. It follows, then, that while rules and guidelines are still important for him, they are less important because of his sense of commitment, the most distinguishing characteristic of a responsible person.

The irresponsible person is, then, the antithesis. Unlike the person who is occasionally careless, the irresponsible one may have said of him, "He comes on strong at first, gives an air of confidence, even sincerity, but he never finishes a job; he doesn't seem to know how to follow through." Even adults who manifest irresponsibility can be retrained, but it is easier to work with the young before their behavior patterns are well set.

OPTIONS: **1** Confront the irresponsible student directly, without rancor, telling him that word is getting around that he is irresponsible. ("Bill, on three occasions within the past two months you have volunteered to lead important committees and in each case you fell short of the mark. Your credibility is being questioned. I think I know some ways that you can regain the confidence of your classmates and maybe bolster your self-esteem a bit. Drop by my office some day this week, and we'll talk about it.")

2 Construct, with the student a "ladder of do's" that will enable him to experience the satisfactions of responsible behavior. An example: Sam, a third grader, shows no responsibility for his school clothing. He's already lost a sweater and a jacket this semester. Devise a check sheet for him similar to the following:

Behavior	Yes	No
Selected jacket for school	x	
Wore it to school	x	
Placed it on the hanger in school	x	
Wore it during recess		x (too hot)
Replaced it on the hanger at school		x
Wore it home	x	
Placed it on the hanger at home	x	
Got a smile from mother	x	

3 Convey to the student the message that a responsible person is independent, that an irresponsible one remains dependent, a sign of immaturity. Being immature is the *last* thing a student wants to be!

4 Give bite-sized lessons or tasks and expect acceptable completion of them before allowing the student to progress to the next phase (see Flight Plan, Appendix).

5 Reward with honest, verbal praise the student who demonstrates responsibility. Emphasize some specific competence, not just competence in general ("Rusty, your committee's plan for the prom is so clear that it is easy to visualize the event," rather than "You've got a great committee there; I'm sure you'll do a great job!") Clinch the feeling of responsibility by having the student tell you why he thinks the committee succeeded.

6 Use an extrinsic reward (see Appendix) to motivate the student. Also try the self-management record (see Appendix), noting that the items listed relate to responsibility. In using this approach the student readily learns that he reaps the consequences of his behavior and that any group of people can be sorted into two subgroups, the responsible and the irresponsible.

J

JEALOUSY

(see also Sibling Rivalry)

CAPSULE: Jealousy is generally the product of feelings of inferiority or feelings that others are favored. Feelings of inferiority come from constant reminders (real or implied) that others are better, more competent, or superior. Feelings of favoritism come when one must share time and attention or give them up to another. A new student in the class, a new teacher on the faculty, or a new baby in the home can stir emotions the individual didn't realize he held. It is useless to tell one he shouldn't harbor such feelings. The person is upset, and his feelings must be dealt with as helpfully as possible. It is easy to identify the overly jealous student because he eyes any newcomer as a threat and expresses his jealousy in hostile ways, often against the very person whose affection he is seeking.

Forever placating the jealous one can be a strain as well as an exercise in futility. There are ways, however, to promote healthy attitudes that will diminish the emotion until the child has a better understanding of himself. Active listening and wise redirection of thoughts are at the top of the list and are implicit in the following suggestions.

OPTIONS: **1** Allow the child to express his jealousy in a noninjurious manner. For example, ask him to show you how he feels about his rival through handling an inanimate object, such as a piece of plasticene or clay, or a stuffed toy.

2 Elicit from the child what he feels are concrete examples of favoritism, using "what" and "how" as keys. ("Let's talk about *what* Mrs. S. does that makes you think she favors Jan over you," or "Let's see if you can show me *how* Mrs. S. favors Jan.") *Note:* Refrain from asking "why" because the typical answer will be "I don't know." However, with the very young a "why" question can provide an opportunity for you to ask, "Will you let me tell you what I think about it?"

3 Empathize with the child. ("I know how you feel. I used to feel that my mother preferred to have my sister serve the cookies when guests came. However, I remember now that she preferred to have me entertain the visitors' children because she said I was so responsible.") This kind of statement may cause the jealous one to recall some note of appreciation to which he has heretofore been blinded.

4 Show the student how he can record the times he feels the victim of partiality. ("Sam, let's stretch this masking tape across the top of your desk and every time you feel something isn't fair make a note of it here and later we'll talk about it.")

5 Suggest to the students that they tell their family about the family council (see Appendix), which can provide an arena for discussing all kinds of feelings, including jealousy.

6 Talk about emotions in class (see Class Discussions, Appendix): "Jealousy is sometimes called the green-eyed monster. I wonder why," or "What do you think of this statement: There are two kinds of people and they look at life in mathematical terms—either they think others are out to subtract from or divide up their lot, *or* they are multiplying and adding to it.")

K

KICKING AND HITTING
(*see also* Acting Out; Anger; Fistfighting)

CAPSULE: Kicking and hitting are convenient, natural responses to something in a person's way—our arms and legs are always with us and ready on a moment's notice. The child who resorts to kicking and hitting will eventually be forced by society to wield more subtle weapons, but between the ages of three and nine these behaviors satisfy his need to get attention, to seek revenge, or to show who's the tough and powerful one. Persistent aggressiveness of this kind reflects feelings of worthlessness. It is up to the teacher and parent to discern how the student is using his weapon and to guide him toward more mature behavior. As an "ounce of prevention," take time to examine your class as a whole, noting particularly the tempo, mood, and freedom to move about. If your schedule reflects long periods of sitting or too long physically active periods, reschedule. You may inadvertently be stimulating the child's conduct.

OPTIONS: **1** Encourage the student to ignore the children he feels like abusing. ("Jon, could you do this? Every time you feel the urge to kick or hit Jeffrey, turn away and walk immediately, *and fast*, to the water fountain and get a drink, then return to the group?") This can teach him to cope by *removing* himself physically for a brief period, *refreshing* himself with a drink, and *returning* to the scene, where the situation has undoubtedly changed since his departure.

2 Establish a reward program for successful handling of kicking and hitting inclinations (see Extrinsic Rewards, Appendix).

3 Have the kicker spend time hitting a punching bag, or kicking a large cardboard box. ("Chris, you have shown us that you have a lot of energy. Yes, it takes lots of energy to kick and hit your classmates. Here's another way you can use that energy.") Give him his choice of hitting the punching bag, or kicking the cardboard box or of using boxing gloves with a friend.

4 Isolate the student until you can talk to him. Then try to elicit the underlying reasons for his kicking and hitting. Pay attention to whether he is seeking revenge, is feeling threatened and scared, or wants attention. Your approach will depend upon his objectives. ("Phil, it seems you were kicking Jim because he knocked Susie down [revenge]. Let's talk about a different way to handle our feelings.")

5 Send the offending students away from the group to finish their kicking and hitting. ("Please go in the vacant room next door if you want to continue your fighting.")

L

LICE

CAPSULE: 'Look! Lice! Count the cooties! See the eggs of the ukus!" Lice, cooties, ukus—they're all the same. The flat, sluggish, wingless arthropod selects the fanciest of homes for himself—the heads of humans. Children sometimes come to school with lice; sometimes they pick them up from their playmates, especially if the children are in the habit of sharing their combs, brushes, barrettes, bobbie pins, or hair ribbons.

One of the first signs of lice is itchiness and excessive head scratching. Another is the sight of tiny grayish-white clusters—the eggs of the lice. Don't panic! The hosts often don't. In fact, in some cultures the detection and extraction of the eggs or the lice themselves is a common pastime.

Most school health programs are equipped to eradicate the lice with proper delousing applications. The problem of getting at the source, which may be among family members not in school, is a constant one. If possible, it is best to treat the entire family or household. To accomplish this may require the finesse of a top-level public relations officer. Some cautions, reminders, and suggestions follow.

OPTIONS: **1** Be cognizant of the fact that the child with lice may be rejected by his classmates. Open discussion and matter-of-fact handling of the problem may be appropriate if there are several cases in the class. ("Some of us have discovered that our heads make cozy homes for lice; today the nurse is here to kill the bugs. Let's talk about what we can do so that they won't want to come back to live on our heads.") With older students, or with a single child, your approach would be quite different. Rely on your tact and common sense to make the incident a learning experience so the infestation won't be constantly repeated.

2 Discuss parasites as part of a regular class lesson. Mention lice. Encourage students who suspect they may have lice to have the nurse check their heads.

3 Encourage the children to refrain from sharing their combs and other personal items. Have a supply of clean combs to sell or give to the children with the understanding that they will not share them.

4 Send the student to the school health department as soon as you see evidence of lice. (If your school has inadequate health facilities, see your administrator about establishing a better procedure for dealing with health and hygiene matters.)

5 Use films, filmstrips, or slides to teach students about contagion and parasites.

LISTENING PROBLEMS

(*see also* Attention Span; Hearing Problems)

CAPSULE: Listening is an art that requires thought and attentiveness; it is not to be confused with hearing, the power of perceiving sound. There are many who feel that listening is fast becoming one of the "lost arts" and that hearing among youth is suffering the ill effects of amplified electronic sounds. Each contention bears sober consideration.

Students learn to be good or poor listeners from their adult models. Consider the impact of the model who announces somewhat boastfully that he's hoarse from talking all day or tired from yelling at the kids all day. That teacher, in addition to complaining of sore throat and fatigue, has just indicted himself as an ineffective listener. (Unless the class is set up to be a lecture course, a 90-10 ratio is a good rule of thumb—90 percent listening and 10 percent speaking per class period.)

Listening provides opportunities to learn something new. Your chances of learning anything new from your own utterances are rather remote. Just for fun, the next time you attend a faculty meeting note the number of active listeners when the principal speaks or when your colleagues give reports. Make another observation: Are the poor listeners the teachers who complain that their students don't know how to listen? Most of us can afford to hone our listening skills a bit. Ideally, from observing you as a good listener your students will learn to empathize with others, to catch significant overtones expressed by the speaker, and to be less self-centered. There's an even chance that they'll become known as "terrific conversationalists" as well.

OPTIONS: **1** Establish a class routine that involves beginning a period or the day with a listening-skill builder. For instance, you might select a brief article (not more than 200 words) to read to the class once, and follow the reading with five to ten comprehension questions. Correct the answers immediately and chart the results on individual graphs. A possible variation would be to ask students to select and administer the listening test.

2 Give directions a limited number of times. Much poor listening is perpetuated by teachers' willingness, despite annoyance, to repeat things innumerable times.

3 Play games that require careful listening. There are several games that require that the student recall not only what the previous speaker said but also what the one before that said, and the one before that. Listening and memory training, then, go hand in hand. Consult library books for appropriate games to encourage better listening.

4 Teach students a listening formula (see Appendix).

5 Use riddles to capture the student's attention before moving into a problem that requires careful listening.

LITTERING

(*see also* Carelessness; Irresponsibility; Messiness)

CAPSULE: Litterbugs are in disrepute everywhere. The beauty of our world is constantly being threatened by the thoughtless citizen who drops and scatters as he goes. Schools struggle daily with the problem of litter.

Students who feel that a custodial staff is employed to pick up after them are just as misguided as the administrators who close their eyes to the care of the buildings and grounds. In fact, a first-time visitor can, by a casual stroll through the halls and a stop-off in a toilet, quickly discern the morale level of a school. Litter, graffiti, and filth proliferate in a climate where indifference (and perhaps incompetence) dwells.

This is not to say that learning activities must be sterile and limited to the use of nonmessy materials. Far from it! It is only to say that thinking and working together do better without litter, and if it can't be totally obliterated, it can at least be markedly reduced via methods that will not only enhance the students' surroundings but teach them how to control their environment. Try some of the following ideas.

OPTIONS: **1** Conduct a no-litter campaign. Sell bumper stickers or notebook stickers. Offer prizes for the best slogan, poster, skit, or song on the subject of litter.

2 Encourage pride in the appearance of the school by recognizing individuals or classes for outstanding efforts to keep the school unlittered. This may be done through a morning bulletin, the intercommunication system, or at an assembly program.

3 Give an "I'm Not a Litterbug" pin or badge to the primary children who fight litter. Making them litter conscious today will assure less litter tomorrow.

4 Introduce the custom of having student guides take visitors around the school. This helps the students become aware of the appearance of the school and generates pride in it.

5 Schedule each class, on a rotation basis, for outdoor litter pickup every morning.

6 Use the subject of litter for discussion, writing, and speaking in the appropriate subject classes, such as social studies, English, speech.

LONELINESS

(*see also* Anxiety; Homesickness; Withdrawn Children)

CAPSULE: Loneliness is universal, but people are lonely for various reasons. Some reject themselves, automatically causing others to reject them. Others feel inadequate or unattractive so withdraw to the realm of loneliness. Whatever the specific subjective reason, the general overall reason for loneliness is *failure*—failure to cope satisfyingly with daily pressures, and more importantly, failure to relate to other people. Some try to conquer loneliness by getting lost in a crowd, becoming part of an impersonal mass. Actually, one of the most difficult kinds of loneliness to cope with is generated by crowds, and the number of friends one has is no index to one's degree of loneliness. The person with one good friend may be far less lonely than the popular public figure. Also, a loner is not necessarily lonely. Simply stated, people must have people to *relate* to, and the people for whom loneliness is an identified problem are those who haven't found such persons. In our crowded schools it is very easy not only to be lonely but to be lost and lonely. The teacher, who is sometimes the lonely student's only friend, is in a position to relieve some loneliness.

OPTIONS: **1** Arrange for the lonely one to tutor a student in a lower grade. This will give him an opportunity to relate honestly to another individual on a nonthreatening basis.

2 Discuss loneliness in a class meeting (see Class Discussions, Appendix).

3 Do a sociogram (see Appendix). Use the information gained to good advantage. One example would be to place the lonely one in a group or on a committee with the student for whom he has indicated greatest preference.

4 Generate communication among students who are not yet acquainted. ("I have your names on these enrollment cards, which I'll hand out face down. Look at the name on your card, then go to another student and say, 'The name on my card is Nancy Blair. Are you Nancy?' The student responds with, 'No, I'm not Nancy Blair, I'm Ellen Kay and my hobby is _____.' Do this until you find the owner of the card. When you do meet the owner, give the card to him.")

5 Have the student list fifteen or twenty things he likes to do. Label each thing with a descriptive code, such as O for "with others," A for "alone," AS for "after school," IS for "in school," and so on. Such an exercise can be very revealing to both teacher and student. It also provides material for discussions.

6 Require participation. Allowing the student to go unrecognized for long periods of time adds to the problem of loneliness.

7 Scrutinize the seating arrangement and make changes to accommodate the student's needs (use your sociogram results).

8 Send the lonely one on an errand with another child. Getting away from the other students is important.

9 Show films that dramatize children enjoying being together. Discuss ways of making meaningful contact with others.

10 Show the student you like him by complimenting him and, at the same time, directing his thinking to why he may deserve the compliment. ("You handle your horse expertly. How did you learn?")

11 Use bibliotherapy (see Appendix). The story of Eleanor Roosevelt, for example, depicts a lonely person who coped courageously.

12 Use a questionnaire (see Appendix) to gather insight into the student's loneliness.

LYING

(*see also* Anxiety; Stealing)

CAPSULE: Lying is as old as Eden. Practiced enough, it becomes reflexive. Many psychologists consider lying an index to a child's feelings of being unloved. From general observation, it can assuredly be said that lying springs from feelings of inadequacy and pressure.

Adults sometimes fail to recognize that there are gradations of truth and falsehoods and that age groups view them differently. The very young child often can't differentiate between fantasy and reality. Also, parents and teachers sometimes make it virtually impossible for older children to tell the truth, as in the case of the student who told his teacher he hated his grandmother, only to be scolded and called a "bad" boy. In the interest of expediency, he turned to saying things that pleased his teacher and made himself a "good" liar.

Threats are poor deterrents to lying. Calling the untruthful child a liar doesn't help either. Dealing with lying is usually an uphill undertaking that requires patience, consistency, and maybe some professional help.

OPTIONS: **1** Appeal to the student's high opinion of himself. ("Bruce, it makes me feel very unhappy when you don't tell the truth, because I've always liked being able to count on what you say.")

2 Arrange for the liar to be paired with a more truthful child when working on class projects.

3 Ask the child a direct question and perhaps you can read in his eyes whether he is lying or not. ("Jimmy, did you take Susie's eraser?")

4 Assure the child that he can depend upon you to tell him the truth.

5 Convey the idea that you are more willing to remember the times he told the truth than the times he lied. ("Phil, I'm sure it was difficult for you to admit you forgot to tell your dad to call me last night, but I'm so proud of you for admitting it." The assumption here is that the teacher and the student recognize the problem and are both working on it.)

6 Deal directly with the habitual liar instead of trying to trap him. ("Jim, you have Carrie's purse. Please return it to her.")

7 Evaluate your expectations of the student and try to discern the areas in which he feels compelled to lie. Does he, for example, lie about schoolwork? His dad's job? His mother's job? His wardrobe? His physical prowess?

8 Ignore those fantasy-oriented tales that probably have no serious consequences. ("My grandpa gives me $5.00 every time I go to see him." Even though you know his grandpa is on welfare, pass this up. Ignore it, but remember it for what it is.)

9 Notify the parents on those occasions when the student chooses to tell the truth, rather than take the easier course of lying. ("Mrs. Brown, I'm calling you to share something about Kathy that I think will please you. Today several students reported late after lunch and it would have been very easy for her to have fibbed about her whereabouts, but she told us the truth and obviously felt proud of herself. The matter is closed as far as the school is concerned, but I thought you would like to know.") The assumption here, of course, is that the school and the parents are working together on what they consider to be a problem and that certain strategies have been worked out, perhaps with the aid of a counselor.

10 Present a hypothetical or real instance of lying for class reaction. For example: "A few years ago I had in my class three girls who were caught shoplifting in the dime store. There were two people who saw them taking lipstick and gum, and the store manager even presented a picture of one of the girls putting a tube of lipstick in her purse. Yet, every girl denied taking anything. How would you handle this?" Such a discussion often begins with hard-and-fast retributive solutions and winds up looking at why the girls felt moved to steal and then lie about it. A simple, "Have you ever found yourself locked into a similar situation?" sometimes elicits some interesting exchanges.

11 Read or tell stories that illustrate the power of truthfulness over falsehoods. Resist the temptation to moralize, because as soon as you do you'll be tuned out.

12 Use normal consequences to help the student learn the benefits of telling the truth. ("You said you had finished _____ and it's clear you didn't tell the truth, so you will have to forego the pleasure of _____." *Caution:* Avoid the "Aha!" attitude.

M

MASTURBATION

CAPSULE: It is not uncommon for the very young to indulge in masturbatory play. In Western culture this practice generates considerable concern, embarrassment, and helplessness among parents and teachers. It cannot be considered deviant behavior unless practiced excessively. A preschooler may masturbate, quite unaware that the act carries any social disapproval. Older children masturbating in school or public places would be showing signs of emotional problems. When it occurs among the older students, the wisest procedure is to ignore it. Don't scold, but seek the advice of a school physician, nurse, or counselor who may be familiar with the child's background. In the case of primary children, some of the following ideas may work.

OPTIONS: **1** Change the activity of the class. Play a record, for instance, and tell the children to march or dance.

2 Check the child's activity schedule. Is he kept seated in one place too long? Is he tired and bored, so drifts into fantasy?

3 Check the child's clothing. Is it too tight and perhaps irritating?

4 Check with the parents and recommend that they receive help from a physician.

5 Keep the child busy with activities that require movement. Ask him to run an errand for you, to stack books, to sort papers, and so on.

6 Take the class out for a run around the playground.

MESSINESS

(see also Littering)

CAPSULE: Teachers and parents express a great deal of concern over the fact that their students or offspring are without a doubt among the messiest, untidiest kids they've ever known. They voice this complaint, aware or not that the child may be using them as a model (or may be responding aversely to their fastidiousness). Of course, the explanation of messiness is not that simple. If it were, we could look at the adult models and, providing they were not pathologically persnickety, conclude that the child would happily emulate them. Or, if the parents were obsessed with being fastidious, families could count on alternating generations of perfectionists and slobs!

Some students are so creative and lost in a world of ideas that they seem oblivious to any array of things around them, orderly or not. Some contribute to messiness as a direct result of their clumsiness or lack of motor control. Others who have always had someone picking up after them just don't know how to curtail messiness.

It doesn't take children long to learn that, in school, things go better with order and that order is a requisite of freedom. "A place for everything and everything in its place" really isn't such a bad idea. It's when having things in their places becomes more important than using them for their intended purposes that the focus becomes blurred. Good housekeeping is essential in a classroom for the mutual benefit of all who work and play together there.

Forced orderliness works in the armed services, but it has rare success in schools. Students rebel when good housekeeping is associated with rancor and caustic remarks ("How can you stand this pigpen?"). They enjoy it as much as anyone else when orderliness is viewed as a common-sense approach to getting their schoolwork done in a more satisfying manner. Perhaps some of the following ideas will help you and your students cope with messiness.

OPTIONS: **1** Agree upon a regular time to have cleanup sessions.

2 Ask the messy student if he would like to be teacher for a period while you are the student. His view of the class from a different vantage point, plus his view of you as a messy student, may give him pause.

3 Exhibit two samples of a child's messy work to show how much improvement has been made since last week. ("This bulletin board is reserved for exhibits of less messy work. What shall we title it?" The students are bound to suggest some clever title, but if they don't, feed their imaginations with some of your own, along the lines of "Lessiness Messiness, Inc.," or "From Sloppy Joe to Dapper Dan.")

4 Give the messy student an important job that will make him more aware of orderliness. Some examples: checking desks for wastepaper; being in charge of collecting wastepaper; straightening bookshelves; sorting things.

5 Have the messy student spend an hour as an observer (see Observation Technique, Appendix), of his class, with the express assignment of noting evidence of neatness and messiness in his fellow students' conduct.

6 Have the students share with the entire class some of their school labor-saving ideas or practices, such as zipper folders for certain kinds of papers, manila folders for others, colored tabs denoting papers in certain subjects, small boxes for clips and erasers, pencil cases, books stacked in the order that they are used during the day, and so on.

7 Keep corrections pertaining to messiness impersonal. (Instead of "John, you're a messy boy!" say, "Messiness keeps us from getting our jobs done.")

8 Praise obvious efforts to be more orderly. ("Jan, it was a pleasure to check your notebook. Not only were there fewer erasures, but every section was in order.")

9 Provide some times, places, and activities in which it's quite all right for the student to be as messy as he likes.

10 Reward obvious attempts to be more organized: Allow primary children to wear a special badge or bracelet indicating their good work; send a note home to the parent praising the child for his efforts to be neater; telephone the parent and praise the child's efforts; reflect the student's efforts to improve by writing meaningful comments on his report card.

11 State clearly what your position is with regard to order. ("So that everyone will have the best possible working conditions, I'm requesting each of you to keep your belongings in your [desk, locker, carton, shelf]. Any items I find on the floor or in my way I'll keep until Friday afternoon, which will be "Reclamation Day." That means that if you leave something out on Monday you will have to get along without it for a week.")

12 Try the extrinsic reward approach (see Appendix). Begin with the simplest requirement, such as handing in *uncrumpled* papers with the student's name written *clearly* on them. Gradually increase the expectations. Develop a hierarchy pertinent to each child's problem.

MIGRANT CHILDREN

(*see also* Bilingual Children; Self-Concept)

CAPSULE: The migrant child follows his parents, who follow the harvest seasons of the nation's crops. He usually enrolls in three or four schools a year. Increasingly, as parents become more education-minded, families try to plan for the child to at least reenter the same three or four schools each year, but the pattern remains an interrupted one. Some schools have made commendable efforts to accommodate migrant families by creating school calendars with fewer months and longer school days.

It would be surprising if a migrant child's ego didn't feel battered when his classmates wryly dub him, verbally or not, a "drop-in," and even the teacher lifts her eyebrows, breathes deeply, sort of smiles, and enrolls the "short-termer." Unless the child is blessed with enough charisma to be quickly accepted, his enrollment period may expire before he becomes part of the group. *Que pena!* Yes, what a pity—when there are ways that his presence can enrich the lives of the class and the class can make his brief stay meaningful and maybe even memorable!

OPTIONS: **1** Arrange an early home visit. If you can't go, encourage someone else (social worker, principal, coach) to call on the family. In addition to clarifying questions they may have regarding the student's program, the caller will be able to discern other needs the family may have.

2 Arrange for a bilingualist to work with the student (and parents) if there is a language problem.

3 Assign the migrant student to another student who will act as a guide, and a big brother, or big sister during the first few days.

4 Conduct a sociogram (see Appendix) to get clues regarding the person or group with which the child might work best.

5 Determine, as soon as possible, the student's academic skills, and assign work on the appropriate level.

6 Establish an NKHR (New Kid Hospitality Routine). Make the ceremony brief, but special! Allow a committee of two or three to plan the routine.

7 Give the student status by making meaningful reference to his travels. Allow him to show on a map where he has traveled and to tell of the family work that necessitates the travel.

8 Invite the parents of the child to visit with the class. This may be an impossibility because of the parents' work hours, in which case a class trip to the migrant's field—a genuine "field trip"— might be possible!

MIMICRY

(see also Attention Seeking; Clowning; Impoliteness)

CAPSULE: The class clown makes open bids for laughs; the mimicker covertly apes others—particularly teachers and administrators. Although he doesn't intend to get caught doing his takeoff, it's often hilariously funny or devastatingly embarrassing when he does.

OPTIONS: **1** Caution and enlighten students who are inclined to cruelly mimic others. ("Today, while Tina is absent, I'd like to tell you something quite important. I noticed some of you mimicking her walk the other day. Perhaps you don't know that a few years ago she was pinned under a car for several hours, and doctors predicted she'd never walk again. She's really something of a miracle.") *Note:* Refrain from reprimanding with, "I don't ever again want to see what I saw you thoughtless people doing the other day!" Children have a high sense of fairness and compassion when "being human" is expected of them.

2 Encourage the mimic to put on a special skit or to get involved with the drama club. His judgment regarding good taste and respect for others may need honing, but his talent shouldn't be overlooked in the process.

3 Laugh with the students if you walk in on an imitation of you. Tell them you think the mimicker could be a first rate actor because he's very observant of details, a sign that he thinks very well.

N

NAME-CALLING

(*see also* Fearfulness)

CAPSULE: Name-calling is a form of aggressiveness meant to hurt the accosted student and to rob him of his uniqueness. It is common among children of minority, racial, and religious groups. It is not limited to these groups, however. The fat; the skinny; the studious; the clumsy; the wearers of glasses, bridges, or braces; the odorous—all are targets for name-calling by fearful aggressors. Unless verbal assaults succeed in getting a response, they can't last long. It is difficult to simultaneously help the aggressor and the target of his aggression, but try to abstain from taking sides, shaming, or preaching, and bend your efforts toward helping the students understand themselves.

OPTIONS: **1** Call the name-caller and his target together for a report of the experience. ("I'd like to have you fill me in on this name-calling episode. Since my memory is sometimes rather faulty, I hope you don't mind if I use the tape recorder." The playback can be very sobering.)

2 Confer privately with the victim and see whether he can itemize reasons why the aggressors might call him names; then encourage him to laugh at himself and take himself less seriously.

3 Encourage a group (student government, parent group) to sponsor an "Ethnic Emphasis Month." ("Next week will be Dago Week, and anybody with a drop of Italian spaghetti sauce in his veins must come to school wearing something red. Lipstick doesn't count! The following week will be Square-Head Swede Week, and all those with a drop of Svenska blood will wear something square.") The possibilities are many, and perspectives are bound to change as students and faculty laugh together.

4 Help the victim ignore those who call him names by getting him busy with something that distracts his attention, such as recording, timing, counting, or checking.

5 Hold a class meeting (see Class Discussions, Appendix) for the express purpose of discussing name-calling.

6 Hold a joint conference (aggressors and victims) to thrash out differences by drawing up a minimal, mutually agreeable plan (see Commitment Technique, Appendix): "You've now all agreed to hold the name-calling down to a minimum. John will report to Mr. Jones after recess on the progress of the gang; Jim will report to Mr. Hurley on his feelings. You say you want to try this for a week and you're willing to sign this contract."

7 Ignore the matter, at least for the time being.

8 Meet privately with the aggressor and state directly that name-calling is an act of aggression that is saying "Help!" Then proceed to elicit the student's fears and the reason that he or she feels compelled to lash out against the victim. ("Jenny, you're a bright girl. I don't have to tell you that calling others names is your way of crying for help. What's bugging you so much that you have to do it?")

9 Meet privately with the victim. Explain that while it is painful to be called ugly names, the caller must be suffering from a pain or he wouldn't have to do what he is doing. Suggest counter-attacks: "Please call me Chicano with a capital C. I'm pretty proud of my Mexican blood." "We niggers feel the same about you whites." (Using the very name they called you can be upsetting to the name-caller.)

10 Show films or use video tapes that deal with forms of aggression, including name-calling.

11 Use role playing (see Appendix). Role playing a name-calling incident will inevitably be raucous, but it can also be highly therapeutic.

NOISINESS

(see also Attention Seeking; Talking)

CAPSULE: The noisy student is accomplishing his goal, which is to make himself heard. He likes the clatter of pencils, the thump of feet, the banging of doors, and especially the sound of his own voice. Assure him that he does not have to be noisy to get your attention—that he is a very arresting person without any fanfare.

OPTIONS: **1** Allow for the student's noisy conduct, without censure, during certain times of the day. Expect *no* noise at other times.

2 Enlist the help of the entire class in designing a classroom arrangement that will keep the noise at a desirable level. Involvement in such a plan may tone down the noisy person or make him aware of others' need for less noise.

3 Experiment with the best location in the room for the noisy one. If placed by a quiet student, he may imitate or contaminate, so sometimes it's better to put all the busy tongues together.

4 Isolate the student until he is willing to work less noisily.

5 Signal the noisy one with a silent cue: blink the lights; write a message on the board; raise your hand; touch your lips; or hold your ears.

6 Speak in a near-whisper to the class. ("May I have your attention?") Repeat yourself until the message has gotten around to the noisy student.

7 Stand at the door as the students enter the classroom. There you can casually remind the noisy one to "turn his volume down."

8 State, simply, what the situation is. ("It's very difficult for the group to concentrate when you're making so much noise, Kathy.")

NONTALKERS

(*see also* Playing Dumb; Withdrawn Children)

CAPSULE: It's not uncommon to find students in the primary grades who will not talk for long periods of time, sometimes for as long as a year or more. It is tempting to conclude that something is drastically wrong, since most children love to chatter. However, the silent child may actually be adjusting to a new situation in a manner very satisfying to himself—the attention gleaned from solicitous classmates and teachers may, itself, be a reward, and the need to perform is often reduced to nil since the child has already been labeled "shy" or "frightened." What may have begun as fear of a new situation could easily have evolved into a most gratifying role. Telling the child that you know his game and that you don't like it is unlikely to bring a change. Likewise, the urge to "shake a child into talking" can be great, but prognosis for success thereby is questionable. It is better to resist punitive action and to exercise patience and fortitude with a consistent approach.

OPTIONS: **1** Be explicit and expectant when asking a child to do something. Resist the temptation to plead, beg, or question. Rather, say, "Billy, tell us by drawing a picture how Baby Bear felt when he found his chair was broken."

2 Become acquainted with the child's family and its history. (Were siblings nontalkers? Does the child talk at home? How do the parents discipline the child?)

3 Clue the class in as to the reasons you work with the nontalker as you do. When the nontalker is absent, ask the students to refrain from speaking *for* the child or explaining his behavior with comments like "He's shy," or "He can't talk." Try to explain that as long as they do that the nontalker won't talk, because he doesn't want to make liars out of them.

4 Consult the family doctor (with permission from the family, of course). You can learn from him whether the silence means organic or psychological problems.

5 Consult a speech therapist.

6 Demonstrate warmth and affection for the child by occasional touching, hand holding, and patting.

7 Exhibit, without comment, the good work of the child.

8 Give the child many opportunities to draw or paint. He will use the pencil, crayon, or brush even if he won't talk.

9 Hold a team meeting (see Appendix) to clarify a consistent strategy to be used with the nontalker.

10 Maintain anecdotal records of the child's conduct for clues to periods of stress, abandon, and unhappiness. Record precisely what the child does, *not* your interpretation of the behavior.

11 Offer a reward (see Extrinsic Rewards, Appendix) to the nontalker. Use a reward that you know is prized by the child. ("Kay, when you are able to say 'good morning' to me you may use my clipboard to write on for a day.")

12 Show a film that deals with a silent child.

13 Surprise the child with a small gift. ("Dona, I'd like you to have this bookmark from Korea.") Don't expect a verbal thank you, but don't collapse if you get one.

NOTE PASSING

CAPSULE: Note passing is a tantalizing student activity. Its secretive nature is mystifying and exciting. A blank piece of paper, carefully folded and surreptitiously passed along can be great sport, but a juicy morsel of gossip makes it even more exciting.

Good teaching allows little time for note writing. Most teachers are not bothered by occasional notes. There will, of course, be times when communications of any kind are taboo (during tests for example). A general understanding early in the semester regarding proper handling of note-writing incidents would be helpful.

Never post personal notes for others to read; such action discredits you more than it does the writer. Resist reading notes carelessly left in books or on desks.

OPTIONS: **1** Accept note writing during class for what it is and ask the offender to delay the practice. ("Tom, please do your math now and write your note when you've finished the assignment.")

2 Intercept, and destroy without reading, any notes passed during tests.

O

OBESITY

(*see also* Dependency; Health Problems;
Physique Problems; Self-Concept)

CAPSULE: Our affluent society has produced an overabundance of everything—including calories—ravenously consumed by a neurotic people. Not only are nearly a fifth of our high-school seniors, according to some authorities, plagued with weight problems, but a high percentage of their parents are also troubled by weight problems.

Up and down the school corridors, kindergarten through high school, we find the overweight child. Along with his obesity, he brings a myriad of well-concealed anxieties. Within a roly-poly physique often resides a withering self-concept. The physical plant that the obese student lugs with him grossly affects not only his own image of himself but also others' views of him. Disposed as we are to stereotypes, we often expect the fat child to be passive and good natured and the skinny one to be active and temperamental. Neither image holds fast, yet just enough credibility supports the pictures to perpetuate their existence. The obese child *is* often passive, for reasons of sheer bulk; he *is* often good natured because sufficient operant conditions (his weight excepted) add up to a good self-concept. It is highly unlikely, in Western culture (where high premiums are put on the "slim line"), that the fat child deliberately sets out to become the biggest kid in the class.

The school has the responsibility to impress upon both lean and fat students that there is a relationship between their food intake and the amount of physical exercise they get. Ideally, every student (from kindergarten through twelfth grade) should be enrolled in a school system in which a well-planned health and physical education program is enhanced by courses in nutrition that emphasize the pleasure to be derived from strong, healthy bodies.

If it is up to you to help your obese student initiate a program for losing weight, you may find an opportunity to share with him the fact that his weight can assuredly be tied to three things: genes (over which he had no control whatsoever), eating habits (which have probably been cultivated by his family and his life style), and lack of exercise (over which he definitely has some control). If you are dealing with a student who knows what it means to assume responsibility for his own actions, you may help him decide whether he wants to lose weight or whether he prefers to remain as he is. You may also want to remind him that crash diets are risky and often harmful—that dieting should be done under the supervision of a doctor. Although dealing with obesity is essentially a medical problem, there are many ways in which the teacher can be an effective agent of change.

OPTIONS: **1** Advise the obese child to consult a faculty specialist (in homemaking, nutrition, or dance, for instance), for help in grooming, dress, health practices, or posture. Steering a fat student to the right counselor can work magic!

2 Consult the child's health record to learn whether there is a history of obesity, whether there is a disease present that reflects itself in obesity, or whether he is under a doctor's care.

3 Consult the physical education teacher with regard to how you can help the obese child enjoy losing weight.

4 Have a junior counselor (see Appendix) assigned to the obese student to encourage him in school. Having a special friend to whom he can report his will power triumph can make a difference. ("Hey, George! Susie offered me a chocolate bar and I *refused* it!" George's smile of pleasure may be all the reinforcement needed.) If the junior counselor wants to incorporate extrinsic rewards (see Appendix) in his effort to help the obese student, show him how to develop a plan that will work.

5 Hold a conference with the child's parents or guardians. Learn the dietary habits of the family, and offer your cooperation in dealing with the problem. You may want to recommend that the entire family consult a physician.

6 Involve the child in physical activity commensurate with his ability to perform without humiliation. Allowing him to sit on the sidelines is a disservice to him. Plan gradual induction into more physical activity.

7 Observe whether the child eats compulsively during times of stress (see *Anxiety*). Refer such a problem to the counselor.

8 Provide opportunities for organizing a club for the overweight students. An adviser who once had a weight problem might come from the community instead of from the school faculty.

OBSCENITIES

(*see also* Attention Seeking; Swearing)

CAPSULE: Obscenities primarily reflect a distorted view of sex and sexuality. They also echo the inner feelings of some students toward school and the rest of life. They have considerable shock power and usually indicate fear. According to some psychologists, girls—once they really let go—use more obscene language than boys. Obscene talk has captivating power and, for many youngsters, a dirty story may provide some comfort, since the teller will sense the presence of those who share the same fears he has about dating, virility, virginity, marriage, child birth, contraception, and so forth. Recognize obscene language as a tension releaser. Avoid thinking of punishment first. Without comment, keep obscenities washed off the walls. Maintain a cool attitude. Unless the behavior is excessive, you may be wise to "let sleeping dogs lie." And do get acquainted with the slang terms used in filthy talk or you'll be sure to be frustrated or embarrassed before the year is over. You need a trustworthy colleague who can enlighten you!

OPTIONS: **1** Build the ego of the offending student in situations not associated with his use of obscenities. For example, in English class: "Greg, you related that incident very well; your choice of verbs was especially effective."

2 Challenge the student by interpreting his or her strategy. ("Jill, it strikes me that you're trying to prove you're tough by using very colorful and offensive language, but I have too much evidence to the contrary. You're really a very sensitive and sometimes frightened young lady.") *Note:* This may lead to some frank discussion and may also provide an opportunity for referral to the proper professional.

3 Help the student take a close look at persons he likes. ("Write down the names of five people you like to be with. Put an O in front of the names of those who use obscene language a lot and an N by the names of those who never use filthy language. Put an S in front of those who swear regularly and an SS in front of those who seldom swear. Put a B in front of those who brag a lot and an SB in front of those who seldom brag. Put an L in front of those who lie and a DL in front of those who don't lie. Put an A in front of those that have been in at least one accident and an NA in front of those who have had no accidents. Put an H in front of those who hate school and an LS in front of those who like school.") *Note:* This kind of exercise will provide for full discussion and review of values.

4 Hold buzz sessions (see Appendix) to discuss such questions as: Why do some people choose to use obscene language? How do obscenities become part of acceptable language, or do they? Why do people enjoy dirty stories? Is it O.K. to use filthy language some places and not others? The level of question should be adjusted to the age group. *Note:* The reports given to the large group will enable the students to speak openly about the subject, and perhaps the teacher will have an opportunity to identify some attitudes and fears heretofore unknown.

5 Praise the student inconspicuously for any obvious effort to diminish his use of obscenities. ("Earl, I can't help noticing how remarkably you've decreased your use of foul language lately.")

6 Remind the student privately that the classroom is not the proper place for obscenities. ("Cathy, may I remind you that the classroom is not the place for the kind of talk you were using today? You will have to decide where it would be more appropriate.")

7 Role play (see Appendix). *Caution:* While role playing focused on obscenities can be embarrassing or raucous, it *can* be carried off, particularly if the teacher is willing to take a role and if the user of obscenities declares himself willing to witness a replay of his behavior.

8 Talk straight and matter-of-factly. ("Ross, your use of the words "fuck" and "shitty" reminds me of my first encounter with a young student teacher who tried for about ten minutes to impress me with his spicy vocabulary, but as soon as he realized I'd heard it all before and would prefer to hear something new, he stopped. I'm going to assume that you will do the same.")

9 Work out, in collaboration with the student, a check or control system for him. ("You have suggested that every time you use a filthy expression you'll pay me a nickel. That's quite agreeable, and we may discover at the end of two weeks that we really didn't have a problem at all—that you were just passing through a 'phase'!") *Note:* The overtones of "I like you whatever you do" are highly important.

P

PARANOIA

(see also Health Problems)

CAPSULE: Paranoia describes a system of defenses associated with feelings of persecution, excessive distrust of others, and irrational suspiciousness. Of course, everybody is a little bit paranoid. Just ask any teacher whose principal has just said "Good morning!" She'll wonder all the way down the hall what he meant by that!

Children with paranoiac tendencies walk the halls of our schools. They must, or we wouldn't have so many paranoid adults. However, it is important not to label a child "paranoid," even though the label might be quite accurate. This is the business of a physician. According to eminent physicians, everyone is mentally unhealthy at some time or another. The human personality is dynamic—constantly changing. Learning to live with reality seems preferable to a life without any tensions. Students who express paranoiac tendencies need help in facing reality and in coping with life on a day-to-day basis. Although the teacher cannot diagnose, he can recognize paranoiac tendencies and help relieve the student of some anxieties.

OPTIONS: **1** Allow the student to talk freely about his persecutions. Respond in declarative sentences. ("You feel that Sue thinks you're not doing a good job as committee chairman.")

2 Help the student who feels that "everybody's picking on him" identify *exactly* what gives him that feeling. If he persists in clinging to a false premise, he may indeed be paranoid and in need of professional treatment.

3 Refer the student to school medical personnel.

PHYSIQUE PROBLEMS

(*see also* Health Problems; Self-Concept)

CAPSULE: One's physical characteristics affect his self-concept from birth to death. Many of the problems that develop in school are physique-oriented. The developing adolescent finds it impossible to appreciate the advantages of a *Schnozzle Durante* proboscis!

The range of physical problems is enormous. Some students enter school with physique problems that hold little or no promise of change—the malformed, the paraplegic, the burn-scarred. The vast majority have fleeting worries regarding their bodies. It is during preadolescence that the internal rumblings begin. Even so-called normal children harbor feelings of inadequacy during this period. The "early blooming" girl, to the dismay of parents, may gain premature social acceptance but secretly wonder if she carries the genes of a Goliath, as well as a Delilah! The "late blooming" boy, aside from being a head shorter than the girls, worries about whether he's temporarily stunted or indeed a dwarf.

The impact of the student's unique physique cannot be denied, so look to it for important clues to his feelings about himself. Question whether the "too tall" child slumps to be more like his friends, or whether the "too fat" child is sedentary just to avoid being teased. These students need positive reinforcement of their obviously excellent qualities and minimal attention to their differentness. Pity is something they do not need or want.

How the student uses his particular physique is complicatedly related to his total social interaction, his attitudes, and that elusive something called "personality." Your attitude toward marked physical differences can provide the impetus for general acceptance of the exceptional student in your class.

OPTIONS: **1** Be sure the classroom furniture is comfortable for the student. Chairs and tables that are too high or too low can precipitate negative behavior.

2 Consult the student's family to learn how they feel and how you can work together on the problem.

3 Cultivate a spirit of delight in people's physical differences. One way to do this is to play the game "Affirmation." In this game, each student states his or her name, mentions a physical characteristic he or she has, and explains an advantage of having this particular characteristic. For example, the first student might say, 'I'm Joe. I'm tall. Because I'm tall I can tip the basketball into the hoop easily.' The next player might say, 'I'm Flo. I'm tiny. Because I'm tiny I can hide under the teacher's desk.' The game continues in this manner until all the students have affirmed themselves in some way.

4 Provide the students with a variety of published materials dealing with the different body types (endomorph, mesomorph, and ectomorph) and the variability in reaching puberty.

5 Refer the student to the school counselor or to appropriate medical personnel.

6 Share stories of people whose unusual size was a determining factor in saving a situation or whose physique problem was no deterrent to notable achievement.

PLAYING DUMB

(*see also* Attention Seeking; Withdrawn Children)

CAPSULE: This role pays off or the student wouldn't use it. Ostensibly the student is miserable, while actually he may be gratified because others are kowtowing to him and relieving him of responsibility. Recognize this role as one often employed by children to wield power or to gain sympathy and attention, as in the case of the child who has an exceptionally bright sibling.

OPTIONS: **1** Challenge the student by interpreting his strategy. ("You know, Marty, I believe you're determined to prove to us that you can't do the work, but of course we're not willing to accept that.")

2 Confer privately with the student and be direct in your inquiry. ("Bill, why do you demand so much attention by playing dumb?")

3 Encourage independence by designing with the student a personalized plan that can denote progress to him. ("O.K., Terry, now we've decided that every time you feel tempted to play dumb and shirk responsibility but play smart instead, you will move one wooden bead over to the other side of this bead bar." A more sophisticated version can be contrived for older students but it should be mutually agreed upon by student and teacher so that it doesn't seem childish [see Commitment Technique, Appendix]).

4 Enlist the help of a peer or an older student (see Junior Counselors, Appendix) to interest the problem student in designing a program that will phase out or extinguish the dumb role. (Monday—Sara will follow all lessons and remain her usual dumb self; Tuesday—Sara will ask a friend to help her when necessary; Wednesday—Sara will ask the teacher for help. Thursday—Sara will speak up in class.)

5 Enlist the help of the class in coping with this problem. ("Students, I have a problem and maybe you can help me. Sara has shown all of us that she can do many things outside of school. She can _____, _____ and _____, but she insists upon playing dumb in school. Can you help me figure out why?") The students may help Sara see that she is engaged in a power struggle with adults.

6 Exhibit, without comment, the good work of the child.

7 Give the student a monitor role, preferably one that keeps him on the move.

8 Ignore obviously foolish questions and respond to acceptable behavior. Refrain from saying, "I'm not paying any attention to your questions when you play dumb"—just *do it*. The student will eventually figure out what brings a dignified, patient response.

9 Set up a program that carries a reward that the student values. Keep the tasks and time durations commensurate with the child's ability to cope. If weight is not a problem, food as a reward is often successful (see Extrinsic Rewards, Appendix).

PORNOGRAPHY

CAPSULE: Every year, usually in the spring, a spate of pornographic "literature" floods some classes. The magazines are surreptitiously passed from desk to desk, and occasionally one is deliberately dropped in the wastebasket or slipped into the teacher's desk drawer—just for kicks. Don't decide that you are going to eliminate the epidemic by denouncing it or by destroying the books in front of the class—there are more where those came from. You are being tested. When the distribution of unsavory material is interfering with teaching the class, the problem is yours, and you must deal with it.

OPTIONS: 1 Keep pornographic material that is handed in to you by someone other than the owner. Put it away and return it to the owner at the end of the day, the week, or the semester.

2 Tell the students that what they choose to read outside of school is *their* business but that how they spend their time in your class is *your* business and that, for this reason, you are requesting that they put their outside reading material away. They will usually comply.

PREJUDICE
(*see also* Arrogance; Bilingual Children)

CAPSULE: Prejudice comes in two flavors—abnormal and normal. The abnormally prejudiced person is looking for a scapegoat onto which to project his feelings of frustration and inadequacy. It is much easier for this person to blame "the whites," "the Japs," "the Arabs," or "the blacks" than to solve his own problem. The normally prejudiced person assimilates a fair share of good attitudes along with the bad ones, and thus has a better chance of conquering his prejudices. Each of us has a storehouse of biases that get more comfortable to live with as the years go by unless we periodically dust them off and reexamine them.

There are some favorable straws in the wind: First, psychologists are finding the subject of prejudice a fascinating one to study and to cast light upon; second, in recent years a number of commercial simulation games have been introduced in the classroom to at least alert students and teachers to their prejudices; finally, there appears to be increased stress on the sameness of people, rather than on their differences.

Of course, instances of vicious, prejudicial attack are upsetting, and the immediate reaction may be to "set the culprit straight." Remember, though, that chances are the attacker is a product of authoritarianism and that his attitudes are firmly entrenched. Depending on the individual, a private conference may deter him in the future, but a sounder approach is in working with a group to which the offender belongs.

In the classroom, you can do much to diminish prejudice by your demeanor. In addition, you have the responsibility of appraising, or "psyching out," the true level of bias among your students. A clever student can mouth acceptable, unprejudiced statements and feel quite the opposite. Go slowly, though, for ignorance and naïveté are handmaidens of prejudice. Don't be too quick to punish the child who ridicules one of another group—he may be totally ignorant of the other's culture, he may have spoken unthinkingly, or he may have acted out of embarrassment. Stamping out prejudice takes time, patience, and insight, with emphasis first on our attitude toward ourselves. This means that it is a fascinating, never-ending venture, to be dealt with at all age levels. The following suggestions for coping with prejudice may elicit even better ideas of your own.

OPTIONS: **1** Conduct discussions (see Class Discussions, Appendix) when problems arise. ("Yesterday we had a fight on the playground because Carl called Tony a 'dirty Dago' and Tony called Carl 'a dumb Swede.' This sounds as though all Italians are dirty and all Swedes are dumb. How correct does that sound to you, Ruth?")

2 Emphasize the positive contributions of particular ethnic groups, and inject an unexpected note. For example, invite a Filipina doctor to discuss aerospace medicine. (Wouldn't they normally expect a male doctor to do that?)

3 Incorporate into regular class assignments (in social studies, literature, and so forth) some opportunities for students to document evidence of discrimination in their immediate society.

4 Role play (see Appendix). After playing the role of a person of another race, ethnic group, or country, a student may want to do an in-depth study of that group.

5 Show, or go to see, films that depict racial stereotypes (the Irish maid, the black butler, the warring Indian), then discuss the movies.

6 Tap community resources for information and personal contacts. Some examples: invite speakers (including parents of the students), make resource files, feature library displays, take field trips, and tape-record interviews with ethnic-community members.

7 Use commercial games that deal with the theme of prejudice.

PROCRASTINATION

(*see also* Homework; Study Habits and Skills)

CAPSULE: The ultimate in polite procrastination is the case of the twins who were never born because each kept demurring, "After you," "No, after you." Whether in the guise of politeness or malingering, the procrastinator is difficult to deal with because there is always the off chance that he *will* do it later. Of course, everybody sometimes puts off doing things that are dull or unpleasant (like correcting papers!), are too difficult, or are overshadowed by more interesting things to do. Show us someone who never procrastinates and we'll show you a mechanical man!

But how annoying the habitual procrastinator can be! Very often he has a poor concept of time and, as long as nothing cataclysmic happens, he floats along quite comfortably. When something that really matters occurs, his respect for time and energy spurts noticeably. With schoolchildren, homework is the object of delay and the source of frantic (and usually futile) efforts on the part of parents to "teach Johnnie how to get his work done!"

OPTIONS: **1** Help the procrastinating student regularize his jobs so that he takes care of things on a schedule instead of trying to do them all at once. (What is best done right after school? Before the evening meal? On Mondays? On Sunday afternoon?)

2 Permit the child to pay the price of procrastinating. If he puts off going to the bathroom, for instance, have him rinse out his soiled pants. Be sure that the matter is treated casually and without saracasm. Don't say it was "just an accident"; it was the result of waiting too long or not holding it well enough.

3 Refrain from bailing the student out of situations that arise due to procrastination. If you do, you are enslaving yourself to a problem that holds little promise of going away by itself.

4 State clearly what is expected by you. "You may do _____ after you have finished _____."

PROTEST MOVEMENTS

CAPSULE: The first concern in dealing with protesters is communication. You must assume that improved communication *is* possible. Some casual reminders: Respect the feelings of the students and maintain an educational, rather than an *in loco parentis,* relationship. Refrain from using threats as deterrents, since such behavior reduces you to a manipulator instead of a motivator. Treat the students courteously at all times, remembering that the psychologically healthy teacher does not need to resort to discourtesies. Avoid jumping to conclusions and thinking of punishment first. Refrain from judging the protesters by the length or cut of their hair or by the mode of their attire. If you feel, for personal reasons, that you are not the one to work optimally with the protesters, muster the courage to acknowledge this, withdraw, and turn the job over to another.

OPTIONS: **1** Acknowledge to the student that in some instances adult standards have been imposed on youth.

2 Anticipate the protest and move in with an activity that carries the message you desire. For instance, if word has leaked that students are organizing to protest taking the English teacher's midterm exam, preempt their action by calling the class together, stating the facts as they appear to stand and eliciting reasons for the planned protest movement, as well as some possible solutions.

3 Arrange for a representative body to meet with a teacher or administrator to mediate/arbitrate.

4 Ascertain where the leadership really lies, and use this information in planning strategy.

5 Ask pertinent questions to redirect anger. ("Before you people became so heatedly immersed in this matter, I can recall some outstanding efforts you made in promoting a project in _____. How do you account for the change?") (see Inquiry Process, Appendix)

6 Avoid taking refuge in "The school rules say . . ." Rather, appeal to the student's sense of justice, which is usually very dependable.

7 Become expert at handling threatening situations coolly, informally, and with dispatch. This may mean meeting the students somewhere other than in the school and at their convenience. Diminish your role as authoritarian kingpin; invite the leading protester to occupy your chair. Sit on the floor.

8 Be realistic about the wisdom of notifying the parents of the protesters.

9 Be willing to change or adjust the curriculum if that is the issue. Through proper channels, adjust it as creatively as you are capable of doing.

10 Be willing to reschedule. If, for example, the protest concerns extracurricular activities, refrain from holding the schedule sacred and investigate possible shifts.

11 Brainstorm (see Appendix) with the protestors.

12 Capitalize on the good ideas of the students. By so doing, some lesser ones will fall into oblivion.

13 Decipher overtones of the protest. Is the movement hinged on one unhappy but charismatic student? Is the teacher really deserving of this protestation? If so, on what basis? Is this the beginning of something that will spread to other groups? Are the parents involved in this in any way? Is an outsider stimulating the protest?

14 Discuss with students the psychology of anger, fear, and hostility. If you can't do this on the level of the students, find someone who can.

15 Empathize with the students. ("I can appreciate your frustration about this because, believe it or not, I was involved in a similar movement some years ago.")

16 Encourage open forums for dialogue and debate. Also, encourage the students to state their anger in the first person. ("*I* am so mad," rather than "*He* made us do _____.")

17 Encourage the students to use the school newspaper to express their controversial views.

18 Enter into a contractual arrangement with the protesters in which time limits and activities are clearly spelled out and are not complicated. ("Your protest has been heard. Now I would like to be heard. Will you agree to submit three good reasons why you feel the schedule should be changed? I will agree to submit three possible changes that could be made. We can then meet here tomorrow at your convenience. If you buy this idea, let's sign this contract.") *Note:* The school representative in this instance acts with precision yet gives the students considerable choice. He attempts to share the burden of preparation. He selects the place and the students select the time. The businesslike approach is added proof that he is taking the problem seriously.

19 Explain school rules that are fixed and state frankly what you feel the chances are for change. At the same time, inform students of the areas in which they may indeed establish their own rules and of the proper channels through which to do so.

20 Include students in curriculum planning. Beware of merely token representation. Be sure you abide by the group's decision.

21 Interpret, when necessary, what you hear the student saying. ("John, what you seem to be saying is that the work in your ――― class is never related to the questions on the exam. Let's consider some ways to get at the facts.")

22 Listen to the students and pay attention to what they say about others; this may be a key to what they think of themselves.

23 Provide the way to organize special-interest and ethnic-group clubs. Be sure to also provide places for them to meet and sponsors, if needed. The sponsors need not be affiliated with the school.

24 Reflect the students' feelings. "You're feeling very angry at this point because . . .")

25 Use examples of natural consequences to help the students view their action more objectively. "If you don't eat, you get hungry." "If you insult others, you incur their anger." "If you don't study, you don't learn." "If you try a new approach, you gain new insights.")

R

READING PROBLEMS

CAPSULE: Poor reading may be a major symptom of a more basic problem. Very often the symptom is persistently dealt with but the problem goes unrecognized. Research indicates a great need for teachers of poor readers and of nonreaders to understand the relationship between the student's reading development and his psychological development. The wise teacher will enlist the skills of specialists (medical and educational) in appraising the status of the student. At the same time that the teacher is seeking professional help, he may want to discourage parents or loving relatives from helping the nonreader *unless they are uniquely qualified.* Reading *to* the child would be a better idea. Parental attempts to have the child read to them after they've read to him may so petrify the child that he won't hear what is read! Almost certainly, poor readers and nonreaders need to be taught an orderly approach to learning. Current research gives the nod to a phonetic approach. Resist the temptation to delimit the child by proclaiming him retarded, stupid, or impossible. Remember that attitudinal change must precede the remedial exercises and that the teacher, more often than not, holds the key to that change. Avoid the extremes of either coddling or neglecting the nonreader—he needs to be treated like the rest of the class. Brisk, varied routines, peppered with smiles and encouraging comments, will help—the opposite could keep him a nonreader for life.

OPTIONS: **1** Capitalize on one of the student's interests (horses, fish, sports) and encourage curiosity, the strongest motivator. ("Why does the chameleon change his colors? Why doesn't it hurt when your hair is cut? Why isn't my skin the color of yours?") Having stirred the student's interest, be sure that pertinent reading materials are within reach.

2 Check, by means of any available valid measuring tool, whether the student *can't* or *won't* read. If the student is willing to try, use an informal reading inventory. *Don't* subject him to the usual standardized test routine if he can't read. If he won't speak, use a nonverbal test. Consult a reading specialist who can help with the selection and administration of evaluative instruments.

3 Check the child's work habits and *systematically retrain* him. If, for example, he hasn't learned to listen, teach him the FALR formula for listening (see Listening Formula, Appendix).

4 Design a flight plan (see Appendix) that will assure the student success and justified reward for accomplishment.

5 Encourage the student to participate in regular singing groups. Reading lyrics provides repetition, rhythm, and obscurity in a nonthreatening setting.

6 Engage the child in making posters, signs, or bulletin boards on which reinforcement of symbols is inevitable. Be matter-of-fact and refrain from "teaching" as you are working.

7 Give him some responsibility, even if it has nothing to do with the lesson. ("Jeff, I'd like you to help with one of two classroom responsibilities. At the end of the period either put the encyclopedias in order or clean the blackboard.")

8 Give the student a part in an operetta or play where a script becomes a prop and a tool. Discreetly help the student become familiar with the script. The need to memorize his role will force him to read correctly.

9 Have the student tell you something that interests him. Tape, or record in shorthand, his story. Print it for his benefit for the next lesson. Reading his own vocabulary makes reading less threatening.

10 Maintain a secure routine, but avoid monotony. ("What shall we do first today—our phrases, the tapes, or a story?")

11 Try appropriate commercial programmed-instruction materials. Use machines, such as the Controlled Reader,* that enable you to automatically or manually control the speed. Children usually enjoy operating mechanical aids.

12 Use comics or anything else the student chooses. Resist the temptation to evaluate the material. Remember that your objective is to help the nonreader learn to read. Content taste is his business.

13 Use materials that are related to the student's life. With teen students, for example, appropriate materials include driver's manuals, restaurant menus, Boy Scout handbooks, Sears Roebuck catalogs, telephone books, and job application forms.

14 Use peer tutors. Make sure that procedures are clearly understood.

15 Use a reinforcement system (see Extrinsic Rewards, Appendix) involving tokens to be traded for prizes. ("James, when you learn five new words, you will receive a yellow token. When you learn five more words, you may exchange your yellow token for a blue one. When you can read five phrases you will receive another blue token. When you can read five more phrases

---

*Product of Educational Developmental Laboratories, McGraw Hill & Co., Hightstown, New Jersey.

you may exchange your blue tokens for a red one. When you can read five sentences you may receive another red token. When you can read all ten sentences [the entire story] you may exchange your red tokens for a toy in the school store.") *Note:* Develop your own token system, keeping the increments realistic and consistent.

REJECTED CHILDREN

(*see also* Loneliness; Self-Concept; Sibling Rivalry)

CAPSULE: The rejected child feels unpopular, unwanted, and unloved. Intense rejection affects one's mental health and one's ability to cope with the demands of schoolwork. For this reason it is in the student's interest that teachers become aware of the rejected child, not only for the sake of the individual but also for the sake of the group. (Research indicates that the presence of a severely rejected member does, indeed, make the group suffer.)

Children are often rejected by immature parents who, not having grown up themselves, don't want to be bothered with the rigors of child rearing. Consequently, they fail to take time to properly care for and train their children. The child thus dealt with feels that he is a burden and a nuisance to the adults around him. In addition to the weight of his school program, he carries unnecessary emotional burdens.

Some children are so threatened with the possibility of being abandoned that they are consumed with worry and therefore cannot function in school. Others are plagued with a need to be popular, and when rejected by a peer group they feel that their whole world has collapsed. To them, being rebuffed by the "wheels" in school is more devastating than parental disownership. The rejected child needs assurance of security.

OPTIONS: **1** Ask the rejected child to do something important for you. Help him to overcome his feelings of rejection by showing him that he is needed. ("Jo, could you stop by the stadium and pick up my football tickets tomorrow?")

2 Assign a junior counselor (see Appendix) to the rejected child. Identifying with someone older can often give the child feelings of security and status.

3 Assure the child, through your consistent friendly conduct, that you do not reject him—that you like him for special reasons. ("Tom, you're the one person I can always count on for . . .")

4 Become aware, through active listening, of the possible reasons why the child feels rejected. Does he feel that you, the teacher, really accept him? Do his peers have a good reason for rejecting him?

5 Conduct a sociogram (see Appendix), which might suggest a possible collaborator from the group who could provide comfort and support to the rejected one.

6 Confer with the parents and the child. You may, on the basis of your conference, want to recommend that the school psychologist be consulted.

7 Hold a team meeting (see Appendix). If teachers who had the child last year are still on the faculty, include them; they will have valuable information to share.

8 Invite the school counselor to spend time in your class to observe the child.

9 Keep anecdotal records of the child's behavior. These are notes regarding significant behaviors (both negative and exemplary), but without value judgment or interpretation, at least for the time being. Simply write down what the child did or said. ("Dale said, 'My puppy got caught in the culvert and that's why I'm late to school.' ") *Note:* It is a good idea to use a format similar to the one shown in Legal-type Note Taking (see Appendix) for recording the anecdotes. This leaves the right side of the page for subsequent notes.

10 Permit the child to occasionally play the role of the teacher.

11 Set up friendly, small-group situations that have maximum chances of success. In planning a class party, for example, the rejected one can be responsible for contributing something that will be appreciated and enjoyed by the entire group and will warrant recognition. ("Thank you, Sandy, for furnishing the pretty centerpiece; it added a lot to our party.")

12 Take the child on a one- or two-hour excursion—just the two of you. (Go fishing, have a Coke, wash your car, go to the zoo.) Out-of-school relationships reveal new sides to personalities.

S

SCHOOL PHOBIA

CAPSULE: A phobia is an abnormally great fear related to a specific situation. The person who experiences excessive fears may be quite aware that it is unreasonable, even foolish, to do so, but he is unable to change his feelings. Many psychologists feel phobias are born of early-childhood experiences associated with shame or embarrassment. School phobia is the result of conditioning that has made the home more comfortable than school. The initial objective, then, should be to wean the child from the preferred environment. Be subtle in your management of seating, pairing of students, and tempo of instruction—all of which can be upsetting to a phobic child. However, don't let the tail wag the dog. A happy, normal setting provides the best therapy. The school counselor can be of inestimable value in planning the approach to be used.

OPTIONS: **1** Be nondirective when you and the student discuss fear of coming to school. ("You sometimes feel as though you'd rather play sick and stay home than come to school.") Abstain from censoring the responses.

2 Develop a hierarchy of fear-ridden steps and lead the child toward being comfortable with his concern. This is sometimes called desensitization and may involve from five to twenty steps, depending upon the case. An effective method of desensitization is to help the student prepare a list of steps he can take to overcome his fear. One such list might start like this:

1. Get books ready to take to school tomorrow.
2. Get clothes ready for tomorrow.
3. [*next morning*] Get dressed for school.
4. Walk with sister to school bus.
5. Get on bus and ride to school.

The list would continue in a similar fashion until the student makes it to the classroom.

3 Discuss with the group (see Class Discussions, Appendix) fears of various kinds. ("It's normal for all of us to have fears. I once knew a girl who was afraid to go to school . . .")

4 Hold a team meeting (see Appendix) of key people, including parents, to gather information and plan appropriate strategy. With a phobic child, consistency is of utmost importance.

5 Show a film that deals with a child who resists going to school. Follow the showing with appropriate discussion.

6 Use a flight plan (see Appendix) to personalize the student's education and to gradually induct him into his academic pursuits so that he sees purpose and joy in these activities.

7 Use extrinsic rewards (see Appendix) to encourage the child to attend school.

SELF-CONCEPT, Poor

(*see also* Arrogance; Underachievers)

CAPSULE:, Simply stated, a person's self-concept is his deep-down, personal view of himself. It is a privately viewed self-portrait—a measure of one's self-esteem.

Idealistic parents and teachers want the child to begin with, and continue through school with, a view of himself that, like fine wine, improves with age. Too often this dream is dashed—for clear, but indefensible, reasons.

The child's portrait of himself is not painted by him. It is the product of innumerable persons who, in one way or another, brush his life and tell him what he's worth. Adding the pluses and minuses, the child comes up with something called a self-concept, good or poor.

Discussions of the child's view of himself remain purely speculative and nonthreatening until it becomes abundantly clear that one's view of *another* seems to be contingent upon his own high or low regard for *himself*! Whether we like it or not, adults must share the responsibility for the child's view of himself. Reckless, and defensive judging, evaluating, and criticizing take from the child his right to evaluate himself.

It is a pity that many responses that contribute to a poor self-concept are proffered in ignorance. The "good-bad" dichotomy is a classic example. Children who are constantly told they are "good" would like to know what for, and children who are told they are "bad" would also like explicitness. Throwing out empty adjectives and using concrete evidence of competence can highlight a child's self-portrait. Following are some other suggestions for the student with a poor self-concept.

OPTIONS: **1** Converse often, and informally, with the student away from the classroom setting. Note his expressions of anxiety, defensiveness, and hope. Don't forget to let him know that you feel he is worthwhile and important.

2 Engage your entire class in strengthening each member's self-concept. ("I'm giving each of you a mimeographed class roll. Next to each name write a complimentary adjective that describes that student. Forget the *un*complimentary ones for the moment! Oh, yes! Write one for yourself too!") The results can provide bases for many kinds of discussions.

3 Help the student identify what he'd like to be able to accomplish, then give him step-by-step assistance in attaining his goal.

4 Permit the student to do something special for an individual or for a class other than his or her own. ("Tina, would you read your story to Mr. Z.'s class?")

5 Permit the student to show his good work to someone he admires (nurse, principal, counselor, custodian).

6 Praise the student's classwork with specifics, not generalities. ("Your poem is both moving and melodic. The meter is perfect in all but the two last lines—or did you purposely decide to end it that way?" Compare such a statement with, "Great poem!" or "I didn't think you could write so well.")

7 Refer to the counselor for a review of the student's test scores. The counselor can point out marked strengths and weaknesses and make recommendations.

8 Refer to the DUSO kit (see Dinkmeyer, 1972).

9 Role play (see Appendix). A student's self-concept is readily revealed in role-playing situations. Insights related to the self can be more freely discussed after a make-believe situation than in a more formal setting.

10 Sit before a mirror when counseling a student. Ask him to tell you what he thinks of himself. Be prepared to have him ask you what you think of yourself!

11 Use a questionnaire (see Appendix) for clues to the student's attitudes toward himself. *Caution*: Be aware that students often record what they feel you want them to say rather than what they really feel.

12 Use a sociogram (see Appendix) to learn the people preferences in the class. Use the findings judiciously.

13 Use the College Board Deciding Program (see Bibliography).

14 Use sentence completion (see Appendix) to evoke expressions of self-worth from the student.

SEXUAL CONCERNS

(*see also* Exhibitionism; Health Problems; Masturbation)

CAPSULE: All schools are subject to problems concerning sex. Chief among these problems are (1) public reaction to sex-education programs, (2) pregnancies, and (3) venereal diseases.

The past decade has seen a series of upheavals related to sex education in public and private schools all across the nation. Individuals and organizations, armed primarily with emotion, have throttled or arrested promising programs. As with sin, the denouncers know that they are "against it," but they haven't found a way to live without it! Of course, when sex education is introduced in schools it is natural to expect some controversy, even among those who are all for its inclusion in the curriculum. In many instances where the intentions were the very best, schools failed to get a program going because of inability to keep a working group together long enough to develop the program or because supposedly qualified teachers could not relate to the students. Many schools have rushed into "crash" programs with insipid results.

Procedures regarding pregnancies among the student body have changed markedly in recent years, with increased leniency regarding students remaining in school during pregnancy and returning after childbirth. And venereal diseases among teenagers have reached alarming proportions, according to medical reports.

While most schools present students with a modicum of exposure to facts related to reproduction, menstruation, and venereal diseases, they seem to skim over or ignore completely the matter of sexuality—the deep delight one experiences simply because one is a human, sexual being. Teachers need no curriculum guide, no written moral code for kindling awareness of this; one's pride in his own sexuality produces natural expressiveness and wholeness—a high state of being.

OPTIONS: **1** Avoid crash programs. Instead, take time to carefully develop the objectives of an all-school sex-education course and to determine how it should be evaluated.

2 Choose sex-education teachers carefully, since the success or failure of the program is dependent upon the teacher's effectiveness. The teacher must be able to relate to the students with naturalness and good taste—not with libertine élan.

3 Consider integrating a sex-education program into the school's regular course offerings, such as health, science, family life, marriage, child care and development, and so forth.

4 Enlist the help of physicians and nurses, but not necessarily as teachers.

5 Include parents, teachers, health and medical personnel, students, and administrators in planning a program of sex education.

6 Keep your teaching nonjudgmental.

7 Maintain dignity in language and handle indiscreet usage, which often finds its way into discussions of sex, with good humor.

8 Suggest to students who confide their pregnancy or V.D. problems to you that they seek aid from recognized agencies, not from quack doctors.

9 Use common sense about mixed-group instruction.

SIBLING RIVALRY

(*see also* Jealousy)

CAPSULE: The term "sibling rivalry" immediately implies the need for family involvement and cooperation. Depending upon the child's freedom to express himself within the family, rivalry will be expressed in a variety of ways, ranging from excessive competitiveness to almost complete withdrawal. Excessive rivalry is the handmaiden of jealousy, which is the core of the intense level. Wherever there are two or more people, competitiveness may become unhealthy. Knowing this, the astute adult capitalizes on opportunities to clarify with children the fact that man's uniqueness is dependent upon differences and that whether we allow differences to *divide* or *unite* men is entirely up to us. Parents and teachers need to remind themselves to suppress temptations to (1) compare a slower child with a fast-learning sibling, (2) to discuss the children's inequities in public, (3) to direct overcompensatory behavior toward the loser, thereby creating dependency, or (4) to connote disappointment, either verbally or via body language. The school and the family can work together on sibling-rivalry problems, and they should, because unresolved hostility in the early years may find dramatic expression in adulthood. Open, honest acceptance of each child for what he is, is preferred to a slavish endeavor to "treat every child exactly alike," regardless of how ridiculous that can get. Sooner or later the child learns that different age groups, people with certain competencies, and others receive certain advantages. Show the child that you accept him for what he is and that because he is unique, he is special.

OPTIONS: **1** Compliment the child on things he can do well, and avoid reference to his sibling.

2 Discuss sibling rivalry in a class discussion (see Appendix).

3 Encourage the siblings to pursue different areas of interest. Instead of watching brothers vie with one another in sports, for example, encourage one of them to excel in a different field.

4 Pair the jealous sibling with one whose needs are dissimilar and who may become a model for the child.

5 Read or tell stories that illustrate sibling rivalry and intelligent resolutions to the problems.

6 Reward *both* siblings for abstaining from overt rivalry. ("Look, girls, half the time I'm not sure who's responsible for the squabbles, so let's just say that if you can settle your own differences for the next four hours there'll be a surprise for both of you.") *Note:* Failure to come through would be unforgivable!

7 Show films that deal with sibling rivalry. Comment where appropriate.

8 Talk frankly about the privileges different age groups can expect. ("When you're Tom's age you, too, will be permitted to _____.")

9 Try games that highlight one's value and make the dominant sibling less threatening. One example might be to list ten things you like to do—five in-school activities, and five out-of-school activities. When each person has listed ten things, take turns sharing the lists, then let each person speak to each other participant, leading with, "We're kind of alike because we both _____." *Note:* Here the emphasis is on being *alike*, not *different*. Another game may emphasize the differences.

10 Use nondirective statements to clarify the student's feelings about his sibling. ("You feel that your sister gets more attention than you do.")

11 Use role playing (see Appendix) to get insights into students' real feelings about their siblings.

SLAM BOOKS

CAPSULE: Students on the junior-high and high-school levels often engage in an epidemic of "slam book" or "truth book" use, through which they express their preferences or hatreds for others. In slam books, a student's name usually appears at the top of each page, and below it statements or expressions about that student are written, the writer being identified by a number only. (The key is usually in the front of the notebook, so it's easy to check the identification of any particular writer). The students who instigate the movement are usually among the very vocal and critical. They are often cruel in their remarks about classmates. (Teachers are not spared, either.) Sensitive students who take these evaluations of their classmates to heart are often deeply hurt. Usually you can wait this one out, realizing that "this, too, will pass," but maybe the following actions will be appropriate.

OPTIONS: **1** Confiscate the slam book if it interferes with the class proceedings. ("I'm sorry, Lou, but I find it very hard to keep my mind on the lesson when that slam book is floating around. I'll keep it for you until the end of the period.") Put it in a drawer and give it to the student at the end of the period with the understanding that it won't show up again.

2 Discourage the circulation of slam books because of the hurt feelings they generate. Discuss in a class meeting (see Class Discussions, Appendix).

3 Use some values clarification exercises (see Appendix) to serve the same purpose that slam books serve, but in a constructive way. One example: Make a list of twenty characteristics you desire in your friends and of twenty characteristics you can't stand in other people. Put an I in front of those characteristics you feel you have. Put an M if your mother has them, an F if your father does, and a BF if your best friend does.

SLOW LEARNERS
(*see also* Self-Concept)

CAPSULE: In education circles, "slow learner" is ordinarily used to describe one in the seventy to seventy-five IQ bracket. Beware, however, of labeling a child "slow," particularly on the basis of only samples of behavior, such as standardized IQ tests. It can be assumed that a high percentage of students classified as "slow" have poor self-concepts. It is here, then, that the teacher's first responsibility lies: Try to determine whether the student is playing a role (helplessness, for instance, or dependency) that serves him better than trying would. Also, be aware of your personality tempo in working with the slow learner. If you are a racehorse teacher and you have a class of pluggers, you had better inquire about another assignment. The slow learner needs an atmosphere of security, but this doesn't mean he needs monotony.

OPTIONS: **1** Arrange for the administration of power (untimed) tests, since school-wide standardized tests are not only invalid for slow learning children but are also shattering to the egos of these students and their parents.

2 Discover the talents of the slow learner and build his ego by going as a class or a small group to see him perform. ("Sally is participating in the roller-skating derby next week. We could arrange to go and root for her.")

3 Enable the student to feel that he has some control over the learning situation. ("What shall we do first today—the numbers, the story, or the blends?")

4 Encourage the student's excellence in something beyond the three Rs, such as riding a bike faster (or slower) than anyone else, putting a basketball through the hoop more often than others, playing a good game of jacks, jumping rope well, and so on. Incorporate references to these skills when dealing with math and reading skills so that the students feel proud for a real reason. ("Janet, if you beat Susan playing jacks every day but Friday during the school week, what percentage of the days do you win?")

5 Establish a program that has bite-sized lessons and carries the lure of an appropriate reward for completion (see Extrinsic Rewards and Flight Plan, Appendix).

6 Get into the habit of calling attention to the student's work that is well done instead of to his mistakes. Throw your red pencil away!

7 Give the student opportunities to tutor younger children or to accompany them as a helper on a field trip. The notion that the slow learner can't afford to be away from his class is a myth!

8 Keep in contact with the child's parents regarding his positive gains. ("Mrs. Greer, I just had to call you to tell you that Nancy has completed her _____ and now she's ready for _____.") After the parents have been retrained to receive positive messages from the school, they are better able to absorb the occasional negative ones!

9 Praise the student within earshot of his classmates. Like anybody else, he likes others to hear good things said about him.

10 Refer to the appropriate curriculum specialist.

11 Seat the slow learner by students who like him and who don't intimidate, coddle, or do his work for him.

12 Use manipulative material to clarify concepts for the slow learner, particularly in math and science.

SMOKING

CAPSULE: Coping with smoking is a concern, to some degree, in nearly all schools. In many private and parochial schools it may be a minor nuisance if strict rules undergird the particular moral code of the institution and if infractions carry understood and immediate consequences. Public schools, as well as lenient private schools, however, operate on a modus vivendi basis. The inability of many schools to control smoking has forced administrators, parents, and students to be more open about smoking and to settle for compromises.

In some ways, these compromises have smiled on the young smoker. For one thing, the advent of pot made tobacco seem like pablum to many previously adamant parents. In some cases, student power has demanded and gotten smoking privileges for high-school students. Some schools provide smoking quarters for students whose parents grant them written permission to smoke. Arising concomitantly with these student privileges has been open acceptance of faculty members' permission to smoke in the teacher's lounge, so the stealthy trips to the boiler room for a puff and a chew of spearmint gum are a thing of the past.

While attitudes toward smoking as a "vice" have relaxed, scientific evidence concerning the threat of tobacco to man's health has increased. Inveterate smokers, dying of lung cancer, beg youth to respect their bodies. Many doctors do the same. The advertising media is, however, undaunted—filter tips still hold glamour. Barnum was right!

However, more and more students are weighing the pros and cons of smoking and making decisions on the basis of study rather than defiance or out of a desire to be like adults or just to act big. Dealing with smoking in schools is easier now than it was a decade ago. Following are immediate and long-range ways of dealing with smoking.

OPTIONS: **1** Allow smoking, but require parental permission, and specify where smoking may take place.

2 Conduct a group discussion of smoking (see Class Discussions, Appendix). Avoid preaching. Talk about smoking in terms of personal decisions, rather than in terms of rightness or wrongness.

3 Encourage a joint faculty-student committee to establish a code of conduct, including expectations regarding smoking. Publicize the explicit consequences of violations. Abide by the decisions.

4 Hold school-wide debates related to smoking.

5 Invite experts on a variety of stimulants (including nicotine) to hold informal talks with your students. Attendance should be voluntary.

6 Involve the class in an analysis of general and specific (in this case, tobacco) advertising. The range of possibilities here is limited only by the teacher's and students' creative capacities.

7 Show films or filmstrips that deal with smoking. Encourage their use on a nonclass basis. Viewing a filmstrip in a library carrel with a friend can be infinitely more beneficial than viewing it with a large group.

8 Suggest to the chain-smoker, who can't go for long periods without a smoke, that he speak to the school nurse or counselor and make an arrangement that will eliminate sneak drags in the restroom.

SOILING

(see also Anxiety)

CAPSULE: Soiling usually occurs among the very young, though it is not uncommon for older students, including teenagers, to have "accidents" during times of excitement or fear. It is humiliating for all concerned, and the best approach is a matter-of-fact one—taking care of the situation as quickly and as tactfully as possible. Soiling can mean several things: organic problems; open rebellion against parents, teachers, or other people; or a case of unexpected diarrhea. Avoid embarrassing the student by asking him why he did it (he doesn't know) or by scolding him. Handle the matter in a low-key manner. He needs to feel that you like him, especially at a time like this, so don't be stingy with a show of affection. The following ideas may be useful.

OPTIONS: **1** Allow the young student to read a book on the toilet if you are trying to develop regularity and want to be sure he's not late to the toilet.

2 Appraise the student's art work—it could give you a clue to his anxiety. If you're not professionally trained to do this, seek help.

3 Change the class activity at the moment of crisis. Send the other students out to play, for example, while you attend to the matter.

4 Consult medical personnel and the school counselor.

5 Establish with the student a routine that will diminish as the problem is conquered. ("This week you will go to the toilet every twenty minutes. Next week perhaps you can wait thirty minutes between visits.")

6 Examine the classroom routines and rules. Do they allow for normal toilet relief without reprisals?

7 Be alert to clues in the student's casual conversation that will indicate concerns or hostilities he may have. Share any clues with the doctor.

8 Seat the student by the classmate least likely to "make a big thing" of a recurrence.

9 Seize the opportunity, *if appropriate*, to talk as a group about embarrassing moments everyone has had.

10 Send the soiled one "on an errand" (a ruse) to remove him from the room with dignity, then act according to your good judgment.

11 Use a variation of the reward system (see Extrinsic Rewards, Appendix) in which you reward the student for not soiling over a certain period of time.

SPEECH PROBLEMS

(see also Stuttering)

CAPSULE: Speech problems are usually the result of either physical impairment or poor speech models. In the case of impairment, specialists will be able to check causes and cures; in the case of the poor models, retraining is necessary, and here the parents and teachers must work together to provide good models. Parents are often excellent behavior therapists and with proper instruction are economical and effective agents. It is important to know that unacceptable overt or covert behavior may be a child's effort to compensate for a speech problem. Inadvertently, the symptomatic behavior might be dealt with, leaving the basic speech problem unattended. Early identification of speech problems can be the "ounce of prevention." In addition to using the skilled services of trained professionals, these practices may be helpful.

OPTIONS: **1** Avoid making mention of the speech problem before a large group. Ask the student when he would like some drill help and arrange to assist him privately.

2 Engage the help of students to cue the soft-speaking student when he can't be heard. ("Jenny, some classmates are telling you by touching their earlobes that they can't hear you.") *Note:* If you and the class had decided during your organizational planning early in the semester that you would cue soft speakers by placing your fingers on your left ear, the statement wouldn't be necessary. Cues may be similarly used for the mumbler, the loud speaker, and others.

3 Send a note to the student's parents, mentioning his improved speech.

4 Surprise the student with a compliment about his improved speech. You might, for example, write him a note (which he can secretly savor) telling him how you noticed that he didn't ——— this morning when he made his report.

5 Use commercial programmed materials (see a curriculum specialist) to handle increasingly complex speech and language patterns.

6 Use extrinsic rewards (see Appendix) to reinforce a correct speech pattern that is gradually increased. In treating a lisper, for example, you might begin by saying,"Jane, repeat after me: 'This is Susan.'" Next, increase to "This is Susan's sister." Finally, increase it to "These scissors are Susan's sister's." After each correct statement, reward the student. Make no comment after an incorrect version. *Caution:* Be alert to the temptation to overwork a drill. Stop when the student feels successful and is not yet tired.

SPITTING

(*see also* Acting Out; Self-Concept)

CAPSULE: Spitting at or on others is a gesture of hostility and contempt. It is the ultimate in bad manners and breeding. It is more contemptible than words or obscene gestures because of its excretory nature.

In certain societies where tissues and toilet facilities are uncommon, expectorating is an accepted cultural behavior.

Certain oral habits, such as chewing tobacco or betel nuts, brought in the use of the spittoon as a regular household accessory. Although spittoons are still proper receptacles for saliva in many countries, spitting on the sidewalk, on the floor, or even into a wastebasket is generally viewed with disgust.

Schoolboys' innocent contests to see who can "make the most spit" or who can spit the farthest are not to be confused with spitting on someone to convey a message of hate. The latter not only insults another, it betrays a deep statement about the spitter himself. He needs help in unraveling some inner conflicts so that he can treat others with respect, instead of with scorn.

It is not easy to be patient with the spitter. The one on whom he spits is certain to be upset, angry, and hurt. Anyone hateful enough to resort to spitting will not willingly accede to being counseled until he cools down, so postpone any thoughts of an immediate confrontation (other than immediate removal from the scene). You may have a bit of cooling down to do yourself!

OPTIONS:

1 Ask the student to tell you *what* he did. Sometimes hearing himself state his action ("I spit on Dona.") helps him to realize more clearly what he did. If he continues with "I spit on Dona *because* . . ." you may elicit further reasons for his contempt by restating his charges declaratively. ("She thinks she's so smart." "She took your notebook." "Her brother stole your bike.") Eventually, not only the venom but also some meaningful information surfaces.

2 Ask the student to write out his feelings of contempt. See whether he can express his feelings as clearly in the written word as in the spitten word.

3 Draw up, with the cooperation of the students, a self-management record (see Appendix) tied to a major reward (see Extrinsic Rewards, Appendix). The spitter would not, for example, earn points under the category "Demonstrates Respect for Others." Note that points are *not* taken away; they are simply not awarded.

4 Ignore the student for the moment, but speak to him in privacy later. ("Pat, I chose not to embarrass you in front of the other students, but I wonder if you realize that by spitting on Jon you were giving a distress signal about yourself." If the student asks what you mean by that, be prepared to explain that by behaving so negatively he is saying that he's dissatisfied with himself and/or very hurt.)

5 Interpret the meaning of the student's act for him. ("Pat, by spitting on me you have just told me that you don't like me very much." Perhaps that is all that should be said at this time; the student may decide that you're too perceptive for him and not try it again.)

6 Order the spitter to wait in an isolated place until someone has time to talk to him. Leave him alone for awhile.

7 Refer the student to the student court (see Appendix) if your school has one.

8 Solicit the help of the class in coping with the spitter. ("Class, right now I am faced with the problem of dealing with Ralph, who has just spit on Eric. Could you help me list on the board some possible reasons he has done that?")

9 State your feelings calmly, and isolate the student for a period long enough to give him or her time to think before counseling him (her). ("Jo, what you have just done makes me very angry, but I'd rather wait to discuss it until I'm not so upset. Please wait here." Notice that you should not say, "*You* make me angry," but rather, "*What you have just done* makes me angry.")

10 Talk to the students about the fragility of the ego, and about how shattering a gesture like spitting can be.

SPITWADS

(*see also* Acting Out; Attention Seeking; Boredom)

CAPSULE: The pellet called a spitwad came in with the little red school-house. Forerunner of the BB gun, it can cause quite a stir, especially when it hits a sensitive area (usually from behind). An isolated spitwad is best ignored; a raid calls for a response. One must always question why the class atmosphere is conducive to such diversion.

OPTIONS: **1** Ask the student to create a generous supply of spitwads for future use on an outdoor target. ("Jo, here is a pint jar. Fill it with spitwads and we'll have a contest later.")

2 Engage the spitwad manufacturers in an after-school contest to see which side can make the most in a given period of time.

The first few seconds are fun, but after a while the competitive spirit wanes and even the saliva runs short, so keep the exercise brief.

3 Include a surprise mention of spitwads in an illustration pertaining to the matter under discussion. ("Class, if we calculated the square root of the number of spitwads Charley has made in the last ten minutes what is your educated guess as to what the answer would be?" The fact that the class can get on with its business without having to give him too much time may be surprising to Charley.)

4 Stop everything abruptly and state your expectations good naturedly. ("Jim, you have just made, aimed, and shot a spitwad that hit the blackboard. I expect that to be the last one.")

5 Warn the student of the possible danger of his weapon. ("It's always fun to try to hit a target, but perhaps you haven't thought of some of the possible consequences of the sport. Last year a child's eye was seriously injured by a spitwad.")

STEALING

(*see also* Lying)

CAPSULE: Remember that stealing is exciting and that children who steal may never be able to fully understand the psychologist's assertion that he who steals has a poor self-image, is asking for love, is seeking attention, or is trying to get even with someone. To assert is easy; to effect change is not so easy. The adults who are faced with helping the student who steals must examine myriad questions before taking action, including: Is this already a pattern of behavior or is it the first time the student has stolen? Is stealing condoned in the child's family? Is he stealing to gain status with his peers? Is he stealing to gratify an immediate need (such as hunger), not having lived long enough to internalize the meaning of property rights?

Use common sense in reducing the temptation to steal. Above all, resist the temptation to preach or to scold students publicly. Rather, concentrate on providing opportunities for the offending student to comprehend that every act brings its own consequences. Once restitution is made, assure the student through actions and words that his mistake is forgotten. The long road toward elimination of stealing begins with two words, "trust" and "attitude."

OPTIONS: **1** Clarify the meaning of "ownership" and implant cultural attitudes through classroom activities. ("This is Jeff's book from his family's library and it is a very special volume—a first edition. We appreciate being able to look at it, and I know I can count on all of you to treat it with respect. You will note that there are several rare coins and feathers attached to the inside of the back cover." At this point you can elicit cautions to be taken when looking at Jeff's book.)

2 Combine admission and reward. ("Terry, you've admitted that you swiped the cupcakes intended for Susan's party, and it takes a pretty big person to do that. Because this is a sign of maturity on your part, how would you like to reward yourself with a privilege?") Some teachers and administrators itemize certain privileges and allow students to accumulate points toward a given one. For instance, ten points for each positive behavior mutually agreed upon by student and adult may accrue to 100 points, which could permit the student to earn a specific privilege.

3 Conduct an inspection (by an impartial adult) on a large-group basis. For instance, if a girl were charged with taking a pen belonging to another girl, the person in charge might summon an impartial adult to inspect every girl's purse. The chances of finding the pen would be slim, but the effort might be worthwhile.

4 Conduct a shakedown or frisking. (Use good judgment!)

5 Confer with parents and professional people and act according to a mutually agreed upon plan (see Team Meeting, Appendix).

6 Elicit suggestions from the offender and then establish a fair payment for the offense, giving preference to work and time over money.

7 Encourage the students to try to identify the thief and settle the matter themselves. (This is applicable from upper elementary grades through high school.)

8 Expect common classroom supplies (scissors, pencils, chalk) to be returned to their proper places and let your conduct reflect only the highest form of behavior. It would be more effective to use statements such as "Thank you for putting the scissors in the box, Don. You might make a count of them, so we know how many we have," rather than "O.K., I know you kids are swiping the scissors! If I catch you, it won't be very funny."

9 Give recognition to students who have had a conspicuous opportunity to steal but have not done so. ("It feels good to live in a community of mutual trust. In some classrooms I would be very foolish or careless to leave my purse unattended.")

10 Give the offending student an opportunity to return the stolen article to a certain unpoliced place, between certain hours, and with no questions asked. The article could even be mailed to a designated place. Generally, it is more important to reclaim the article than to identify the thief.

11 Reduce stealing through preventive efforts, such as emphasizing self-concept building techniques (see Dinkmeyer, 1972).

12 Report the incident to the police and cooperate with them.

13 Retain all students in the room until the stolen article is found.

14 Role play (see Appendix) incidents that demonstrate that in our culture stealing has strong consequences. For example, take a current story from the news media to dramatize—every issue of the newspaper has ample material!

15 Try bibliotherapy (see Appendix) using stories about Honest Abe or other, less pointed, material.

16 Use class discussions (see Appendix) to explore reasons people steal. Identify constructive ways to meet people's needs. The discussions could conceivably lead to a unique plan to decrease thievery in your class or school.

STUBBORNNESS

(see also Argumentativeness; Compulsiveness; Fearfulness; Immaturity)

CAPSULE: Stubbornness is sometimes called the debatable virtue. Take for example, the mother who confers with the teacher: During their discussion the mother refers to the child's stubbornness as being tinted with independence, resolution, and stalwartness, and may even coyly volunteer that she "was a bit like that" herself. Later on, the father of the child confers with the teacher and refers to the mulish stubbornness of the child, tainted by "the other side of the family." Tinted or tainted, the behavior exists.

One thing is certain, it is foolish to set out to "show the child who is the boss." This would only worsen the situation, as the student has already shown you that *he* is. Stubborn people are often highly intelligent and extremely competent in certain areas. When they are uncompromising within their particular realm of excellence, they receive support for behaving on a "matter of principle." When they habitually control others through stubbornness, they are not only difficult but also very unfair to others. Consider the stubborn student a challenge. Chances are that under the cloak of obstinacy resides someone who very much wants sincere friendship, which you ought not to stubbornly withhold.

OPTIONS: **1** Acknowledge obvious efforts to be less stubborn. ("Sue, you're to be commended for changing your mind and coming to the meeting. Your suggestion at the end really saved the day.")

2 Appeal to the stubborn student's classmates to help you deal with him. ("Class, Jess is refusing to _____. I'm going to be in the library for the next ten minutes. I'll ask the class chairperson to engage you in a discussion of Jess's dilemma.") Peer-group discussion and the teacher's withdrawal from the scene may lead to a resolution of the student's stubborn conduct.

3 Ask the student to put into writing the reasons he feels that he must stubbornly resist _____ .

4 Avoid calling undue attention to a stubborn child for awhile. His stubborn conduct may soon pass. If too much is made of it, however, it may become his badge of distinctiveness.

5 Be willing to wait for the child who stubbornly refuses to act. Waiting and silent periods are not devoid of thought. When the student does make a statement, empathize and reflect. ("I think I know what you mean when you say you won't play the game their way because _____ .")

6 Challenge the student by interpreting his strategy. ("Pat, it looks to me as though you're trying to drag me into battle with your stubbornness, but I refuse to acquiesce." Keep your word.)

7 Deny the student certain privileges but offer him alternatives, then be aware of opportunities to reinforce his cooperative behavior.

8 Help the student see the difference between being stubborn and "standing up for his rights." ("Pat, as soon as you mention "rights" you are implying that others have them, too, and that means that you're traveling a two-way street. Let's focus on the *issue* and consider it a problem to be solved rather than a battle to be won.")

9 Present a hypothetical case of extreme stubbornness and discuss it with the class.

10 Reinforce, at fixed intervals, the child who stubbornly refuses to finish his work (see Extrinsic Rewards, Appendix).

11 Role play (see Appendix) an incident of obtuse stubbornness, such as a student refusing to move from a seat. Follow this activity with a class discussion.

12 Show films dealing with stubbornness and follow them with discussion.

13 Transfer the stubborn student to another class. Sometimes such a move brings about an unexplainable change in attitude and conduct.

14 Use listing (see Values Clarification, Appendix) to focus on things or ideas that stimulate strong feelings. ("List ten things that make you feel very stubborn." "List ten people from whom you resist taking suggestions." "List ten things about which you wouldn't change your mind." "List ten things about which you couldn't care less.")

STUDY HABITS and SKILLS, Poor

CAPSULE: Some students seem to intuitively develop good study habits and skills, and some stumble upon them, but the vast majority never fully master the art of studying. Teachers and parents can assume some of the blame for this because of their nagging pleas to "try harder" or "study more," without first undergirding the child with concrete, supportive help—physical and psychological.

A good student, like any craftsman, knows the skills of his trade. A carpenter knows how to use his tools; and so does a serious student. A carpenter knows he must begin with the foundation; and so does the student. The carpenter will complete his house if he needs it as his home or if someone else wants it and will pay him for it. He is not building it aimlessly; he has a purpose. The student, too, must have a purpose in studying what he does. Without a goal, he is likely to flounder with those who never master the art of studying. Teachers have the awesome responsibility of making the student's studies and life goals relevant.

Librarians, both school and public, can be of enormous assistance in showing students how to achieve maximum use of libraries. With the advent of learning (or resource) centers and the like, teachers as well as students must be constantly brought up to date on facilities and materials that are available to enhance learning. It is hardly necessary to state that staff members in charge of libraries and learning centers must themselves be curious, vital people, more committed to learning than to silence and order.

In addition to acquainting your students with the study skills described in the Appendix and mentioned in the Bibliography, you may want to try to make studying more attractive to your students by using some of the following suggestions.

OPTIONS: **1** Develop student listening skills (see Listening Formula, Appendix) through regular, brief daily exercises. ("Beginning tomorrow, we'll have a three-minute listening test at the beginning of the period. Today I'll show you how to record your scores on graph paper.")

2 Discuss study skills in class. Have your students share clever ways they have devised to learn and retain their lessons. Allow them to teach the skill to their classmates. They might prepare a booklet called "Tips on How to Study".

3 Encourage the student to build a reward system into his study schedule. ("After I've memorized ten words on my vocabulary list I'll treat myself to a ten-minute telephone conversation with Susie, then resume study.")

4 Have students record on 3 x 5 cards (which they can slip into their pockets), important formulas, words, dates, names, quotations and so forth, to be memorized. These cards will enable them to study while riding the bus, waiting for a train, and so on.

5 Hold a general parent meeting at which you can share the study skills you are teaching. Many parents are perennial students and may find your suggestions personally helpful.

6 Offer to teach a small group (two or three) specific skills that they obviously need. Have each of them then teach the skills to another student who needs help. In teaching another, they will reinforce their own learning.

7 Teach a specific skill in connection with a given assignment. ("Today I'll introduce you to legal-type note taking [see Appendix]. We'll use our social-studies assignment for practicing.") Remember, though, that one-shot lessons are worthless. The skill must be honed through regular use.

STUTTERING

(*see also* Speech Problems)

CAPSULE: Stuttering is a stress signal. There are many misconceptions about stuttering. One of these is that a stutterer never speaks normally, even when he talks to himself. But this is not true; just as it takes two to tango, it takes two to stutter. It is also believed by many that physical weakness or emotional maladjustments cause stuttering, but neither position is scientifically supported. A stuttering problem usually begins when the child is about three years of age. Parents may become overanxious about the lack of smoothness in their child's speech and convey this concern to the child, who in turn becomes concerned that he is not speaking right, and the cycle continues. The parents and teachers working with the stutterer need to learn to appreciate how children develop normal speech patterns and to be encouraged to leave the child's speech alone. Under no circumstances should the stutterer be ridiculed or forced into humiliating situations. Nor should his ideas be anticipated and stated for him. If you have little or no experience with stutterers, it's best for all concerned to consult a speech therapist, who can advise you. Following are some suggestions that may help the stutterer enjoy school more as well as improve his speech patterns.

OPTIONS: 1 Assure the older stutterer that he is making gains. ("You're speaking smoother all the time. Remember, it's okay to be hesitant in your speech. Everybody else hesitates, so why shouldn't you?")

2 Enlist, with sincerity and discretion, the cooperation of the other students in not ridiculing the stutterer and in listening when he speaks.

3 Provide many opportunities to increase confidence and decrease self-consciousness through group work, such as choral reading or glee club. By himself, the stutterer can read along with

taped editions of good models, such as Basil Rathbone's recordings of classic poetry and prose.

4 See that the stutterer has many opportunities, separated by brief time intervals, to talk to people he *really likes* in situations where he is *comfortable.*

SWEARING
(*see also* Attention Seeking; Obscenities)

CAPSULE: Swearing, to a child, is a sign of being big. Active response to his bad language is what he is seeking, so prepare yourself to ignore him—at least in the beginning. The release power of swearing is short-lived, but it does say, "I'm upset about something" or "I need help." Examine your own language. If you've been a poor model, perhaps you can solicit the help of your students to reprogram your own language habits!

OPTIONS: **1** Ask the elementary-school student privately to list all the swear words he knows. You contribute a few, too, so he'll know you're speaking the same language! (Use good judgment, of course!) Make it a learning experience by having him alphabetize the list.

2 Devise a private and mutually agreeable method of checking the habit. ("Here is a 3 x 5 card with your name and the word "swearing" at the top. The M, T, W, T, and F down the left-hand side stand for the days of the week. I have a card just like it. We'll place a checkmark next to the day every time you swear. We've agreed to keep our separate records and compare notes at the end of the week. Let's see how it works out.") *Note:* The particular technique is insignificant; the fact that the student is *systematizing* his attempt to solve the problem *is* significant.

3 Ignore the swearing. If you convince the student that you like him no matter what, the swearing will probably diminish without comment.

4 Remind the student that what may be acceptable in other places is not acceptable in school. ("Even though you say your dad says it's O.K. to swear at home, I'm reminding you it's not O.K. here.")

5 Repeat, in jest, what the student has just said. It sounds different, coming from you. ("John has just said he doesn't want to do 'the goddamn assignment' but I believe you'll all remember we agreed last week to do this assignment before taking the field trip to the museum.")

T

TALKING, Incessant

(*see also* Talking Out)

CAPSULE: The nonstop talker behaves as he does because he doesn't know what else to do. As long as he's filling the air with verbosity, he is staving off counterattacks. And there's always the off chance that his syllabic marathon may spawn an idea others will actually heed. He's a menace to everyone in the classroom. He differs from the student who blurts out or talks at inappropriate times because his behavior is diarrhetic.

OPTIONS: **1** Use the student court (see Appendix). Sometimes this procedure is risky, but it is often very effective.

2 Hold a team meeting (see Appendix) with the student and all his teachers, administrators, and counselors present.

3 Isolate the student, after a warning.

4 Recognize (with a smile or a nod, for instance) the student's obvious attempts, if not actual success, to break his own habit.

5 Role play (see Appendix).

6 Tape-record or videotape a regular class period for review and discussion.

7 Use background music at times to mute, if not eradicate, the talking.

8 Use the observation technique (see Appendix). The results can be eye-opening for the most myopic!

9 Use peer pressure. Class-determined consequences are more conducive to change than teacher limits. ("Class, we have a problem to resolve. Eric likes to talk more than our time together will allow. Should we exercise some controls? How?") Better still, take time at the beginning of the school year to collectively determine what the consequences of divergent behavior will be. Such action will reduce needless confrontations.

TALKING OUT

(see also Blurting out; Talking)

CAPSULE: Talking out differs from blurting out only in degree—the blurting being more like an explosion. Assume that the problem is solvable. Consider the possibility of a hearing problem. (Sometimes hard-of-hearing people speak compulsively to fill the void.) Consider the balance and pace of the class structure: Are there ample periods of quiet? Of movement? Of group activity? Of discussions? We all need variety and spice in our lives. Perhaps the student decided to take it upon himself to provide the spice because you had somehow overlooked it. Consider what he is trying to tell you by talking out. ("I'm overstimulated by my neighbor." "I want to be liked." "I want attention." "I want to control you.") Consider also whether he could function better in another class. Such a move should be made through the proper channels, with the student participating in the plan. Be decisive. The student will readily understand that interference with class routine has to be dealt with because you have goals and needs that have to be met, just as he has.

OPTIONS: **1** Anticipate when a student is going to talk out. Say, "Jim, you had something to contribute."

2 Ascertain which other student the offender has selected as a model to emulate. Ask the model to be a member of your team to diminish the problem.

3 Ask another teacher to observe your class. He may note something that has escaped your attention in dealing with the student.

4 Ask the right questions. Well-phrased thought questions instead of fact questions may help to eliminate talking out (see Inquiry Process, Appendix).

5 Assure the student that his talking out has nothing to do with his academic standing beyond the fact that the talking out keeps him from accomplishing more academically. Conquer the temptation to lower his academic grade because of his conduct.

There are other ways of recording this, since it is common practice to report citizenship ratings.

6 Avoid statements like, "Jim, you're always talking out." (He already knows that.) Instead, try "Jim, I've noticed several John Steinbeck books in your hands lately. Is this a new interest?"

7 Enlist the student's help in programming a hierarchy of goals to help him break the habit, then go along with it even though it may not be your way. A typical program might begin: "Monday: five talk-outs allowed; Tuesday: four talk-outs allowed; Wednesday: three talk-outs allowed . . ."Find some way to build an intrinsic reward element (a smile, a nod) at a time when you recognize he is deliberately holding his tongue.

8 Establish an easy-to-make record of how much the student actually does disturb proceedings by talking out (see Observation Technique, Appendix). This technique can help you chart the student's pattern of talking out.

9 Examine the class seating arrangement. Is the offending student perhaps sitting by a subtle contributor to the problem?

10 Ignore the student's attempts to get attention. Ask yourself, "Does this really interfere with the class's performance?"

11 Interpret for the talker what he has done. ("Jim, do you realize that by talking out just now you deprived Monica of a chance to tell us what she thinks?")

12 Introduce competition and reward. Peer-group pressure may prove an effective deterrent. ("The team that talks the least during the next thirty minutes may be excused five minutes early for lunch.")

13 Keep a tally on the board of the talker's behavior from 8:00 to 9:00 on Monday, 9:00 to 10:00 on Tuesday, 10:00 to 11:00 on Wednesday, and so forth, in order to determine what his "high" times are.

14 Provide the student with opportunities for talking within an acceptable framework.

15 Set aside ten minutes each day for *absolutely no talking.*

16 Speak frankly and unnaggingly to the entire class about your concern, and enlist their cooperation. ("Class, quite frankly I'm up against a problem that I find difficult to solve: Jim talks out a lot and I'd like to find a way to work with him so that he can still talk—since he enjoys talking and we enjoy him—but still provide a climate that will allow the class to work undisturbed.") Solicit ideas from the class, and formulate a plan of action, paying reasonable attention to the person's offense and the consequences thereof.

17 Try an approach that does not flatly deny the privilege of talking but that limits it. ("Jim, try to limit your talking out to supportive and unsarcastic comments for the next half-hour.")

18 Try role playing (see Appendix). It is not difficult for the offender to gain some behavioral insights when his role is taken by another. *Caution:* A vindictive teacher can ruin the effectiveness of this technique, but a wise one can use it to everyone's advantage.

19 Use buzz sessions or class discussions (see Appendix) to uncover why there is so much talking out.

20 Work on a plan specifically designed for the offending student. Talk to him privately and ask him if he is aware of speaking out indiscriminately. Listen to him. Try to work out a reasonable plan to help him control talking out. ("I'm aware that we don't break old habits instantly, but we can try to make some changes a little at a time. Suppose I agree to ignore the first two times you talk out, but on the third time simply write your name on the board. Would that help?") Better still, encourage the student to suggest his own plan of control.

TARDINESS

(see also Absenteeism)

CAPSULE: The chronic latecomer is saying something through his behavior, and the message can easily be misread. He might be seeking attention or revenge; he might be frightened of the day ahead because of his failure to complete his assignments; he might have been temporarily wooed away from school by a persuasive friend; or he might (heaven forbid) be delaying exposure to aversive behavior on your part. There's a reason for tardiness, as there is for everything else, so scrutinize your clues and carry on.

OPTIONS: **1** Allow predecided consequences to effect changes in the tardy student's behavior. Class members or an all-school committee could, for example, create a plan for earning special privileges. Punctuality would earn x number of points, (see Self-management Record and Extrinsic Rewards, Appendix).

2 Arouse the student's ambition to realize an attainable goal. ("Bonnie, you've been tardy six times in ten days. Are you interested in setting up a goal for yourself? Let's begin by recalling why you weren't tardy on those four days" [see Commitment Technique, Appendix].)

3 Assure the student that you recognize his tardiness as a symptom of something but that you're not sure what it is. Maybe he can tell you!

4 Consider a flexible schedule (see Appendix), which may expunge, or at least make less conspicuous, the student's habit of tardiness.

5 Enlist help from the student's peer group. ("As we all know, some of us have a hard time getting to school on time. Let's list some things that make us late." Probe the validity of the excuses.)

6 Explore the possibility of using the student's habit of coming late as a topic for written assignments in regular courses. Under proper guidance such an effort might yield insight to the writer, as well as credit in a course. In an English class, for example, you might say, "Develop this topic sentence: 'I'm a nocturnal person, and reporting to homeroom interferes with my dreams.'"

7 Show films dealing with tardiness.

8 Show your pleasure when the student is punctual, but don't overdo it, and never be sarcastic. One foolish remark like "So you decided to join us on time since we're having a party," means only that you're a loser.

9 Study the student's past performance and attendance records for clues. Don't fall into the trap of those who don't want to clutter their minds with any negative information from the student's past! If you're that easily persuaded, you had better try a new profession. Little clues can be big helps.

10 Use an occasional surprise reward for punctuality. ("Jack, since you have been on time for five days in a row, I'm going to let you go to lunch a minute early today.")

11 Use the student in needed extra capacities that will draw him to school on time: assistant cameraman, audio-visual assistant, timekeeper for athletic events, and so on.

TATTLING

(*see also* Loneliness; Rejected Children)

CAPSULE: It's reasonable to assume that the tattler is a lonely child. Tattling is common among the very young because it is an almost sure-fire attention getter, for the tale bearer is hard to ignore. The tattletale loves to curry favor by peddling juicy morsels. Some will desist when peer pressure gets to them, but the persistent tattler says, in effect, that the scorn he gets from his peers is a small price to pay for the attention and reinforcement he gets from the adults. Sometimes the tattletale in school is looking for a parent figure to respond to him; he will even tattle to incur punishment, which he feels he deserves. It is almost certain that the tattler feels unnoticed and unappreciated. Check your response to the tale bearer; it's possible to unwittingly convey the notion that we not only expect but actually enjoy the tales!

OPTIONS: **1** Become aware of the student's social status with his peers (see Sociogram and Observation Techniques, Appendix) and when possible, redirect antagonistic behavior. If, for instance, the tattler is on the same team with someone who dislikes him, make a change.

2 Interpret for the tattler what his behavior has done. The consequence of this behavior may impress him. ("Tim, while you used your time to tattle on May, your bus left.")

3 Join a minus with a plus. ("Susie, I *didn't* like to hear your tale about the boys, but I *did* like the way you said, 'Excuse me' when you passed in front of Mr. Doe.")

4 Keep a mental record of the tattler's tales and when appropriate, praise him for tattling less and less.

5 Remind the student that tattling is unacceptable behavior in school and that it is different from reporting. ("Susie, see if you can tell me which of these statements is tattling and which is reporting: 'James pulled Jan's braids'; 'Mrs. Brand said to tell you the bus is here.' ")

6 Role play (see Appendix) a tattletale incident.

7 Show a film that deals with tattlers.

8 Show the student you appreciate him at a time when he hasn't borne tales. Refrain from mentioning tattling!

9 Turn your attention to something else when the tattler approaches you with a tale—do not talk to him. Marshal the cooperation of colleagues and parents so there is unified resistance. What doesn't succeed won't continue.

10 Use tattling as a topic for class discussion (see Appendix).

TEASING

(see also Attention Seeking;
Physique Problems; Prejudice)

CAPSULE: Teasing is a common form of attention seeking. In its milder forms, it is an innocuous annoyance, but when it becomes persistent and overdone, it is considered harassment. Some schoolchildren are taunted to the extent that they resist going to school because of the teasers they will encounter there. The students who have physique problems are most vulnerable. "Fatty, Fatty, two by four, can't get through the kitchen door" rings in the ears of the fat child long after he leaves the schoolground. Good natured teasing, like asking the tall boy "How is the weather up there?" is usually enjoyed. Boys teasing girls (and vice versa) is usually secretly relished by the teased one if he or she happens to like the one he has been teased about; if he doesn't, he can become livid.

OPTIONS: **1** Agree with the students on something they can do when they get teased. ("We've decided today that when someone starts teasing us we'll stare them down.") This way the tables are turned and the all-class agreement gives support to the victim.

2 Discuss the teaser in a class meeting (see Class Discussions, Appendix). ("Ron, I won't say anything about what you have been doing all during recess; we'll discuss it at the class meeting tomorrow.") Peer-group pressure will probably help him.

3 Isolate the teaser and the teased after the incident and allow them to "talk things over." This can be effective with small children who are quick to forget superficial troubles. Being alone in a closed room without supervision, and with no questions asked afterward, can make them feel quite responsible for their own behavior.

4 Role play (see Appendix) a teasing incident.

5 Speak plainly about the degree of common courtesy that is expected from the students. Elicit from the class ways in which they should handle themsleves when someone decides to tease them.

TEMPER TANTRUMS

CAPSULE: The temper tantrum kid is sounding an alarm in more ways than one! Everything else stops when he screams, and the audience is agog with fascination and wonder at how the drama will end. The adult in charge has to be concerned with the immediate and long-range goals. Tantrums usually occur among the very young (four- and five-year-olds) but they occasionally occur among older children as well. At any age, if they continue it is because they work. Of course, it is difficult not to acquiesce to a child who screams and flails his limbs about, particularly if there is an audience. However, the surest cure for tantrums is ignoring them. In the schoolroom, be prepared to have your corrective strategy complicated by oversolicitous classmates who will want to respond to the tantrum thrower in one way or another. If this is the case, a quiet comment or two will normally elicit cooperation. Remember that tantrum behavior was learned and that it must now be unlearned via consistent, constructive treatment.

OPTIONS: **1** Appeal to the child's ego with a matter-of-fact statement. ("Barbara, nobody enjoys the Barbara that throws tantrums, but everybody enjoys the helpful Barbara.")

2 Apprise the child of what he can expect from tantrums. ("Billy, tantrums are bothersome to everyone. Don't expect to get favors with them.")

3 Discuss with the student harmless ways of having a tantrum. ("The next time you feel a tantrum coming on you may use the punching bag in the gym.") Solicit other "harmless ways to throw a tantrum" from the student and his peers.

4 Explain to the child, at a time when he is calm, what the consequences will be the next time he has a tantrum. ("Jerry, perhaps this situation will never happen again, but I want you to know what will happen if it does: I will leave you alone until you stop screaming.")

5 "Sniff out" the impending tempest and redirect it by engaging the rest of the class in singing, clapping, or marching.

6 Use nonverbal modes of coping, such as signaling the other students to quietly follow you out of the classroom and closing the door behind you.

7 Write, with the student's help, a note to the parents, telling them what took place. ("Dear Mr. and Mrs. Black; Today Leslie had a tantrum. This is the way he behaved: [Insert the child's precise description of his conduct here]. He says this will not happen again because [Insert the child's commitment here]. I believe Leslie.") Have the student hand-carry the original to his parents. If after two days you have not had a response, mail an additional copy to the parents. Place a copy in the child's record.

TEST PHOBIA

(*see also* Fearfulness)

CAPSULE: Fear of taking tests is common among those considered very normal. When it becomes highly acute, however, it can be labeled a phobia. No amount of ridicule or pooh-poohing will eradicate the problem. It must be dealt with straightforwardly, sympathetically, and systematically if it is to be conquered. The wise teacher will, of course, try to become well acquainted with the student's school record, noting such items as incidence of absences, marks in the different subject areas, and various potentiality indicators.

OPTIONS: **1** Administer nonverbal tests to the phobic student in order to get a more accurate measurement of intelligence.

2 Administer power (untimed) tests in order to eliminate timing frustration.

3 Allow the student to feel he has some control over the situation and solicit suggestions from him for conquering his problem.

4 Check the child's reading ability. (Gray's Oral Reading Test is one of several short-form tests that will give you pertinent information quickly.)

5 Consider the use of appropriate background music during testing.

6 Consult a doctor regarding the advisability of medication to calm the student during tests.

7 Contact the student's parents for further information and cooperation.

8 Help the student work through an objective test, just for practice.

9 Remember to reinforce good performance on essay tests with written comments or verbal praise.

10 Show films on how to take tests.

11 Talk to the student privately. Discuss fear of testing, reflecting his feelings. ("Taking tests really frightens the daylights out of you.") As a result of your discussion, design a plan to attack the problem. It may involve steps in which the intensity gradually increases so that success is built into the program: (1) Take oral tests until able to handle the written. (2) Stay in the room, merely observing classmates taking a test. (3) Take bite-sized tests, then work up to more substantial ones.

12 Teach the child how to keep an assignment book.

13 Teach legal-type note taking (see Appendix) to help the student be better prepared for tests.

TICS

(*see also* Anxiety; Eye Problems)

CAPSULE: Tics are small involuntary muscle spasms that sometimes evoke smiles, if not laughter, from the uninformed who think the person is trying to be funny by lifting his eyebrows, blinking, jerking his head, or even clicking his tongue. Such behavior is not uncommon during adolescence, which one might expect, since pressures are high at this time of life. Actually, the tic operates both as an indicator of tension and as a safety valve. Be alert to the kinds of circumstances and types of personalities that seem to trigger the tic. If possible, exercise control of situations so that the behavior does not increase. Refrain from calling undue attention to a student's tic. Ordinarily, it's best to abstain from any action, but under certain circumstances it may be appropriate to try one of the following.

OPTIONS: **1** Arrange for a family consultation in order to learn the student's history.

2 Discuss (see Class Discussion, Appendix) people's needs to release tension, and hold group sharing of different forms of adjustment. ("Today we are discussing some of our individual ways of coping with tension and nervousness. Betty, you told me the other day that when you get nervous you move your left shoulder up and down and it's hard to stop it.")

3 Introduce a graduated and less-threatening approach to classwork. If, for instance, Bill is anxious about speaking before the class, try having him privately record his speech on tape, then delivering it in a room by himself, then to a classmate, and finally to the entire class.

4 Refer the student to health specialists.

5 Show the student you like him and that you don't even notice the tic.

TRUANCY

(see also Absenteeism; Fearfulness)

CAPSULE: In some schools today truancy has ceased to be a problem because they operate on an open-campus, individualized-assignment basis. There are still many schools, however, that hold to recording attendance and conventional schedules. Consider the ridiculousness of suspending or expelling a student for truancy! By his conduct, the student has already stated that he prefers something else over school, so the sensible approach is to seek out the reasons he cuts out. Some of the reasons are obvious (learning problems, fear of someone, irrelevancy of schoolwork, a penchant for drugs), but others are more difficult to pinpoint. Preaching to the student is useless, as is retribution. About the only things one can be sure of are that there *is* a reason for the truancy and that, unless there is an attitude of discovery without blame and intimidation, no real change will take place. There are several courses of action one should avoid in dealing with the truant. Avoid taking refuge in "The schools rules say . . ." unless, of course, the student has had a part in the shaping of the applicable rules. Instead, appeal to the student's sense of right and wrong, which is usually quite dependable. Avoid sarcastic, aversive behavior. A comment like "So you decided to come to school today!" only reassures the student that you don't expect his best, so why should he bother? More than anything else, the student wants to feel welcome in school. Depending on your philosophy, the kind of school in which you teach, and your understanding of the total problem, you may wish to try your version of some of the following suggestions.

OPTIONS: **1** Counsel with truants in a group setting, stressing values. Elicit from the students ways of decreasing truancy. Respect and try their suggestions, even if they sound crazy to you (see Simon, Howe, and Kirschenbaum, 1972).

2 Demonstrate to the student that you are glad he's in school *without saying so.* Possible methods include asking him to take a message to an important person, displaying his work without fanfare, using his name frequently, and being courteous when you address him.

3 Detain the truant in school after hours. *Caution:* The risks are great, since after-school jobs, clearance with parents, sports, and club activities are common reasons (or excuses) for not staying. Too often, detention halls become places to put in time or just to sit. In a quiet setting supervised by a nonhostile person, a detention hall *can* be a good place for a truant to study and to take the consequences of his voluntary misbehavior.

4 Discuss truancy freely in class (see Class Discussion, Appendix). Be alert to expressions of fears that cause student to play hooky.

5 Empathize with the student and at the same time remind him of his responsibility to others, ("I appreciate the urge to skip school on a spring day like yesterday, but your absence curtailed the activities of Joan and Sig, who depended upon you for their panel presentation. Please talk to them and reschedule your panel discussion.") *Caution:* Refrain from a put-down, crybaby attitude; be matter-of-fact.

6 Engage junior counselors (see Appendix) to work with truants as individuals or in a group. High-school junior counselors working with students younger than themselves can be very effective. Encourage them to devise their own motivating techniques.

7 Establish a new kind of relationship with the truant. Extend a personal invitation to your home, for example, or hire him to wash your car, mow your lawn, or pick your berries. Resistance breaks down when teachers are observed in a nonschool setting.

8 Establish a short-term reward system (see Extrinsic Rewards, Appendix). ("Jim, your records shows that you're truant between six and eight days a month. Could you cut your truancy 50 percent if there were a privilege or a reward for you at the end of the month?")

9 Evaluate with the student his academic work. Point out that his truancy had nothing to do with the marks, but mention that the marks might have been higher, had he been in class.

10 Examine the pattern of the truant's absences and use it as a topic for discussion with him. If, for example, the absences are always on exam days, try "Tom, I've observed that your last three absences were on days Mr. Hill had a chemistry test scheduled. Does that mean anything, or is it just a coincidence?"

11 Explain the school rules that are absolutely firm. At the same time, tell the student the areas in which *he* can establish rules and how to go about doing it (such as through the student council, petitions, or lobbies).

12 Hold a team meeting (see Appendix) with the truant present. The adult who has the best relationship with him might chair the meeting. Open discussion should precede formulation of a reasonable plan of action.

13 Individualize the truant's instruction (see Flight Plan, Appendix). Individualization might not diminish the truancy, but it can make it less crucial. Personalizing the lessons is one way to keep the schoolwork relevant to the student's life.

14 Make available to the truant responsible jobs that will demand his presence in school (handling physical education, audio-visual, or stage equipment, for example).

15 Make the subject of truancy a matter of research and a bona fide part of a course.

16 Refer to a ladder of offenses and their corresponding results. (First offense: student is warned by school personnel; second offense: parent is notified by telephone in the presence of the student—(a letter is sent if there is no phone); third offense: the student, the parents, and a teacher [s] confer and agree upon a plan of action.) Such ladders can be constructed by a representative committee, can be circulated among students and parents, can be referred to when a course of action needs to be taken.

17 Require the student to be responsible for work missed during his absences. Some teachers gripe about having to give extra time to a truant outside of class, while others welcome this opportunity to get some insight into the student's problems. Administrators can help their faculties by seeing that make-up work guidelines are carefully thought out and circulated.

18 Suggest voluntary withdrawal. ("Bill, you and your parents have decided you will withdraw temporarily. There will be no damaging notation in your cumulative record, and you may return when you are ready to work.")

19 Threaten the student with consequences of further truancy. *Caution:* It's risky, but sometimes inevitable and effective. People who threaten usually overuse the technique. Occasionally, however, a threat, with follow-through, is quite correct.

20 Use a demerit system. If such a system is already in existence, be sure it is fully explained. If a demerit system is being set up, include student representation on the planning committee. Students are more inclined to accept the consequence of an offense if they were involved in naming the price. (This plan is more popular in military schools than in other types of schools.)

21 Use a student court (see Appendix). *Caution:* Students often tend to be too severe. This procedure *can* be highly effective, however.

U

UNDERACHIEVERS

(*see also* Anxiety; Discouragement; Fearfulness;
Reading Problems; Self-Concept)

CAPSULE: Underachieving describes most of us. In school jargon the term is used to describe a discrepancy between the mental age (as reflected in an IQ score) and the educational age (as reflected in standardized achievement-test scores). For instance, a student with an IQ of 100 whose achievement test scores are in the 30th percentile is underachieving. Chances are, his underachievement is related to socioeconomic factors, family factors, unrealistic goals, or a poor self-image. The reasons could also be physical, in which case referral to the school or family doctor is appropriate. In American culture, boys outnumber girls as underachievers until they enter college or other advanced training institutions. Cultural taboos, such as labeling fields of study more appropriate for one sex or another, still prevail—but they are gradually being lifted, thanks to liberating movements.

Research does not discount the fact that teachers' and parents' attitudes and expectations affect the performance of the student. Sometimes the underachiever is fulfilling the expectations of those around him as in the case of the boy who constantly hears that he couldn't possibly perform as well as his brother, who was in that room last year. After checking the difficulty level of the subject matter and the pace that you adhere to in your classroom, you might help the underachiever by (1) focusing on activities that help him establish attainable goals, (2) reinforcing what is already admirable in his performance, and (3) undergirding his self-image with pride. Being a motivator instead of a manipulator is one of your first responsibilities. The following ideas can be cut to size for all ages.

OPTIONS: **1** Assign the underachieving student to another teacher for a segment of a day, week, or term so that different ideas and stimuli can be generated regarding his problem. A student limited to a single environment may have little encouragement to upgrade his achievement.

2 Become aware of any exaggerated fears the student may have related to schoolwork, and lead him gradually through a process that conquers the fear (see Option 11 in *Test Phobia*).

3 Check the student's ability to read by administering, or asking the reading specialist to administer, an informal reading inventory that will indicate his frustration, instructional, and independent reading levels.

4 Confer with the parents and urge them to converse with their underachieving child about school. Caution them to avoid asking questions like, "What did you learn in school today?" He is sure to say "Nothing." Instead, suggest something like, "You kids played hard in that after-school game." This kind of statement opens the spigot, instead of turning it off.

5 Consider adjusting the curriculum to better serve the underachiever—after all, what is so sacred about the one that exists if it isn't serving the student? ("Instead of insisting that you take a foreign language, here are some other options.")

6 Encourage the underachiever to commit himself (see Commitment Technique, Appendix): "I agree to check all of my math before handing in my assignments. I further agree to meet Mrs. Smith, my math teacher, for a conference every Thursday at 2:00 for the next three weeks." *Caution:* It is easy for a student to be extravagant when drawing up a contract, so encourage realistic goals or he may perpetuate his underachievement.

7 Have the student maintain an assignment book. The teacher initials this book each time the student has entered an assignment correctly; the parents initial it each time the student has finished an assignment.

8 Have the underachiever tutor another student. *Note:* Don't be fooled by the idea that because he is not performing up to par he would be a poor teacher!

9 Have the underachiever write his autobiography. It may give you clues to his pattern of underachievement.

10 Hold a case conference (see Team Meeting, Appendix) to discuss the best strategy to be used with the student. Be sure the student is accountable to the person who can work best with him.

11 Learn, through the use of values exercises (see Values Clarification, Appendix) how the underachiever feels about his pattern of underachievement. Ask him to list five reasons why he feels he is underachieving and five things that could be done to change the situation. Based on this information, help him outline a plan to improve his achievement. *Note:* This is recommended for both individual and group activity.

12 Note the underachiever's outside-of-school interests and relate his academic work to these. Construct a flight plan (see Appendix) based on the student's interest areas. This plan enables the student to see the total assignment and adjust his work schedule accordingly.

13 Refer the underachiever to the school counselor.

14 Reflect the student's feelings about his achievement. ("You don't feel satisfied with your work in English, but you're at a loss as to how to improve.") If the student indicates that at last he's found someone who knows how he feels, you may have your first opportunity to give him specific assistance. Don't flub your chance!

15 Reinforce the underachiever's bite-sized lessons with honest, substantive praise. ("Ted, in only ten minutes you have finished three out of four problems. Get youself a drink, and let's see what you can accomplish in the next ten minutes.")

16 Teach the student some study skills (see Legal-type Note Taking and Listening Formula, Study Skills, Appendix).

17 Use an extrinsic reward (see Appendix) to motivate the underachiever. ("Every time you improve your performance in [name the subject or skill] you will receive a token. When you accumulate twenty tokens you may exchange them for [a prize or privilege appropriate to the age level] .")

18 Use a student self-rating technique. Once a week, for example, the student evaluates his progress with an adult. Encourage the student to devise his own self-rating tool, such as a chart or graph that registers change in achievement.

19 Use buzz sessions or brainstorming (see Appendix) to collect the students' ideas regarding effective class-as-a-whole motivation. ("In the next seven minutes each buzz group will list as many ideas as possible that could be used to motivate learning in this class.") Next, share, thrash out, and agree upon some viable steps for implementing the best ideas. Follow this with evaluation.

VANDALISM

(see also Gangs)

CAPSULE: Vandalism is on the increase. Inside and out, many schools and other public and private buildings bear the scars of ruthless disregard for others' property. This fact poses some questions, two of which are, "Are the schools indeed breeding this hostile behavior?" and "Can the schools rectify the situation?" The respective answers are, "Quite possibly," and "Of course!"

Unlike the arsonist, who prefers to work alone or with one accomplice, the vandal usually goes with a gang. He may be the leader, which requires decision-making skills ("What do we wreck tonight?"), or he may be an obedient follower. He may work with Vesuvian passion or with the stealth of an adder, but he is *always* destructive. He dwells in a world of ambivalence, for in his bid for attention he fears getting caught yet hopes he will be.

Flagrant abuse of property raises the ire of thinking, feeling people. Sympathy for the vandal runs thin when smashed windows, rifled safes, jammed typewriters, besmirched walls, defaced books, damaged statuary, and slashed tires are left in his wake. The immediate impulse, and doubtless the correct move, is to contact the police. However, the school cannot rest the case there; it must examine possible factors within the school that might be contributing to such aggressive conduct. In other words, the disease, not the symptom, must be treated. This calls for a united faculty-student effort that emphasizes restitution instead of retribution.

OPTIONS: **1** Ask the student to suggest what he feels is appropriate compensation for his misdemeanor. Keep the compensation appropriate to the offense, preferably in terms of work rather than of money. ("Tom, you defaced the flagpole and you feel it is fair to expect you to paint it," or "You scratched the table and now you will sand it.")

2 Ask the student to write a description of his vandalism venture. Tell him it's for him, not you. Place the description in his file and agree to remove it at the end of the school year when it is clear that he has not repeated vandalistic acts.

3 Befriend the vandal. You may be his best friend or the only one who has hope for him.

4 Challenge the student by interpreting his or her strategy. ("You know, Dee, by scratching notes all over the outside of the building you must be giving a distress signal. Perhaps you can tell me what it is.")

5 Confer with the principal. He may enlist the cooperation of the law-enforcement officers.

6 Consult the guidance counselor.

7 Discuss values informally. ("Today we are going to consider the subject of property. First, list ten items of property that you take good care of. Next, list ten items that you are careless with. After each listing, put an M if the property is yours, an O if it belongs to others, and a P if it is public property.")

8 Emphasize career guidance. The student who has a constructive world-of-work goal will have little time for vandalism.

9 Engender a spirit of pride in the school by making different individuals, classes, or clubs responsible for some of the building and ground care. Primary-grade children can select a bush to plant and nurture, for example. They can put name tags on trees or near flowerbeds to personalize and generate pride in responsible acts that give pleasure to the entire school.

10 Fine the offending student so that repairs or replacement can be made.

11 Have the student body, with the aid and supervision of the head custodian, sponsor an annual "Spring Housecleaning Day." The student council could plan and execute the activity, and chairmanship could be on a yearly rotating basis (this year the seniors, next year the juniors, and so on). A field-day event could climax the day.

12 Invite professional persons (such as psychologists, and psychiatrists) from the community to speak to your class about destructive, aggressive behavior.

13 Notify the parents of the vandalous student. Arrange a conference with the parents and the student. *Note:* Your particular school policy will determine who notifies the parents and who holds the conference.

14 Recognize, and give credit for, obvious efforts to resist temptations to deface property and obvious efforts to discourage others from vandalism. ("I saw you discourage Sue from dragging her pencil along the hall wall. Thank you!")

15 Use a student court (see Appendix) to deal with the vandal.

16 View and acknowledge scribbling and scratching activities for what they are. One cannot label the schoolboy who scratches his and his girl's initials on his notebook a vandal. He is a distracted, moonstruck lad, expressing *love* for his girl. When the scratches become other four-letter words and are carved on public property, *that* is vandalism!

WASTEFULNESS

CAPSULE: It is not surprising that our nation has spawned, along with Nobel Prize winners and space travelers, a people that takes *plenty* for granted. While the schools (public, particularly) may have unwittingly contributed to the belief in a bottomless storehouse by providing ample tax-paid supplies, in light of current shortages it now behooves the school to conquer wastefulness by teaching conservation and frugality. It is to the credit of teenagers that they are ecology minded and on their own have instituted many worthwhile projects. The younger students need prudent training and good examples to follow.

OPTIONS: **1** Discuss shortages of all kinds (gas, water, toilet paper) and encourage the students to speculate on the consequences that might ensue if the present trends continue unabated.

2 Discuss signs of gluttony in today's society (eating and drinking habits, for example).

3 Encourage your students to think of as many ways as they can to use wastepaper, pencil shavings, stubby pencils, wrappers, and boxes. While engaged in such divergent thinking, they may become fascinated with the possibilities for other kinds of leftovers.

4 Lead the students into the habit of salvaging bits and pieces of things. Store things in a categorized manner (crayons, fabric, and string, each in separate boxes) so the students will have ready access to them.

5 Limit the students to a specific quota of supplies, and devise a fair, efficient way of dispensing them.

6 Show, by products you make, how things others might throw away can become part of an attractive display or a functional product.

7 Urge the student who crumples a little-used piece of paper to build his own supply of scratch paper for working his math problems.

WHINING

CAPSULE: Whining is the sound and sign of an unhappy person. Few people outside the school setting have the courage to denounce whiners; they simply avoid them. This leaves the teachers and parents with the burden of effecting behavior changes, if any are to be made. The problem is doubly difficult if the child's model happens to be a teacher or a parent! Hopefully, casual disregard for the whining will eventually eliminate it, but if it doesn't, try some of these ideas.

OPTIONS: **1** Assign roles in creative dramatics that call for low-register voices and forceful delivery. (In primary grades: Papa Bear or the Old Troll. In upper grades: serious, authoritarian characters.)

2 Award tokens for diminishing whining (see Extrinsic Rewards, Appendix).

3 Discuss whiners in a class meeting (see Appendix). ("The other day, when Mrs. Z. substituted, she said several children whined. Can we talk about why they did that?")

4 Have a student, with the permission of the whiner, record the times he whines during a given day. Compare several recorded days and talk about the evident changes.

5 Have the whiner imitate the sounds of drums, tubas, or low notes on the piano to help him appreciate his voice range.

6 Reinforce nonwhiny behavior with a compliment. ("Sara, did you realize that when you spoke to me just now you didn't whine at all? Beautiful!")

7 Talk to the whiner about his habit and agree upon a silent, secret reminder to help him break it. ("I'll put my pencil on my ear when I hear that unpleasant sound.")

8 Write the student's name, followed by a smiling face, on the board at the end of a nonwhiny day.

WITHDRAWN CHILDREN

CAPSULE: To withdraw to a safe place when threatened by anything is normal defensive behavior. To spend most of one's time in this manner is not normal. In a secure nook of withdrawal, a person can dream and fantasize, perhaps for long periods of time without detection. It can happen in the classroom, and it does. Take note of the child who is described as "so good," "never gives anyone a minute's trouble," or "very shy and sweet." That student could, in fact, be very well adjusted but, on the other hand, excessively passive behavior could be expressing such feelings as "I want to be liked," "I'm afraid of being hurt," "I feel inferior to others," "I can't do the work," "The work is dull," "The courses have no relevance to my life," "I don't understand the teacher's speech pattern," or "I'm sick." There is always the possibility that withdrawn behavior has a physical basis; explore that. By comparison, the student who acts out is much healthier than the withdrawn one, who may be stockpiling emotions for an eventual explosion that even those closest to him might find incomprehensible.

Don't diminish your effectiveness with the withdrawn student by feeling sorry for him. Remember that since this student dwells in a fantasy world, much of his activity will be covert. He may indeed be very destructive. Such a student usually functions best in a classroom environment that is uncluttered. Swift movements and sharp declarations on your part are upsetting to him. Neither mollycoddling nor caustic treatment will help him come out of his shell. The behavior pattern, so well learned, will now have to be *un*learned, and gradual movement out into the arena he fears is essential.

If you are serious about helping the withdrawn child, you will learn as much as you can from the usual sources: records, parents, teachers, counselors, observation, and so on; you will carefully assess the difficulty and amount of work for the student, remembering that work too easy or too difficult encourages withdrawal into less threatening realms; you will check into his dietary habits, since research indicates that many tuned-out students overindulge in carbohydrates and sweets; you will find ways to show the student that you believe in the need to dream and fantasize but that you are convinced of the need for a healthy balance between dreaming and doing; and you will be alert to young children's tendencies to overprotect the withdrawn one and to older students' inclinations to ignore their apathetic peer.

OPTIONS: **1** Arrange to involve the withdrawn student in puppetry, if not as a puppeteer (where he has the security of a backstage station), then as a viewer of a story about a character who is tuned-out, dreamy, passive, and so forth.

2 Ask the student to tutor a younger student and help him with the proper procedure. ("Eric, I've been asked by the second-grade teacher to find tutors for several children. May I submit your name to her?")

3 Capitalize on the child's chief interest, allowing him to pursue it in seclusion; seize the right time to help him move into a small-group activity.

4 Design a flight plan (see Appendix) with the student. This approach enables him to emerge gradually.

5 Enlist peer judgment in the presence of the student. ("Susie has a hard time continuing her work. I wonder if we can help her.")

6 Exercise skill in preparing the student for shifts in lesson emphasis, since abrupt changes frighten him. ("Those who have finished reading the science directions may go for a drink and then join Jan's group to do the experiment.")

7 Find ways for the student to make a genuine contribution. ("Tom attended the horse races last month. I see a model of the winner on his desk. Can you tell us about his records, Tom?")

8 Get him started by physically placing him in position with paper, book, pencil, and his posterior squarely on the chair (a dubious strategy with older students!).

9 Give the student a task that both teaches and requires physical movement. (Putting away cards in numerical order, for instance.)

10 Give the student many opportunities to develop self- and critical judgement by selecting his own best work (best page, best picture, best letter, best anything). *Variation:* Help the student compare this month's record with last month's.

11 Give the student some responsibility, even if it has nothing to do with the lesson (collecting things, distributing things, counting things).

12 Have a fellow student work with the withdrawn child and reward the helper when the tuned-out one tunes in (see Extrinsic Rewards, Appendix).

13 Have a designated student check on the dreamer. ("Time's up for Terry.") This will alert the student to the fact that other students, as well as the teacher, are trying to involve him.

14 Help the student dramatize or talk about his daydreams by having the entire class share fantasies. ("Sometimes I have a daydream that takes place in a gymnasium. I'm watching a thrilling basketball game. Three of our best players foul out and the coach calls me out of the bleachers to substitute—and I save the game! Imagine a girl saving a boy's game!")

15 Hold out a simple reward. ("Tina, as soon as you finish this you may _____.")

16 Question the student after successful participation in a task, with "How does that make you feel?" This may prompt a feeling that withdrawing is not his only means of coping.

17 Show films that depict children enjoying each other's company. Let the medium be the message.

18 Solicit suggestions from classmates when the withdrawn student is absent. ("Boys and girls, sometimes Sandy prefers to daydream instead of getting her work done. Can you give me some suggestions for helping her?") Such an exercise can be a learning experience in humaneness.

19 Suggest something positive. ("Rick, tell me how far you've gotten in your math," instead of "Rick, stop daydreaming!")

20 Talk to the student privately about his tendency to daydream. Restate his ideas nonjudgmentally. ("You like to dream about a world without schools.")

21 Use a reward system (see Extrinsic Rewards, Appendix) that encourages participation. ("Each time you work with another student you will receive _____," or "Each time you participate in class you will be credited with _____.") *Note:* Every plan must be tailormade for the student and tempered with common sense.

22 Use a timer to keep the student's interest focused on a task. A simple egg-timer model can be constructed for five- or ten-minute periods. *Variations:* Establish time limits in odd minutes. ("Greg, see how much you can finish in seven minutes.")

WOLF WHISTLES

(*see also* Attention Seeking)

CAPSULE: This is one of the oldest attention-getting devices known to man! It may mean that the student is disinterested in the lesson, that he is desperate for attention, or simply that he is temporarily diverted by a "celestial body." Make a mental note of what has evoked this response (halter too loose, sweater too tight, skirt length provocative?). Why not assume that it won't become too disruptive a habit and try to anticipate and avoid circumstances that lead to this kind of response? Ask yourself, "Does this *really* interfere with this student's or anyone else's performance?" If the answer is "no," why do anything? Avoid responding with anger or sarcasm. This only reinforces the notion that the method works.

OPTIONS: **1** Be decisive about calling a halt to the behavior if your better judgment dictates. Make clear what you want. ("Terry, please turn this way so you can see the map," instead of "Terry, cut that out!")

2 Engage the entire class in learning how to do a tremendous wolf whistle in unison, then incorporate it into an original choral reading! The students can help you create it. At the conclusion of the "rendition" move briskly back to business.

3 Ignore the wolf whistle and, at the same time ask the student to do an errand for you. ("Jim, please deliver this book to our principal. Thank you.") Remember to be matter-of-fact in this.

4 Respond to the wolf whistle with, "Jerry, you have an eye for beauty." Then drop the matter.

APPENDIX

ANN LANDERS TECHNIQUE

This technique was initiated when one of the authors was employed as a counselor in a large junior high school in Colorado Springs. It was a technique that sprang from necessity—the guest speaker failed to arrive and the auditorium was packed with expectant students. Acting on an impromptu basis, the counselor took the mike and said, "Until our guest speaker arrives, how would you like to fill in by posing a problem you have to the audience and getting some immediate response from the other students?" There was a resounding "Yes!" The counselor then established four ground rules:

1. The questioner must come to the platform and use the mike.
2. The responders must come to the platform and use the mike.
3. The responders must take their place in line at the side of the platform.
4. The responders may speak one minute.

The first session was a huge success. Someone dubbed it Ann Landers Day—a name that stuck. When the guest speaker finally arrived, the students were reluctant to stop their parley. The technique thereafter became part of the all-school guidance program.

BIBLIOTHERAPY

Bibliotherapy is a technique designed to provide therapy through reading. The literature used is specifically selected to reinforce positive feelings about the self. Students with serious personal problems often gain courage to face them when they can identify with someone who has become a legend because of inordinate courage in facing a handicap, a hazard, or an emotional crisis. There is some comfort in feeling that "He and I are alike because . . ."

Several excellent recommended lists of stories and books are available from commercial companies. They are complete with teacher's guides. The librarian in your school can be of enormous help in obtaining such a list for you, or in compiling a recommended list from the existing library collection. The school counselor will also be able to assist you, since bibliotherapy is often used in working with parents.

BRAINSTORMING

Brainstorming is a technique used to get people to share wild ideas without feeling foolish or self-conscious. Rules of the game include the following:

1. No censoring of ideas is allowed. Every idea is accepted.
2. Rapid-fire participation is encouraged. This relieves the temptation to sort out ideas, and it also keeps people on their toes.
3. The participants are encouraged to work on others' ideas. The group soon gets the feeling that while there may be "nothing new under the sun," new arrangements of old ideas spell creativity.

Suggested topics for brainstorming:

1. What are some ways we can stop kids from acting out in the classroom?
2. Let's think of all the kinds of things that make us angry.
3. Without speaking, how can we help someone get over being mad?

BUZZ SESSIONS

The buzz-session technique was developed early by group-dynamics scholars to provide optimum participation of large-group members by increasing the numbers of people who could speak and be heard during a short period of time. The technique is implemented by a regrouping of the large group. A class of thirty students, for instance, would be broken into groups of five or six members each. Each small group selects a chairman, who also serves as the feedback person to the large group. The leader of the large group explains the task of the small group (to explore the problem further, for example, or to raise further questions or provide optional solutions). As soon as the interest of the small groups seems to be waning, the large-group leader calls for feedback from the small-group leaders.

CLASS DISCUSSIONS

The total range of the daily behaviors and concerns of students, teachers, and parents can be dealt with through effective class discussions, described in detail by Glasser (1969) and Dreikurs, et al. (1971). The requirements are simply stated but require patience and practice. They are: (1) the content must be important and relevant, (2) the leadership must be nonjudgmental, and (3) all participants must be seated in a circle. (This provides face-to-face relationships and is a movement in the direction of equated power.) For the teacher, the second requirement is the most difficult. A study of the relevant sections of the two books cited above will be helpful. Three professional films have been produced to facilitate learning the techniques: *The Class Meeting*, available from Education Training Center, 2140 West Olympic Boulevard, Los Angeles, Calif., 90006, and *Behavioral Group Counseling* and *Carl Rogers on Facilitating a Group*, available from the American Guidance and Personnel Association, Film Dept., 1607 New Hampshire Ave. N.W., Washington D.C., 20009.

COMMITMENT TECHNIQUE

The commitment technique of working with classroom behaviors is one of the approaches developed by William Glasser to implement his reality therapy. The major differences between this approach and other disciplinary approaches are that (1) it focuses on individual responsibility rather than punitive measures; (2) it directs attention to conscious behavior instead of unconscious thoughts and feelings; (3) it emphasizes the present, not the past; (4) it stresses the child's need for value judgment (morality) with regard to his own behavior; and (5) it actively teaches responsible behavior (via the plan and commitment) as opposed to allowing the child to find his own way.

A simplification of the commitment technique follows an eight-step sequence:

1. Be warm, friendly, accepting, open, and honest.
2. Emphasize present behavior—"*What* are you doing?" *Why* is not important.
3. Insist on *value judgment*. Does what you are doing help you? Your class? Your school? Your home? Your community?
4. Plan better alternatives and make the plan feasible. ("Can you avoid fighting until noon?")
5. Get commitment, either oral or written; if written, get the person's signature.
6. Get feedback, and accept *no* excuses.
7. If necessary, make another, more viable commitment. Repeat, repeat, repeat, if necessary.
8. Do not punish.

Those who wish more detail on the technique are encouraged to read Glasser's books (see the Bibliography).

EXTRINSIC REWARDS

Experience and research have demonstrated that student behavior can be positively motivated by the use of extrinsic rewards. For example, pupils who find it impossible, under the traditional motivations (teacher, peer, or parent encouragement; approval, pressure, and punishment systems), to stay with the tasks of learning to read or learning to control their classroom behaviors *have* learned to read or behave better when rewarded with tokens: marbles, candy, toys, stars, emblems, titles, and so forth. Some schools set up citizenship awards based on points.

In addition to "things" awards, privileges can be strong motivators. Short-term motivations may include such rewards as free time or a longer recess or lunch period; longer-term procedures could include a cumulative point (or token) system that would lead to the privilege of attending movies, field trips, carnivals, and so on. The system that is used can be built by the teacher *and* the students based on a self-management sheet, listing mutually agreed upon important behaviors, such as punctuality, care of school property, completed assignments, courteousness, and so forth.

Awarding is more effective than taking away.

FAMILY COUNCIL

Some school behaviors are direct derivatives of behaviors learned in the home, and most behaviors in school are influenced by home values and attitudes. It will often be helpful for teachers to suggest that parents develop a formalized discussion period—a family council. In such councils, all members of the family are present and all participate; written minutes are kept, rules of procedure are developed, and chairman and secretary responsibilities are rotated. The first meeting must be held on the planning of a family fun event. Succeeding meetings could include such plannings but should also include concerns or problems of individuals or of the family as a group. See Fullmer (1971), for family consultation.

The attitude must be (1) *open*—each person must be listened to, and the entire range of concerns must be family fare; (2) *"we" oriented*—individual or multiple suggestions of solutions must finally be "we" *supported* and "we" *agreed-upon*; (3) *specific*—solutions must be in simple, understandable terms; (4) *committed*—solution implementation must be responsibly assumed by each concerned person; and (5) *credible*—the adequacy or inadequacy of the agreed-upon solution should come out at the next meeting. The pervading atmosphere must be one of mutual respect and shared helpfulness. See Dreikurs, *et al.* (1971).

FLEXIBLE SCHEDULING

Flexible scheduling was invented to increase educational effectiveness via the individualization of student instruction. The Stanford School Scheduling System, which features the use of computers to cope with the complexities involved, has been successfully tested in a large number of schools. If you are in one of those schools, or a similar one, your student who is frustrated or bored by his academic activities can readily be reassigned. In other schools, less formidable scheduling arrangements can be made. For example, outstanding students can be released from "required" classes and can be provided with advanced texts and study materials, with only occasional contacts with the regular teacher. Students who need simpler materials and more time to learn can be taught effectively by older students or adult aides.

FLIGHT PLAN

The flight plan is an approach to lesson planning that evolved over the years as the authors worked with high-school, junior-high, and elementary-school students. An outgrowth of the "contract plan," which had its genesis in the 1920s and 1930s, it is an effort to personalize, as well as to individualize, assignments in a manner that follows important principles of learning.

The flight-plan approach is hierarchical. The teacher works as an artist-technician. As such, he begins lesson preparation by first finding out two things: what the student has to learn (to read better, to compute, to organize ideas) and what the student's interests are. This information enables the teacher to meaningfully weld individualizing and personalizing. The trained teacher has the skills to detect, via formal and informal means, the present level on which the student is functioning. Next, he must thoughtfully identify the behavioral objectives he and the student have as their common goal. Having done this, a close look must be taken at the skills needed to accomplish the goal. A good motto in lesson planning is "first things first," or as our good friend J. Louis Cooper used to say, "Remember, he can't jump high if he can't jump low!"

A sample flight plan is not included in this book, but a check board delineating the skeletal structure is provided on the following page. It indicates the segments of the plan and briefly describes the emphasis on each level of operation. You will note that there are four flights, but there could be more. The check board could be duplicated on a large board for planning purposes. For instance, after the objectives are clearly in mind and the skills identified, the box under Flight I, Number 2, could be used to make notes regarding the books, exercises, and so on that will be used in teaching the skills. As new ideas occur to

Name of Class or Individual Student _____

Behavioral Objective _____

A FLIGHT-PLAN CHECK BOARD

Emphasis	Flight I — Ground Crew Work	Flight II — The Take-off	Flight III — Flying High	Flight IV — On the Moon
1. Who's in charge?	Teacher directs	Student works with teacher as helper	Student works with other student or alone	Student Solos
2. What's the nature of the work?	*Basic:* skill drill	*Augmented:* skills application	*Divergent:* activities with many choices	*Culminating:* unique creative products and activities
3. How can the learnings be categorized?	Simple	Complex	Compound	Sophisticated
4. How can the learnings be described?	*Cognitively:* knowledge and comprehension	Application	Analysis	Synthesis and evaluation
	Affectively: awareness and responding	Valuing	Organizing	Internalizing values
5. What are some suggestive titles of flights that will help the learner comprehend the natural sequences involved in every learning endeavor?	"The Egg"	"The Larva"	"The Pupa"	"The Adult"
	"The Overture"	"Opus I"	"Opus II"	"The Finale"
	"Change: In General"	"Change: In Me"	"Change: In My School"	"Change: In My Neighborhood"
	"Change: In My Community"	"Change: In My State"	"Change: In My Country"	"Change: In the World"

the planner, he can make note of them, always being careful to put them in their logical place on the continuum.

The plan is duplicated, and each student has his own copy. This way he knows what is ahead and can plan accordingly. Evaluation is continuous, with the teacher or an aide usually in charge. The parents are made aware of the plan and are encouraged to become involved, particularly in Flights III and IV when divergent thinking and creative activities are emphasized.

A plan such as this incorporates certain safety measures. For one, with clear objectives it makes meaningless, isolated assignments virtually impossible; second, the subsequent parts must be constructed so that they reinforce previous learnings; third, the possibility of failure is eliminated because Flight I is equated with a D, Flight II with a C, Flight III with a B, and Flight IV with an A, in systems that use letter-grade evaluations. Being relieved of the possibility of failure is one of the greatest motivators there is!

The flights may be long and involved or extremely brief and simple. In either case, the principle is the same. From the incubation stage the learnings unfold until there is a resultant creative product.

We have experienced success with this mode of planning. We pass this idea on to you, not for your adoption but to encourage you to combine and recombine old and new ways so that your teaching remains vital and you and your students continue to enjoy learning.

INQUIRY PROCESS

The inquiry process in learning is designed to maximize the student's capabilities in learning a new concept. Closely allied to "discovery technique" and "the divergent thinking strategy," it can be applied as easily to a student's learning about his own behavior and its modification as to academic conceptualizations. The key lies in the teacher's skill in questioning. Nonthreatening, matter-of-fact questions will be most productive when they (1) isolate the elements of the situation, (2) devise hypotheses about them, (3) pursue what might be true (consequences) if the hypothesis were correct, (4) keep the whole situation in mind, and not only isolated aspects, (5) consider, accept, and reject a variety of possibilities, and (6) are climaxed by thinking about the thoughts developed during steps 1 through 5.

Your questions could well pursue the following areas, from the simple to the complex: sensory observations; recalling; comparing-contrasting; classifying-grouping; analyzing; interpreting; inferring; generalizing; hypothesizing; predicting; evaluating–value judging; synthesizing.

JUNIOR COUNSELORS

While serving as dean of girls in a large junior high school, the senior author developed a leadership training program for ninth graders who were interested in becoming a part of the total guidance and counseling program. Forty students who, according to their homeroom teachers, had leadership qualities were recommended for the training, which would prepare them to work with individuals and small groups. The trainees came to school one hour before the opening of school one day a week for twelve weeks. During that time they explored the differences among democratic, autocratic, and laissez faire procedures. They examined the roles they themselves habitually assumed in groups (interrogator, clarifier, antagonist, peace maker, and so on). They studied active listening, questioning and clarification techniques, parliamentary procedure, and regard for confidentialities. Of the forty who began the training, only two dropped out.

The thirty eight junior counselors not only assumed the role of confidante and helper to individuals and small groups who had problems with study habits, weight, skin, truancy, and loneliness, but they also assisted in the total orientation program of the school, assisted with career guidance that went on all during the year, and infused the total school with an atmosphere of friendliness and good will. At the end of the year they were awarded a small token of recognition for their accomplishments, but throughout the year it was evident that the satisfaction of helping others help themselves was their highest reward.

LEGAL-TYPE NOTE TAKING

The authors have used and taught many students to take notes using what is called legal-type note taking, since it is somewhat imitative of legal briefs. The approach is very simple. Instead of using traditional outline format or hit-or-miss note taking, it sticks to questions and answers. Preferably, one section of a notebook is allocated for a given subject. To implement this kind of note taking, have the student do the following.

Begin by opening the notebook to the second page. At the top of the left-hand page write "class notes." On the opposite page write "reading notes." Under that write the name of the subject, the chapter number, and the date. Take a ruler and draw a line down the center of the page on your right. At the top of the first column write "question"; at the top of the second column write "answer." Begin reading your text. Each paragraph should contain one or two main ideas worth remembering. Identify the significant fact or idea in your head. Now convert that fact or idea into a question. If you can't do that, you may not understand the material. Formulate the question in as brief a form as possible, and after number 1, write it out. On the other side of the center line place another 1, followed by the answer in very brief form. Keep the numbers in line with each other as you work down the page. See the sample below.

CLASS NOTES	READING NOTES	
	Biology	Date _____
Place here any	Chapter 8	
pertinent teacher's		
notes; reminders	QUESTION	ANSWER
for tomorrow;		
new assignment;	1. What was	1. xmxmxmx xmx
diagrams	. . . .?	xx x x xxxxxx
	2.	2.

You will note that the left-hand page is free for class notes during the teacher's lecture, a student's report, or slide or transparency showings. You may draw arrows from your notes to the diagrams or reminders, and vice versa. Remember, you fortify your learning every time an idea is reinforced.

This method of note taking is especially helpful when reviewing for exams. A friend or a relative can ask you the questions from your notebook and the answers are right there. No need for time-consuming hunting for the answers. And, by the way, don't make the mistake of throwing your notebook away at the end of the course! It may come in handy later.

LISTENING FORMULA

The FALR formula for listening has been very useful for a large number of students. The letters refer to:

1. *F*ocus your attention on the speaker.
2. *A*sk yourself what you might or should learn from the speaker.
3. *L*isten carefully, all the while relating new material to what you already know about the subject. Listen for main ideas, key words, particular points of interest.
4. *R*eview what you have learned in the way that works best for you—perhaps by making notes for future reference, relating new ideas to a friend, or pursuing the subject through independent study.

OBSERVATION TECHNIQUE

The peer observation technique is useful in providing opportunities for pupils to make decisions regarding their own behavior. A rotation plan is used in which three to four pupils are given an opportunity to make observations of the activity of their classmates for a period of ten to twenty minutes. At the end of the observation period the observers feed back the behavior of the pupils observed by relating, with help from their notes, the behaviors that took place. All of the pupils discuss these observations from the standpoint of profitable use of time, of social relationships, and of other factors. The students who have been observed and their peers are then given an opportunity to suggest better ways of behaving during future classroom periods. A class roster is useful for making notations and a code for making notations is also helpful. A possible code would be *wh:* working hard; *ah:* asking for help from Teacher, *w:* whispering; *t:* talking out; *s:* singing; *pn:* passing notes; *dd:* daydreaming; *wa:* wandering around.

CLASS ROSTER

1. Brown, Suzy   t, dd
2. Dropper, Jim   dd, w
3. Farmer, Jill   wh, ah, pn
4. Riugy, Sally   t, pn, ah

ORGANIZING A CLASSROOM

This book is addressed to teachers who want to find the best possible ways to cope with a wide range of student behaviors. The authors feel that many classroom behavior problems are the direct result of inadequate or poor classroom organization. The following approach to beginning a semester was suggested by a good friend and gifted teacher, Mary Lombard, whom we learned to know and appreciate in Connecticut in the 1950s. We have used this approach many times and have recommended it to many colleagues and student teachers over the years. We pass it on to you with good wishes for enriched teaching.

The underlying assumption of this approach is that the classroom will be the students' as well as the teacher's. Whether the students are in your room for only a period or for the entire day, it should be a place they look forward to entering. This feeling or attitude is seldom achieved, particularly on the upper elementary level, if the teacher has everything lined up, neat and orderly, when the students arrive.

Try this. Have on hand a rich collection of materials, textbooks, library books, paperbacks, reference books, old and new magazines, puzzles, games, furniture that no one else wanted, paper, paints, scissors, string, junk. If the students act as though they are in the wrong room, tell them that you thought they ought to have something to say about their own room and that since you didn't know what they'd like you've waited until now. Watch their faces light up!

Immediately you all have a problem to solve. Your lesson plan is made! Before you know it, priorities will be established by the group, leadership will emerge, imaginations will take flight. The students will, of course, bring their previous class organization ideas with them, but given latitude they are almost certain to want to create something entirely different from anything they've had before. Stand back and watch, listen, help when needed, and step in, if necessary; after all, you're a member of this group, not an onlooker. Do encourage them to come up with something unique, but if they opt to try the same old thing they've had in another school, go along with it for the time being. Capitalize on opportunities for students to use math skills, as in plotting the arrangement of the furniture using graph paper. Encourage competition for stimulating creative ways to solve problems. Sooner or later they will see the need for some management. Perhaps they will want to choose leaders or officers. All the while they are working through ways to make their room the most interesting one in the school, they are putting the books in order, sorting the supplies, getting to know each other. And at the same time you have been closely observing the kinds of books they pick up and mull over, the level of book that they stay with, their preferences in friends, their dexterity, their voices, their attitudes toward one another, and their feelings about themselves. Before you know it, they will be making lists of things they want to accomplish before the year is over. The year will be gone much too soon!

QUESTIONNAIRE

The questionnaire is a widely used technique for collecting information or statistical data. Many samples can be found in professional books and periodicals; others can be purchased commercially.

When working with children on a particular problem in school, adaptations or self-made questionnaires have distinct advantages. First, they will be relevant—the children use their own topics and terminology. Second, the purposes and meanings become clear to the users. Third, there is pride in "something that is mine."

SELF-MANAGEMENT RECORD

TEACHER ——————

CLASS PERIOD —————— SUBJECT ——————

EVALUATION TIME PERIOD —————— TO ——————

NAME OF STUDENT	IS PUNCTUAL	IS COURTEOUS	IS HONEST	IS FRIENDLY	RESPECTS SCHOOL PROPERTY	PERFORMS MONITOR DUTIES ACCEPTABLE	USES ACCEPTABLE LANGUAGE	COMPLETES CLASSROOM ASSIGNMENTS	DEMONSTRATES RESPECT FOR OTHERS	HAS REASONABLE TABLE MANNERS	WORKS WELL IN CLASS	BRINGS BOOKS TO CLASS, PENCILS TO CLASS	PERSONAL PROPERTY RESPONSIBLE FOR	COMMENTS

A questionnaire "About Me" might include such questions as: What are the names and ages of my brothers and sisters? What are the names of my three best friends? What do I do when I have time to do as I please? Do I listen to the radio? When? What are my favorite programs? Do I watch TV? When? What are my favorite programs? What hobby do I have? Which subjects in school do I like best? If I could be granted three wishes, what would they be?

ROLE PLAYING

In role playing, pupils reenact behavior episodes for the purpose of studying their own behavior and learning how to control it.

Suppose two pupils want a single copy of a book at the same time, and conflict results in physical blows. After the teacher resolves the immediate conflict and the emotion has subsided, the pupils may change roles or other pupils may play one or both of the roles to reenact the conflict from its beginning, recalling as nearly as possible the words and actions of the episode. The class then discusses why the conflict took place.

When the motivations and causes of the conflict seem to be defined, the entire class offers suggestions as to how the conflict could have been avoided by another way of behaving. Then the two pupils are given an opportunity to practice the new way of behaving.

SENTENCE COMPLETION

The sentence completion technique is a procedure in which the teacher and his student may learn about the latter's attitudes toward specific people, relationships, and experiences. It can easily be designed to elicit feelings toward school, work, play, authoritative figures, joys, and fears. Forms are available from test publishers, or a teacher may develop his own by using a variety of structures. Examples of sentence completion items include:

I feel_____ .

Teachers are _____ .

My problem is_____ .

I hate_____ .

My father's greatest mistake was _____ .

Mary is_____ .

The fight was_____/_____.

The situation is_____.

SOCIOGRAM

The sociogram is a procedure useful in studying relationships within a group. Teachers use the information to assign seating, to suggest leadership, and to make plans for individual pupil growth. The class or group is informed of the purpose of the procedure. Each student is then asked to write his name in the upper right-hand corner of a 3 x 5 card and to put in the center of the card the name of one of his peers in the group he would choose in answer to *a* question, such as: Which person would you like to sit near? Who is your best friend in this class (or group)? Which person would you choose as a helper in arithmetic? Which person would you like to work with on a committee? Like all other very personal information, the results must be kept confidential. The teacher collects the cards and arranges them according to the choices. The resulting arrangement is finally transferred to a sheet of paper, with arrows indicating choice direction (sometimes they are reciprocal), triangles representing boys, and circles representing girls. The usual pattern looks something like this:

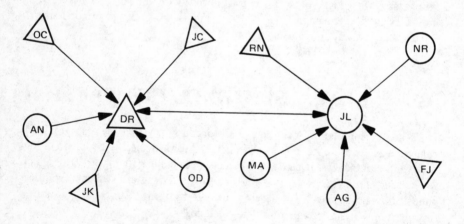

STUDENT COURT

Student courts can provide a meaningful learning experience for the defendant, judge, jurors, lawyers, clerks, and witnesses. Student courts are most effective in schools where the morale is high and where their sphere of control is in the area of minor disturbances and infractions. Major violations of acceptable behavior norms often invite student courts to make the defendant a scapegoat; their punishments are often too harsh and severe. The offender may threaten or jeopardize student privileges, or members of the student court may be morally rigid. Students need to be carefully trained so that the experience of the defendant is one that provides growth and not resentment and bitterness.

STUDY SKILLS

There are specific study skills that can be taught by any teacher and learned by any student. The following guidelines are taken from Myrtle T. Collins' *How to Study* (Big Spring, Texas: Gamco Industries, 1972).

1. Don't study on an empty stomach—or on one too full.
2. Have your vision checked once a year.
3. Learn to listen (see Listening Formula).
4. Take a diagnostic test; then improve your reading.
5. Use the following *SQ4R* study formula; Scan, Question, Read, Review, Recite, Reinforce.
6. Learn to concentrate.
7. Make a daily activity schedule.
8. Identify the time of day you work best.
9. Select the same quiet, neat place to study daily.
10. Take good notes.
11. Use loose-leaf dividers.
12. Give yourself lots of time to prepare for examinations.
13. Reward yourself for jobs well done.

TEAM MEETING

The team meeting is a regularized procedure designed to provide optimum help for a teacher and a student. The teachers and the principal of the school select a time each week when all special-service personnel serving the school (counselors, nurse, psychologist, and so on) meet with the principal and any teacher(s) concerned about the developmental behavior of a particular student. The agenda is made by the principal from teacher or special-service personnel referrals. A copy of the agenda is placed in all professional staff mailboxes prior to the meeting so that all who want to help may come prepared. Data are shared and an optimum action plan is agreed upon. Follow-ups are provided in the plan.

The plan will work best if the meetings are held *regularly*. Called meetings are generally held too late to be of significant help.

VALUES CLARIFICATION

All behaviors are influenced by values. Teachers have long made random attempts to influence the values of students by moralizing, sermonizing, modeling, and curriculum selection. Research suggests that the direct teaching of moral behavior is not very effective.

It has been demonstrated, however, that one effective way of developing moral behavior is the use of a system known as values clarification. The system is more concerned with the process of valuing than with the contents of students', teachers', or parents' values. Actually, teachers have made valiant, if sporadic, attempts at helping students clarify their values, using such exercises as listing famous people and their most admirable qualities. More recently Simon *et al.* (1972) have systematized the approach. Their book contains seventy-nine values clarification activities that students enjoy doing and that require a minimum of supplies—generally only pencil and paper.

BIBLIOGRAPHY

Ackerman, J. Mark. *Operant Conditioning Techniques for the Classroom Teacher.* Albany, Ore.: Linn County Mental Health Clinic, 1972.
This guide offers the teacher many suggestions for preventing disruptive behavior and for encouraging growth in learning.

Addicott, Irwin O. *Constructive Classroom Control.* San Francisco: Chandler, 1958.
This brochure includes suggestions for organizing the classroom to secure good teacher-pupil relations, some tested principles, some pitfalls to be avoided, and some practical techniques that many have employed with success.

Allen, Dwight W., and Seifman, Eli. *The Teacher's Handbook.* Glenview, Ill.: Scott, Foresman, 1971.
A compendium of the views of eighty-six specialists. Sections 2.5, 3.1, 3.2, 3.5, 3.12, 3.14, 4.16, and 7.13 should be helpful to the teacher as he works with misbehavior in the classroom.

Almy, Millie, and Cunningham, Ruth. *Ways of Studying Children.* New York: Teachers College, Columbia University, 1959.
A manual and comprehensive guide to specific techniques and approaches to the understanding of the ways children feel, behave, and think.

Bandura, Albert. *Principles of Behavior Modification.* New York: Holt, Rinehart and Winston, 1969.
Presents basic psychological principles governing human behavior within the conceptual framework of social learning.

Bany, Mary A., and Johnson, Lois V. *Classroom Group Behavior: Group Dynamics in Education.* New York: Macmillan, 1964.
Actual incidents of classroom group behavior as reported by more than 300 teachers are analyzed. The latter parts of the book describe group decision techniques, problem-solving techniques, and preventative measures applied to specific classroom situations.

Baruch, Dorothy. *New Ways in Discipline.* New York: Whittlesey House, 1949.
Even though written several years ago, this brochure is very much "alive" today. The "new ways" in discipline include ascertaining the underlying causes of behavior, helping the child to know you understand how he feels, helping the child to express his "badness' in acceptable ways, and channeling his feelings into other emotions and activities.

213

Becker, W. C.; Thomas, D. R.; and Carnine, D. *Reducing Behavior Problems: An Operant Conditioning Guide for Teachers.* Urbana, Ill.: Educational Resources Information Center, National Laboratory on Early Childhood Education, 1969.
Brief and helpful pamphlet on methods and results of research on operant conditioning. Preschool and elementary levels.

Benson, Arthur M., ed. *Modifying Deviant Social Behaviors in Various Classroom Settings.* Eugene, Ore.: College of Education, University of Oregon, 1969.
The titles of the two parts indicate the contents of this brochure: Part I, "Teachers, Peers and Parents as Agents of Change in the Classroom," and Part II, "Special Class Placement as a Treatment Alternative for Deviant Behavior Children."

Blackham, G. and Silberman A. *Modification of Child Behavior: Principles and Procedures.* Belmont, Calif.: Wadsworth, 1970.
Dealing with grade-school children, the authors describe and analyze more than forty problems that concern teachers, counselors, and parents.

Brown, Anthony M. *Discipline Concepts in Education.* Boston: St. Paul Editions, 1964.
The author analyzes the similarities and differences in the methods and aims of discipline in Catholic and public school organizations.

Brown, Duane. *Changing Student Behavior: A New Approach to Discipline.* Dubuque, Iowa: William C. Brown, 1971.
The book is designed to help the reader implement a classroom atmosphere, discipline, punishment and a personal philosophy toward the mental, emotional, and behavioral development of school children.

Carter, Ronald D. *Help! These Kids Are Driving Me Crazy.* Champaign, Ill.: Research Press,1972.
This book gives teachers some knowledge of workable techniques for humane classroom control.

Chamberlin, Leslie J. *Effective Instruction Through Dynamic Discipline.* Columbus, Ohio: 1971.
The author's years of experience in ghetto areas of a large city is combined with sound professional orientation and his own humaneness to illustrate how teachers can prevent many behavior problems and can correct others in an acceptable manner. He lists scores of corrective, therapeutic, and undesirable techniques.

Clarizio, Harvey F. *Toward Positive Classroom Discipline.* New York: Wiley, 1971.
The author examines five major classifications of discipline techniques: (1) rewards, (2) modeling and observation, (3) extinction, (4) punishment, and (5) desensitization. Concrete examples are given.

College Entrance Examination Board. *Deciding.* Princeton, N.J.: College Entrance Examination Board, 1972.
Deciding is a course of study (junior and senior high school) that incorporates such activities as decision-making exercises, discussion guides, role playing, and decision-making simulations.

Cuban, Larry. *To Make a Difference: Teaching in the Inner City.* New York: Free Press, 1970.
>This book presents a studied and experienced approach to successful teaching methods that cope with many of the problems faced by teachers in the inner city school.

de Cecco, John P. and Richards, Arlene K. *Growing Pains: Uses of School Conflict.* New York: Holt, Rinehart and Winston, 1974.
>The authors analyze conflict data gathered in high schools from 1969 to 1973 and conclude that both absence and presence of choice lead to classroom conflict. They then develop a three-step model of ameliorative negotiation.

de Zafra, Carlos, Jr.; Mitchell, Elizabeth B.; and Berndt, Richard L. *Effective Classroom Discipline.* Rochester: The Mohawk Press, 1963.
>Describes succinctly twenty-four "techniques for disciplining the group" and fifteen "techniques for disciplining the individual."

Dinkmeyer, Don. *Developing Understanding of Self and Others (DUSO).* Circle Pines, Minn.: American Guidance Service, 1972.
>DUSO is a program of interesting activities and materials designed to help children understand themselves and those around them.

"Discipline Symposium," *NEA Journal* 52 (September 1963), 8–22.
>A symposium presenting diverse points of view.

Dreikurs, Rudolph; Grunwald, Bernice; and Pepper, Floyd. *Maintaining Sanity in the Classroom: Illustrated Teaching Techniques.* New York: Harper & Row, 1971.
>Based on the psychology of Alfred Adler and heavily case oriented, this text applies techniques of motivation modification to classroom problems.

Educational Research Associates. *A Handbook of Personal Growth Activities for Classroom Use.* Amherst, Mass.: Educational Research Associates, 1972.
>This handbook describes a variety of personal growth activities—games, role playing, simulation and brainstorming—that purport to improve communication, decision making, problem solving, and interpersonal relationships.

Educational Research Council of America. *Dealing With Aggressive Behavior.* Cleveland, Ohio: Educational Research Council of America, 1972.
>This brochure describes ways to cope with violence and aggression using games, media, and readings.

Elder, Carl A. *Making Value Judgments: Decisions for Today.* Columbus, Ohio: Merrill, 1972.
>Teachers and counselors will find this resource book useful to themselves and their students as they cope with problems of smoking, drinking, drugs, prejudice, premarital sex, pollution, and career goals.

ERIC ED 025 084. *Research in Behavior Modification: New Developments and Implications,* 1965.
>Excellent summary of research to 1965 by nineteen researchers. Implications for application are described.

Fargo, George A.; Behrns, Charlene; and Nolen, Patricia. *Behavior Modification in the Classroom*. Belmont, Calif.: Wadsworth, 1970.

A book of carefully selected writings by proponents of behavior modification. They are designed primarily for teachers and students in teacher training who seek practical answers to classroom management.

Fullmer, Daniel W. *Counseling: Group Theory and System*. Scranton, Penn.: International Textbook Co., 1971.

The author describes how school personnel can help the family develop "a learning environment capable of influencing behavior formation."

Glasser, William. *Schools Without Failure*. New York: Harper & Row, 1969

The author presents many specific ideas on reaching negatively oriented children, including no punishment (but discipline), no excuses, positive involvement, and individual responsibility. Among the most important innovations he proposes is the use of the class, led by the teacher, as a counseling group that daily spends time developing the social responsibility necessary to solve behavioral and educational problems of its members.

Glasser, William. *Reality Therapy: A New Approach to Psychiatry*. New York: Harper & Row, 1972.

The requirements of reality therapy are an intense personal involvement between teacher and pupil, the facing of reality and responsibility, and learning better ways to live. The basic human needs are to love and be loved and to feel worthwhile to oneself and to others. The book contrasts reality therapy with traditional procedures, then shows it in successful practice with individuals and groups.

Gnagey, William J. *The Psychology of Discipline in the Classroom*. New York: Macmillan, 1968.

Written like a classroom novel, this eighty-page brochure brings together authentic classroom incidents and the findings of scientific investigations.

Gnagney, William J. *What Research Says to the Teacher about Controlling Classroom Misbehavior*. Washington, D.C.: National Education Association, 1965.

This thirty-page pamphlet reports to classroom teachers the most important suggestions that have been produced by research on classroom discipline. Suggestions for on-the-job applications dominate the text.

Haring, Norris G., and Phillips, E. Lakin. *Analysis and Modification of Classroom Behavior*. Englewood Cliffs, N.J.: Prentice-Hall, 1972.

Specific procedures describe how to deal with children with behaviorial disorders, how to arrange an instructional program, and how to maintain adaptive behavior in the classroom.

Hart, Leslie A. *The Classroom Disaster.* New York: Teachers College, Columbia University, 1969.
> Pages 209, 269–72, 315, and 332 state that "open" schools bring about "reduction, often to the vanishing point, of 'discipline' problems within learning groups."

Hipple, Theodore W. *Secondary School Teaching: Problems and Methods.* Pacific Palisades, Calif.: Goodyear, 1970.
> This helpful book is composed mainly of descriptions of problems that classroom teachers have actually encountered. Proposed alternative solutions range from the most traditional approaches to the most modern. They are presented by the use of a unique technique of involving the reader in creating additional solutions.

Holt, John. *What Do I Do on Monday?* New York: Dutton, 1970.
> An intensely human and caring book of practical ways to help children learn better and of techniques that minimize the development of discipline problems.

Homme, Lloyd, *et al. How to Use Contingency Contracting in the Classroom.* Champaign, Ill.: Research Press, 1969.
> This manual for teachers, written in a programmed format, gives step-by-step procedures for developing and using the behavior improvement contract.

Hunter, Madeline. *Reinforcement Theory for Teachers.* El Segundo, Calif.: TIP Publication, 1967.
> Written in programmed style, this brochure is written for daily classroom use by the elementary teacher.

Hymes, James L., Jr. *Behavior and Misbehavior: A Teacher's Guide to Action.* Englewood Cliffs, N.J.: Prentice-Hall, 1955.
> It is a book for teachers, with suggestions on what to do and how to cope with classroom problems that arise.

Jessup, Michael H., and Kiley, Margaret H. *Discipline: Positive Attitudes for Learning.* Englewood Cliffs, N.J.: Prentice–Hall, 1971.
> A variety of classroom situations and possible alternatives for dealing with them are presented.

Kounin, Jacob S. *Discipline and Group Management in Classrooms.* New York: Holt, Rinehart and Winston, 1970.
> The authentic descriptions used in this report of the author's latest study are taken from classes that were videotaped. Specific classroom managerial techniques are researched.

Krumboltz, John D., and Thoresen, C., eds. *Behavioral Counseling.* New York: Holt, Rinehart and Winston, 1969.
> Although the target readers are counselors, these carefully selected readings will be of interest and use to the teacher in the classroom.

Krumboltz, John D. and Krumboltz, Helen B. *Changing Children's Behavior.* Englewood Cliffs, N.J.: Prentice-Hall, 1972.
> The authors present 227 behavior problems found in the school, home, or community. Each behavior is provided with a behavior modification procedure that is based on recent psychological research and uses a common-sense approach.

Kujoth, Jean Spealman. *The Teacher and School Discipline.* Metuchen, N.J.: Scarecrow Press, 1970.
> This book contains forty-six articles from twenty-eight journals. It includes principles, guidelines, comparisons, psychologies, lessons from experience, test cases, research findings, and practical experiments relating to school discipline.

La Grand, Louis E. *Discipline in the Secondary School.* West Nyack, N.Y.: Parker Publishing, 1969.
> The book presents practical information on the important place of discipline in the learning process; on the traits that are essential for the teacher to develop if he is to establish a meaningful relationship with students; on how discipline problems can be reduced; on what requisites are indispensable to classroom management; on teaching image; and on principles of student-teacher relationships.

Larson, Knute G. *School Discipline in an Age of Rebellion.* West Nyack, N.Y.: Parker Publishing, 1972.
> This book addresses itself to: (1) How can we work with militant groups to improve our schools? (2) How can we help the youth "rebellion" to build a better nation?

Larson, Knute G., and Karpas, Melvin R. *Effective Secondary School Discipline.* Englewood Cliffs, N.J.: Prentice-Hall, 1964.
> The introduction of the book states, "This is a book of answers; it brings together some of the best contemporary thinking on the subject of secondary school discipline . . . it does present practical and logical approaches which actually work in schools of all sizes in rural, suburban and urban settings."

Lyon, Harold C., Jr. *Learning to Feel—Feeling to Learn: Humanistic Education for the Whole Man.* Columbus, Ohio: Merrill, 1971.
> Teachers, administrators, and counselors will find in this book a rich storehouse of specific suggestions for improving the affective lives and behavior of their students.

McDonald, Blanche, and Nelson, Leslie. *Successful Classroom Control.* Dubuque, Iowa: William C. Brown, 1959.
> The authors describe scores of do's and don'ts in classroom management that will minimize negative classroom behavior.

Madsen, Charles H., Jr., and Madsen, Clifford K. *Teaching Discipline: Behavioral Principles Toward a Positive Approach.* Boston: Allyn & Bacon, 1970.
> A teacher's guide relating behavioral principles to classroom discipline and subject matter presentation. Over half the text contains specific applications to real classrooms.

Mancusa, Katherine C. *We Do Not Throw Rocks at the Teacher.* Scranton, Penn.: International Textbook,1966.
> A book that goes into its third printing obviously meets some of the needs of many readers. The author shares years of thinking, innovation, and experience as a successful classroom teacher. The text is enriched with scores of anecdotal illustrations of the author's approach to discipline.

Meacham, Merle L., and Wiesen, Allen E. *Changing Classroom Behavior: A Manual of Precision Teaching*, New York: International Textbook, 1969.
> Part I outlines the specific principles of learning that can be applied by the classroom teacher to enhance learning and improve behavior. Part II provides additional applications in normal classrooms and also includes applications to retardation, social deprivation, and severely deviant behavior.

Neill, A. S. *Freedom—Not License!* New York: Hart, 1966.
> The headmaster of Summerhill replies specifically to letters from parents and children (mostly American) on what to do about a host of behaviors that worry them.

Neisworth, J. T.; Deno, S. L.; and Jenkins, J. R. *Student Motivation and Classroom Management.* Newark, Del.: Behavior Techniques, 1970.
> The book describes numerous techniques designed to stimulate students and to systematically manage classrooms.

Parody, Ovid F. *The High School Principal and Staff Deal with Discipline.* New York: Teachers College, Columbia University, 1958.
> This monograph deals with a positive approach to the problems that youth face. It reports verbatim case conferences in which a variety of specialists join the local school staff, presents check lists of improvement techniques for principals and teachers, and provides procedural guides for working with student problems. The work of the "Discipline Committee" and the "Discipline Study Group," which most schools could emulate, is described.

Patterson, Gerald R., and Gullion, M. Elizabeth. *Living with Children: New Methods for Parents and Teachers.* Champaign, Ill.: Research Press, 1968.
> The book is written in the form of programmed instruction and provides material for planning what parents can do to change "problem" behaviors into more constructive behaviors.

Phillips, Ewing L.; Wiener, Daniel N.; and Haring, Norris G. *Discipline, Achievement, and Mental Health.* Englewood Cliffs, N.J.: Prentice-Hall, 1960.
> Two psychologists and an educational consultant "proceed on the basis of giving suggestions and advice" for the solution of discipline problems in order to make learning in the classroom possible.

Polk, Kenneth, and Schafer, Walter E., eds. *School and Delinquency*. Englewood Cliffs, N.J.: Prentice-Hall, 1972.

After establishing a position that the school experience may actually be a determinant in the generation and maintenance of delinquent careers, the authors suggest several well-studied remedies.

Redl, Fritz. *When We Deal with Children*. New York: Free Press, 1966.

In a paper titled "Discipline in Classroom Practice" Redl expands the material of Part II in *Discipline for Today's Children and Youth* (see Sheviakov, Redl, and Richardson, 1965.) The paper contains "live" cases and specific ways of resolving them. It is an excellent analysis of group psychological factors in discipline problems.

Sarason, Irwin G.; Glaser, Edward M., and Fargo, George A. *Reinforcing Productive Classroom Behavior*. New York: Behavioral Publications, 1972.

The authors of this pamphlet interpret ideas about behavior modification that are relevant to the classroom. "Putting Principles into Practice" and "Four Classroom Case Studies" are especially helpful.

Shaftel, Fannie, and Shaftel, George. *Values in Action: Role-Playing Problem Situations for the Intermediate Grades*. New York: Holt, Rinehart and Winston, 1971.

The program consists of a series of ten discussion and problem-solving filmstrips and accompanying recordings designed to challenge intermediate-grade students with dilemma situations.

Sheviakov, George V.; Redl, Fritz; and Richardson, Sybil K. *Discipline for Today's Children and Youth*. Washington D.C.: National Education Association, 1965.

A most helpful and useful publication that develops working principles of classroom discipline, with excellent illustrations of classroom application. Written in a delightful style, it is today as it was in 1944 (first edition) a classic in its field.

Simon, Sidney; Howe, Leland; and Kirschenbaum, Howard. *Values Clarification: A Handbook of Practical Strategies for Teachers and Students*. New York: Hart, 1972.

Designed to engage students and teachers in the active formulation and examination of values, this handbook presents seventy-nine practical strategies to implement the engagement.

Skinner, B. F. *The Technology of Teaching*. New York: Appleton-Century-Crofts, 1968.

One of the great scholars of behavior modification rethinks the whole educational enterprise in terms of reinforcement. Three chapters are of special interest to readers of this book: "Discipline, Ethical Behavior and Self-Control," "Why Teachers Fail," and "The Science of Learning and the Art of Teaching."

Stenhouse, Lawrence, ed. *Discipline in Schools.* Elmsford, N.Y.: Pergamon, 1967.
> The book includes papers by five British educators. They are designed to provide a basis for discussion (by teachers or teachers in training) of discipline in schools. It presents discipline as a central problem of human relations in the school, calling for insight rather than rule-of-thumb methods.

Stouffer, George A. W., Jr., and Owens, Jennie. "Behavior Problems as Identified by Today's Teachers and Compared with Those Reported by E. K. Wickman," *Journal of Educational Research* 48 (January 1955): 321-31.
> Comparisons of current data are made with Wickman's study (1926), which compared the gravity rankings of student behaviors by teachers versus those done by psychiatrists, psychologists, and psychiatric social workers.

Sunshine, Lakeside, Calif: Interact, 1971.
> Sunshine provides a simulation game related to racial problems and has demonstrated its effectiveness in helping solve some control problems and in reducing apathy.

Walch, J. Weston, ed. *Elementary School Discipline.* Portland, Maine: J. Weston Walch, 1957.
> In response from the readers of *Successful School Discipline* (1955) editor Walch developed another compendium for elementary school discipline only. Over 300 specific techniques are described as used by teachers, principals, and other professional school personnel.

Walch, J. Weston, ed. *High School Discipline.* Portland, Maine: J. Weston Walch, 1960.
> The editor states that the book contains a collection of 308 successful disciplinary methods contributed by teachers, principals, and superintendents. 140 additional methods were selected from current educational periodicals.

Walch, J. Weston, ed. *Successful School Discipline.* Portland, Maine: J. Weston Walch, 1955.
> The editor states that the book contains a collection of 530 tested disciplinary techniques chosen from the contributions of hundreds of practicing teachers and school administrators.

Webster, Staten W. *Discipline in the Classroom: Basic Principles and Problems.* San Francisco: Chandler, 1968.
> Following the author's presentation of his posture toward discipline in Part One of his book, he presents ten case examples of student behavior problems. An initial analysis of each child is made by four experienced educators. Then, after supplementary information is provided for each case, the evaluators present their second reactions.

Weiner, Daniel N. *Classroom Management and Discipline:* Itasca, Ill.: Peacock, 1972.

> "Goals must be set, and then the means sought that will best achieve them. Good management, classroom discipline, and self-discipline are our methods," states the Preface, and the book guides the teacher to do just that.

Woody, Robert H. *Behavioral Problem Children in the Schools: Recognition, Diagnosis and Behavioral Modification.* New York: Appleton-Century-Crofts, 1969.

> The book provides an introduction to the psychology of behavioral problem children and to the means of coping with the behavioral difficulties. The author provides assistance to teachers and other school personnel in working with a wide range of child behavior and proposes that virtually every child at some point in his life could be considered a "behavioral problem child."

Wrenn, Gilbert C. and Schwarzrock, Shirley. The *Coping With* books. Circle Pines, Minn.: American Guidance Service, 1970.

> In a series of 32 monographs the authors describe scores of interests, concerns and problems of young people, then suggest relevant guidelines and useful techniques for coping with them.

BIOGRAPHICAL DATA

Myrtle and DWane Collins, Assistant Professor of Education and Professor of Educational Psychology respectively, at the University of Hawaii, bring a combined 112 years of student, teaching, counseling, and administrative experience to the writing of this Survival Kit. They have studied, researched, and coped with student behavior at elementary, junior-high, high-school, and university levels in such diverse locations as New England, New York City, Iowa, South Dakota, Texas, Colorado, Hawaii, Brazil, and Laos. Other individual and co-authored articles and chapters by the two have appeared in professional journals and books.

Myrtle Telleen Collins received her B.A. in speech and English from Iowa State Teachers College (now University of Northern Iowa), Cedar Falls, Iowa, and her M.A. in counseling and guidance at Colorado College. Prior to returning to Laos, she was a coordinator of practice teachers, University of Hawaii. Among her publications are research studies on the effect of contract teaching on the creativity of students and a textbook on the teaching of English to children in Brazil. She has had experience as a teacher of English, drama, reading, and social studies on the secondary level, as a teacher of elementary grades, as a dean of girls in junior highs, as a counselor on all levels, and as a principal of an American school abroad. In addition, she was, at one time, secretary to the late Dr. Ruth M. Strang. She is a member of the Delta Kappa Gamma Society.

DWane Collins was awarded an Ed. D. degree at Columbia University in student personnel administration. His experience includes teaching and counseling at elementary, high-school, and university levels and serving as chairman of a department of educational psychology. His honors include: Fellow, American Psychological Association; Kappa Delta Pi; Francis E. Clark Award for outstanding service in guidance, State of Hawaii; and member of the Hawaii Legislative Task Force on Guidance and Counseling. His publications include several articles in the professional journals of the United States, Brazil, and Southeast Asia, monographs, and chapters in two textbooks.

Currently Collins and Collins are serving in Laos. Myrtle is elementary school principal and all-school counselor at the American School of Vientiane. DWane is a member of the University of Hawaii/USAID/Lao Ministry of Education Contract Team.